EVERYMAN'S LIBRARY
EDITED BY ERNEST RHYS

REFERENCE

A DICTIONARY OF NON-
CLASSICAL MYTHOLOGY
COMPILED BY MARIAN EDWARDES
AND LEWIS SPENCE

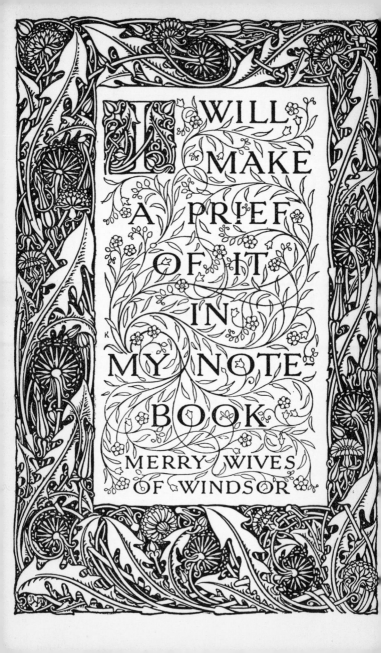

I WILL MAKE A PRIEF OF IT IN MY NOTE BOOK

MERRY WIVES OF WINDSOR

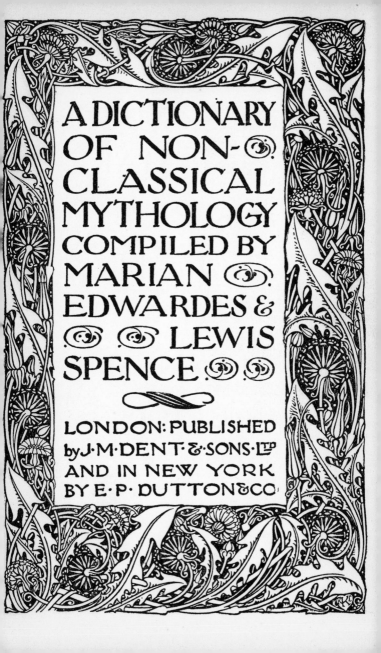

A DICTIONARY
OF NON-
CLASSICAL
MYTHOLOGY
COMPILED BY
MARIAN
EDWARDES &
LEWIS
SPENCE

LONDON: PUBLISHED
by J. M. DENT & SONS Ltd
AND IN NEW YORK
BY E. P. DUTTON & CO

INTRODUCTION

Not one mythology, but several, will be found concentrated within the pages of this volume, which embraces, as Ymir did in himself a whole race of giants, the great imaginations and divine beliefs of the races of the East, North, and extreme West. The difficulty of the subject is not only in the world-wide extent of the area covered, but lies too in the comparatively recent advance of our knowledge in many of its regions and literatures. Only within the past year or two have some of the facts it tables been made good. A collection of Egyptian relics and objects was exhibited at University College, London, this summer of 1912, brought back by the British School of Archæology in Egypt from its last winter's work under the direction of Professor Flinders Petrie, which told us of a city older in its foundation than Memphis. This was but 35 miles south of Cairo, which one might think was well within the lines of recorded antiquity, yet there a cemetery was unearthed (now known as Tarkhan—the name of the nearest village), whose burials ranged over five dynasties, from the earliest time to the Pyramid era. Out of one of those tombs came four seals of a king, Narmer-Mena, the fourth of which was the great seal of the Fayum, with the shrine and sacred crocodile, and more crocodiles in rows on the curly waves of a lake; while a reliquary from the same ground was carved in the shape of a beetle, showing that the sacred beetle was then already venerated. At Memphis itself, a new gigantic alabaster sphinx was unearthed, and statues in red granite of Rameses II. and the god Ptah, who, as we read in the following pages, was another type of the " All-Father "—Father of Beginnings, Architect of the Universe.

Comparative mythology has led the way to a new and a larger understanding of the old deities like Ptah, or Tlaloc of the Mexicans, or Pillan of the Araucanian Indians who was the "Supreme Essence" in their belief; and it has taught us that the religious and symbolic forms, here set down in brief, are not dead, but vitally and indestructibly

significant if we read them aright. It is when we relate
the Classical Mythology of Greece and Rome to that of Egypt,
and see behind Zeus the forms of a succession of Eastern
and Celtic divinities, or behind Bacchus the Vedic Soma, that
we begin to grasp the creative idea in man, and learn how
nearly the old myths touch the essence of our humane and
divine philosophy. We see in Krishna the evolution of a
hero into a god, and may compare him if we will with the
Celtic figure of an Arthur who some mythologists say is a
devolved deity.

In preparing this volume its authors have striven to keep
the wider interests of comparative mythology in view; but
that is a science which is growing, which has new evidences
yet to collect from cemeteries like Tarkhan, books like the
" Popol Vuh," and the inscribed stones of Britain, France,
and elsewhere, and the pages must be looked upon as a memoir
or a dictionary to serve now, and to be revised from time
to time hereafter.

CHIEF AUTHORITIES

J. G. FRAZER, The Golden Bough. New Edition, 1912.

A. LANG, Myth, Ritual, and Religion; Custom and Myth.

G. W. COX, Mythology of the Aryan Nations.

P. D. CHANTEPIE DE LA SAUSSAYE, Lehrbuch der Religions-geschichte, 2 vols., 1905.

S. REINACH, Orpheus: A General History of Religions (trans.), 1909.

P. HINNEBERG, Die Kultur der Gegenwart, theil i. abt. iii. (Die Orientalischen Religionen), 1906.

BUEHLER, Grundrisz der Indo-Arischen Philologie, bd. 3, heft i., Vedic Mythology by A. Macdonell, 1897.

A. BARTH, The Religions of India (trans.), 1882 (Trübner Oriental Series).

J. MUIR, Original Sanscrit Texts, 1859.

A BERGAIGNE, La Religion Védique, 1878-83; Les Dieux Souverains de la Religion Védique.

H. OLDENBERG, Die Religion des Veda, 1894; Ancient India: Its Language and Religions (Rel. of Science Library), 1898.

W. J. WILKINS, Hindu Mythology, 1901.

L. D. BARNETT, Hinduism (Religions Ancient and Modern), 1906; The Heart of India (Wisdom of the East), 1908.

J. GARNETT, Classical Dictionary of India, 1871-73.

J. DOWSON, A Classical Dictionary of Hindu Mythology and Religion, etc. (Trübner Oriental Series), 1878.

E. MOOR, Hindu Pantheon, 1864.

M. WINTERNITZ, General Index to the Names, etc., of the Sacred Books of the East, 1910.

L. E. POOR, Sanskrit and its Kindred Literatures, 1881.

MAX MÜLLER, Books of the East; Translation of the Rig Veda; Origin and Growth of Religion, as illustrated by the Religion of India, 1878; Chips from a German Workshop.

H. H. WATSON, Translation of the Rig Veda.

THOMPSON, Bhagavad Gita.

R. V. LANZONI, Dizionario di Mitolgia Egizia, 1881-88.

G. RAWLINSON, Religions of the Ancient World, 1882.

A. WIEDEMANN, Religion of the Ancient Egyptians (trans.),
    1897; Realms of the Egyptian Dead (The Ancient East),
    1901.

G. MASPERO, The Dawn of Civilisation (Christian Knowledge
    Society), 1910; Etudes de Mythologie et d'Archéologie
    Egyptiennes, 1893-98.

E. A. W. BUDGE, The Gods of the Egyptians, 2 vols., 1903;
    and Guides to the Egyptian Rooms in the British Museum;
    Books of Egypt and Chaldea, 28-30 (The Egyptian Heaven
    and Hell, etc.); and Translation of the Book of the
    Dead, 1901.

E. NAVILLE, Das Aegyptische Totenbuch der xviii.-xx. Dyn.,
    1886; The Old Egyptian Faith (trans. C. Campbell),
    1909.

W. M. FLINDERS PETRIE, The Religion of Ancient Egypt
    (Religions Ancient and Modern), 1905.

A. GERMAN, Handbook of Egyptian Religion, 1907.

G. STEINDORFF, Religion of the Ancient Egyptians (American
    Lectures on the History of Religions), 1905.

H. BRUGSCH, Religion ŭ Mythologie der alten Aegypter,
    1884-88; Die Aegyptologie, 1891.

A. H. SAYCE, Religion of Babylon and Assyria; Hibbert
    Lectures.

M. JASTROW, The Religion of Babylonia and Assyria (English
    trans.), 1898.

P. JENSEN, Die Kosmologie der Babylonier, 1890.

T. G. PINCHES, Religion of Babylonia and Assyria (Religions
    Ancient and Modern), 1906.

L. W. KING, Babylonian Religion and Mythology (Books on
    Egypt and Chaldea), 1900.

R. W. ROGERS, Religion of Babylonia and Assyria, 1908.

Guide to the Babylonian and Assyrian Antiquities in the
    British Museum.

H. PAUL, Grundrisz der Germanischen Philologie (Northern
    Mythology, by E. Mogk), vol. iii., 1896.

P. H. MALLET, Northern Antiquities, 1847.

H. A. M. BERGER, Nordische Mythologie, 1834.

E. H. MEYER, Germanische Mythologie, 1891; Mythologie der Germanen, 1903.

W. GOLTHER, Religion und Mythus der Germanen, 1909.

F. KAUFFMANN, Northern Mythology (trans., Temple Primers), 1903.

E. S. BUGGE, Studies in Northern Mythology, 1884; and Home of the Eddic Poems (trans. by Schofield, Grimm Library), 1899.

RYDBERG, Teutonic Mythology (trans. R. B. Anderson), 1889.

GRIMM, Teutonic Mythology.

THORPE, Northern Mythology.

DASENT, Popular Tales from the Norse.

COX AND JONES, Tales from Teutonic Lands.

WAGNER, Asgard and the Gods.

THORPE, Translation of the Edda.

SQUIRE, Mythology of Great Britain and Ireland.

Sir JOHN RHYS, Celtic Heathendom: The Arthurian Legend.

*D'ARBOIS DE JUBAINVILLE, Cours de Litterature Celtique, 1883.

SIR EDWARD ANWYL, Celtic Religion (in Constable's Religions series).

ALFRED NUTT, The Voyage of Bran.

M. LEFLOQ, La Mythologie Gauloise.

H. OLDENBERG, Die Iranischen Religion. *See* Hinneberg.

W. JACKSON, Die Iranische Religion, in W. Geiger and E. Kuhn, Grundrisz der Iranischen Philologie, ii.

V. HENRY, Le Parsisme, 1905.

H. A. GILES, A Glossary of Reference on Subjects connected with the Far East.

A. G. ASTON, Shinto, The Way of the Gods, 1905; Shinto, The Ancient Religion of Japan (Religions Ancient and Modern), 1907.

K. FLORENZ, Die Religionen der Japaner, *see* above, Hinneberg.

B. H. CHAMBERLAIN, Things Japanese, 1905.

E. PAPINOT, Historical and Geographical Dictionary of Japan, 1910.

E. SATOW, The Mythology and Religious Worship of the Ancient Japanese (*Westminster Review*, July 1878); Handbook for Travellers in Japan (Murray), 1881; third revised edition by B. H. Chamberlain and W. B. Mason, 1891. Referred to as " Murray."

LAFCADIO HEARN, Japan, an Attempt at Interpretation, 1904.

F. BRINKLEY, Japan, its History, Arts, and Literature, 1901-2.

D. G. BRINTON, Myths of the New World.

Sir CLEMENTS MARKHAM, Rites and Laws of the Incas.

L. SPENCE, The Mythologies of Mexico and Peru, Lond. 1908; The Popol Vuh, 1909.

Handbook of American Indians North of Mexico.   Bulletin of the United States Bureau of Ethnology, No. 30.

Mexican Antiquities.   Bulletin of the United States Bureau of Ethnology, No. 28.

NON-CLASSICAL MYTHOLOGY

A

God A. In the MS. of the Mayan Indians of Central America this deity is represented as a figure with exposed vertebræ and skull-like countenance, being drawn in the Dresden Codex on several occasions with large black spots on his body, apparently symbolical of corruption. Sometimes he is depicted with swollen abdomen, another sign of mortality. He is decorated with a stiff collar or ruff, perhaps analogous to the collars worn by the dead in the Dresden Codex. Upon his head he wears an ornament bearing some resemblance to a snail, the Aztec symbol of birth, perhaps to illustrate the connection between the cradle and the grave. There are several variations in the pictures of him occurring in the Dresden Codex, whereas in the Codex Tro-cortesianus but one type is presented. He is also distinguished by the bells which he wears on his hands, feet, collar, and panache, and the pair of cross-bones which he wears. His symbol is that for the day, Cimi, "death." His hieroglyph is a representation of a corpse's head with closed eyes, and of a skull, in front of which stands a sacrificial knife of flint. The constant appearance of the god in the codices is proof that he was a figure of great importance in Mayan mythology. That he was practically identical in almost every respect with Mictlan, the Aztec god of death and hell (*q.v.*), admits of no doubt, but whereas the Aztec deity presides over the north, his Mayan prototype presides over the west. Although the north is often regarded by American aboriginal peoples as the home of death and famine, the west, the place of the setting sun, is also regarded as an abode of rest.

The owl is fittingly enough the symbolical bird of the god of gloom, and indeed in some representations of the death-god he is depicted as having an owl's head.

Aah (Ah). An Egyptian moon-god, connected with Thoth, figured at times with the ibis-head, surmounted by the crescent and the disk, which also symbolically represent him.   In other representations he has the figure of a man.

Adad (Ramman).   Babylonian and Assyrian god of storm and thunder, at whose command the rains fell or were withheld. He was introduced into Babylonia by the Amorites, and there became synonymous with Ramman.   Flood, famine, and lightning were the weapons he wielded against his enemies. An Assyrian king, Hammurabi, invokes the wrath of Ramman with the words, " May he overwhelm the land like a flood, may he turn it into heaps and ruins, and may he blast it with a bolt of destruction " (*see* slab in British Museum, Bab. and Ass. Room).

Adad completed the second great triad of gods with Sin and Shamash.   The storm god was associated with the great cosmic event of the flood.   Before it rose to destroy mankind " the whirlwind of Ramman mounted up into the heavens, and all light was turned into darkness " (King, " Bab. Rel. and Myth.," 1899).   To the Assyrians the storm god was also a god of war, and a substantial ally against their enemies.   A temple at Ashur was dedicated to him in conjunction with Ashur, the supreme national deity.   Ramman is identified with the Rimmon of the Old Testament.

Adad had a wife, Shala.   He was also worshipped in Canaan, where he bore the titles Martu (the Amorite) and Kur-Gal (Great Mountain), and he was probably the Ba'al or local god of Mount Lebanon.

Adapa.   A myth preserved in one of the Tel-el-Amarna tablets, which relates how Adapa lost his chance of immortality. He had broken the wings of the South Wind in anger at having his boat capsized, and in consequence the processes of life ceased for lack of the wind's fertilising breath.   Anu, hearing complaints of this, sends for Adapa.   The latter's father, the god Ea, warns him not to accept any food or drink offered him by Anu, as it would be food and drink of death.   However, Anu does not keep his anger for ever, and as he knows Adapa has learnt much divine and secret wisdom from Ea and had now been admitted into heaven, he determines to make him immortal.   So he offers the food and drink of life to Adapa, but Adapa, mindful of his father's counsel, refuses them, and so misses becoming as one of the gods.   Adapa is, perhaps, a Babylonian Adam.

Adar.   *See* Ninib.

Aditi. Hindu goddess. Her name represents the idea of " infinity," of something free from all bounds. She was " that which is born, that which is to be born," " the mighty mother of gods " and one with all the gods. There was about her apparently " a confused and imposing notion of a sort of common womb, a substratum of all existences " (Barth) ; or, as Muir writes of her, " she may best be regarded as a personification of universal, all-embracing Nature or Being." Daksha (*q.v.*) was both her father and offspring ; Vishnu occurs as her husband, and in his dwarf incarnation as her son, his father being Kasyapa. Aditi was the mother of the Adityas. It is related in the Rig-Veda that she had eight sons. Seven she presented to the gods, and the eighth, born imperfect in shape, she cast out. The Adityas altered his shape and produced Vivasvat (the sun); the pieces they cut off and threw away turned into an elephant.

Adityas. In Indian mythology sons of Aditi, gods of the ineffable light beyond the realm of phenomena. " They are the inviolable, imperishable, eternal beings " (*see* quot. from Roth, Muir, v. 56). Their number varies from six to twelve ; it included the two great Vedic gods Varuna and Mitra ; others of this class of abstract deities specified in the Rig-Veda were Aryaman, Bhaga, Daksha, Amsa ; Indra, Savitri, and Surya are also named as Adityas. When the number was enlarged to twelve they were interpreted as personifications of the sun as he appears in different aspects during the succeeding months of the year. The Adityas, with Varuna as their chief, were looked upon as chief upholders of the moral law, and the Vedic hymns contain prayers to them for forgiveness of sins.

Adsullata. A goddess of the continental Celts, who was supposed to preside over the River Savus, in Noricum.

Aegir (Hlér, Gymir). Chief of the Scandinavian sea-giants. Symbolic of the peaceful ocean (Kauffmann). He had friendly relations with the gods, who received him as a guest at one of the feasts in Asgardh, on which occasion Bragi related to him tales of the gods. Aegir in his turn entertained the gods in his gold-illumined hall, and brewed drink for them in the huge cauldron that Thor had carried off from Hymir (*q.v.*). Loki disturbed the peace of one of Aegir's feasts by entering and vilifying the gods, after having been previously turned out for killing one of the servants ; not till Thor arrived and threatened him with his hammer did he finally turn and flee.

Aegir had a wife, Ran (robbery), the goddess of the deep,

who spread her net to catch the seafarers, and drew the drowned, whom she considered her spoil, down to her dwelling beneath the waves, where, from all accounts, she treated them well. Their nine daughters were the storm billows or tempest. The Danish island of Hlesey (Lesso) was supposed to be Aegir's home.

Aeshma. An archdemon of Zoroastrian belief, the Asmodeus of the Book of Tobias. He is the spirit of anger and violence.

Aesir. Generic name given to the gods in Scandinavian mythology; the number of the Aesir, stated at twelve or more, is uncertain. In the Gylfaginning (prose Edda) it is related that the Aesir, led by Odin, invaded Svithjod (Sweden) and the land of Gylfi, and there took up their abode.

Af. The form of the Egyptian sun-god as he made his nightly journey through the underworld.

Agni. One of the chief gods alluded to in the Indo-Aryan Vedas or sacred books. A personification of the three forms of fire—sun, lightning, and sacrificial fire. He was an omniscient and immortal god, ancient yet ever young, daily born afresh on the altar. He was both son and begetter of the gods, and in him were comprehended all the gods. The circumstances of birth, however, are uncertain; he was the son of Heaven and Earth (Dyaus and Prithivi); he was begotten by the sky, the clouds, the dawns; born among men, in heaven, in the celestial waters; and Tvashtri (*q.v.*) is referred to at times as his father. He is also sometimes numbered among the Adityas. Threefold also was his dwelling, in heaven (or ocean), earth, and waters. The gods owed him their splendour, and to him or to Savitri their immortality; his divine spark was latent in all things and could vivify the dead. He was the first to kindle the sacrificial fire,[1] and as himself the sacrificial fire, he passed between the gods and men as mediator. But he had a less priestly character as the " guest of men," and " lord of human clans," as the beneficent god of the household, a giver of good things, a healer, a furious opponent of darkness and evil. His destroying power is uppermost in some legends, but he chiefly appears as a god of light, a being by whom all things exist, a beloved god, with the dawns for his spouses. Agni (or Pushan) conducted the souls of the deceased to the abodes of bliss. With Indra (or Vayu) and Surya, Agni

[1] Other persons and families were also supposed to have first kindled the sacrificial fire, among them Manu. (Muir, v. 209, note.)

formed a triad of deities, lords respectively of wind (or Indra), sun, and fire; Indra or Vayu's element was the air, Surya's the sky, Agni's earth. He was identified with other gods: with Varuna in the evening; in the morning with Mitra; at other times with Savitri and Indra (Muir, v. 219, note). Descriptions of Agni are symbolic of his fire-like attributes. His luminous chariot is harnessed with ruddy horses; he, the charioteer, is golden-haired, with ruddy limbs; he is seven-tongued, and seven-armed, with double face, and armed with bow and arrows. In an early myth of this god he is represented as hiding himself in the waters, the grass, or in a tree, and the gods have to search for him. The epics contain other myths associated with him, the burning down of the Khandava Forest being a leading incident of the Mahābhārata. As one of the eight guardians of the universe he presided over the south-east. Agni presents all the attributes of a sun- and fire- god, and bears a close resemblance to (among other deities of that class) the Celtic Lug, the Greek Apollo, and the Aztec Huehueteotl. As typifying the three kinds of fire, too, we can trace a resemblance to the Hurakan of the Kiches of Guatemala. Like the American fire-gods, too, Agni is described as red in colour. Like other fire-gods—Vulcan and the Mexican Xolotl for example—Agni has a domestic significance. He is the household priest who rises before the dawn and who personifies all the various Hindu sacrificial offices in one. It is he who preserves the communication between gods and men, and he accompanies the gods when they visit the earth. In some respects he may be regarded as the genius of the home, watching over its inmates and registering the events in their lives. Some myths ascribe to him the highest functions, even creative power, but these we may regard as due to the homage paid to the manifold functions of fire. He has also his saturnine side as the devourer and destroyer.

NOTE.—Sacrifice was the chief rite in the worship of the Vedic period. An " embodiment of all mysteries, the symbol of all the most important and profound of the phenomena of life " (Oldenberg, "Ancient India"). Chief of all sacrifices was the " Açvamedha " (horse sacrifice) (see Rig-Veda, i. 162). The preparation for it was long and strict, the horse itself being kept apart for a year beforehand, watched over by a band of 400 youths. According to Lehmann, the idea of this sacrifice was to provide the sun-god with a new horse for his chariot, thereby securing in return a blessing on the kingdom.

Ahriman. The modern Persian form of the name of the evil principle in Zoroastrian theology, given in the Avesta as Anra-Mainyu. He is apparently co-existent with Ahura Mazda from the beginning, but his reign is not eternal as that of the latter. His power has a term (*see* Zoroastrianism). He is the king of evil and unclean spirits, the dævas and drujs, and is surrounded by his archdemons and demons as Mazda with his angelic host. His figure and that of Satan have much in common.

Ahsonnutli. The principal deity of the Navaho Indians of New Mexico. He is regarded by the tribe as the creator of the heavens and earth, and tribal legends state that he placed twelve men at each of the cardinal points to uphold the sky. He is regarded as possessing the attributes of both sexes, and is styled "The Turquoise Hermaphrodite."

Ahura Mazda. The good principle of the Zoroastrian belief, which was based on the dualistic conception of two supreme antagonistic powers (*see* Zoroastrianism). Ahura Mazda is the one eternal being (*see* Cosmology), who is finally to overcome the evil adversary, when this world will pass away and a new one arise. He and Ahriman (*q.v.*), as they appear in the Avesta, had co-existed from the beginning. An idea of later development pre-supposes a primal cause of "endless time" whence they both proceeded. Mazda is father and creator, endowed with all the attributes of the highest divinity, but not entirely omnipotent, for the evil principle remains in power till the 12,000 years of the world's existence are accomplished. He is the source of light, upholder of the universe, the judge of the world, all-wise, all-knowing, and of all time. Of all the gods of the Aryan people, writes Prof. Jackson, he stands nearest to Jehovah. Around his throne are six archangels (Amesha Spentas), representative of abstract qualities and genii of the elements, etc.: Asha-Vahista (righteousness), the genius of fire; Vohu-Manō (good thought), of living beings; Khshathra-Vairiya (loyalty or majesty), of metals; Spenta-Armaiti (modesty and piety), a female genius of earth; Haurvatât (health or integrity), of waters; Ameretât (immortality), of trees and plants. Subordinate to these are angels, of which one was Mithra (*q.v.*) and another Sraosha (*q.v.*).

Airavata. In Indian mythology the name of Indra's elephant.

Aizen Myō-o. Japanese god of love, figured with three eyes and six arms (Murray).

Aka-Kanet. A grain and fruit god of the Araucanian Indians of Chili, who presides over harvest. He is supposed to dwell in the Pleiades, and is worshipped as the guardian of the race.

Alaghom Naom. " Mother of Mind," otherwise called Iztat Ix, a goddess of the Tzental Indians, a Mayan tribe dwelling in Mexico. She was the spouse of Patol, their chief deity, and was credited with the creation of mind and thought, in fact with the higher part of man. This fact rather disposes of the idea that females were regarded by the red race of America as inferior beings.

Albiorix. Often called Rigisamos or " King of the World," a war-god of the continental Celts in France. By the Roman writers, from whom our only knowledge of him is obtained, he is equated with the Roman war-deity Mars.

Alfar. The elves of northern mythology. In the Edda they are represented as of two kinds—light elves, with their dwelling in Alfheim, and dark elves ; but at an early period this distinction seems to have been forgotten, and popular belief knew of them as spirits haunting house and field, water, forest, etc., dexterous and helpful little beings, but occasionally mischievous and harmful, even kidnappers or exchangers of children. So their favour had to be gained, and at certain seasons offerings were made to them, and as they appear to have sometimes sought aid from mortals, any service that could be rendered them was readily accorded. The dwarfs were closely allied to the elves, the name of the famous dwarf, King Alberich (Ælf-Ric = Elf-King), being evidence in itself of this; but dwarfs were not represented as pleasing in appearance, whereas elves were delicate and attractive. The latter dwelt above ground, the dwarfs under earth or within the mountains. Neither class of fancy-born creatures belongs so much to mythology as to heroic legend and folk-lore. It is not unlikely that the conception of a dwarf-folk originally arose from contact with a prehistoric people of inferior physical development, like the Pygmies of Central Africa. The idea is common to nearly all countries, and is too persistent to be merely traditional. Moreover, discoveries of dwarfish remains in many lands substantiate the theory.

Alfheim. Dwelling-place of the northern god Freyr and of the Alfar (*q.v.*).

according to
.y, or to sacrifice.

Allatu, or Ereshkigal. Babylonian goddess of the nether regions (*see* Nergal and Ishtar).

Her realm is described as dark and drear; her minister was the demon of pestilence, and her scribe the " Lady of the Desert."

Alviss (All-wise). A dwarf to whom Thor's daughter was promised in marriage during her father's absence. Thor objected to the union, but allowed Alviss to come from his underground home to fetch his bride. Then he kept the dwarf plied with questions all night, for Alviss was a traveller and versed in knowledge, until the morning dawned, when the dweller in darkness turned stiff and cold as dead stone beneath the first rays of light. Uhland interprets it as a nature myth, Thor's daughter being the corn seed confided to earth, which rises into the light again with the advent of spring, *i.e.*, when Thor comes into the land.

Amaethon. The British Celtic deity of agriculture. He was brother to Govannon, and son of Don. His theft from the Otherworld, the domain of Annwyn, of a white roebuck and a puppy hound precipitated a battle with Arawn, lord of that realm, at Cad Goddeu, or Battle of the Trees, known in the Mabinogi or Welsh traditional books as one of the " Three frivolous battles of Britain." With Govannon he reclaimed the waste territory of Yspaddaden Penkawr, a task which had before appeared beyond the wit of man or deity.

Amaravati. In Indian mythology Indra's celestial city, built by Visvakarma, the architect of the gods. It is an abode of all delights, of gold palaces, gardens of delicious shade, and flowers, nymphs, and music.

Ama-Terasu. Japanese sun-goddess and the ancestress of the imperial house of Japan. She was born from the left eye of Izanagi (*q.v.*). The chief myth concerning her is in connection with her brother Susa-no-o (*q.v.*). The latter having affronted her in the most flagrant manner, the goddess withdrew to a cave, of which she closed up the entrance. Then complete darkness fell upon the world. The myriad host of gods assemble outside and exercise all their powers of allurement to entice her out. It is described how they employ every possible fascination, but nothing was apparently sufficiently tempting to cause Ama-Terasu to leave her hiding-place, until a goddess outside, who is said to have been dressed in a curious

(Amon):
with the dia....
a child. At Thebe...
Amen-Ra, and " Mistr....

costume, began to dance and caused great merriment among the onlookers, which led Ama-Terasu to peep out for curiosity. Soon after she was induced to come forth bodily into the open. The myth, of course, relates to the daily disappearance of the sun. The famous shrine of this goddess is in Ise, and to it thousands make yearly pilgrimage. It is called the Mecca of Japan. Her sacred mirror was at one time always placed under the guardianship of a virgin of the royal household. The sun-goddess has a bird for her messenger.

Ambika. In Indian mythology a name of Uma (*q.v.*), referred to both as sister and wife of Rudra.

Amen (or Amon). A god of ancient Egypt, usually found in conjunction with Ra or Re, and seldom alone. The name signifies " The Hidden One." His cult was practically universal in Egypt, but was almost invariably blended with that of some other deity. Originally he was probably a god of the dead, but later he became patron of Thebes, and chief god of the empire. As Amen-Ra he was worshipped as the supreme " King of the Gods," a creator and soul of the universe, inscrutable and eternal, and the divine father of the Pharaohs. He is usually figured in human form, with two long upright plumes rising above his head, holding a sceptre and the symbol of life. The ram was sacred to him, and in this animal he was believed to be incarnate by his Theban worshippers; the goose was also associated with him. The multiplicity of his divine attributes is symbolised in a figure with the body of a beetle, several wings, arms, and rams' heads, feet of a lion, etc. (*see* Lanzoni). An immense number of temples were erected to him. His oracle was on the oasis of Jupiter Amon, where a sacred stone was held in honour as his symbol. The Greeks identified him with Zeus. Her-Heru, the high priest of Amon, seized the supreme power on the death of Rameses XII., and was the first of the priest-kings of Egypt (twenty-first dynasty). Amen is probably a nature or earth deity, the generative and universal power of whom is exhibited in his many attributes. The fact that he is connected with death points to a subterranean and thus probably an agricultural significance.

Ament. Female counterpart of the Egyptian god Amen. Figured with a sheep's head, or human head crowned ⸱dem of Lower Egypt, and also seated and suckling ⸱es she was equated with Mut, the wife of ⸱ress of the Gods."

Amentet. "The Hidden Land," the Egyptian Otherworld, like most places of the dead situated in the west with the setting sun. On the tomb of Seti I. (*circa* 1366 B.C.) is illustrated the "Book of that which is in the Underworld." It depicts the nightly journey of the sun-god Ra through the Egyptian Hades, which is divided into twelve sections watered by a stygian stream down which the sun-boat drifts towards the eastern horizon. The chief dweller in Amentet is Osiris, in his form of a mummy. With him the dead are identified, and trust, like the sun-god, to pass through Amentet to the blessed paradise beyond (*see* Ba). The conception of life whilst in Amentet is similar to that passed by the dead in the Greek Hades—a nebulous and shadowy existence, wherein folk forget the past and become careless of the future.

Amida (Mida). A chief Buddhist deity of Japan, supposed to dwell in the west, in some far-off paradise. At Kamakura, near Yokohama, stands the famous bronze image of this god, 49 ft. 7 ins. high, known as the Great Buddha. "Originally he was an abstraction, the ideal of boundless light" (Chamberlain). He is generally figured seated cross-legged on a lotus flower. The spot on his forehead is said to be emblematic of wisdom.

Ammit. An Egyptian fiend, known as the "Eater of the Dead." He is figured as a terrifying monster, with the jaws of a crocodile, and a body, part lion, part hippopotamus. Ammit waited for prey near the scales in the judgment hall of Osiris, and those whose heart was weighed and found wanting he devoured.

Amrita (Gr. Ambrosia). The nectar of the Hindu gods and the draught of immortality. By drinking it the gods who had lost their vigour in their struggle with the evil powers, renewed their strength and became immortal [1] (*see* Churning of the Ocean).

Amset. *See* Horus, Children of.

Amsi, Amsu. *See* Min.

Anahita (Anaïtis). A goddess worshipped by the Persians. She is found invoked side by side with Mithra and Ahura Mazda. The Greeks associated her with Cybele. Lehmann states that her name is similar to one of those given to Ishtar (*q.v.*).

[1] Legends differ as to how the gods became immortal; different views they owed it to Agni, to their own austeri

Angiras. A chief Prajapati or Rishi (*q.v.*), the reputed author of some of the Vedic hymns. His poetical works are designated his "daughters." The name is sometimes applied to Agni, as the two names are said to have the same root.

Angirases. A class of beings in Indian mythology who have attained to a heavenly state and worshipped by their descendants are stated to dwell in the third or highest of the three heavens, and to be divided into races, namely, Angirases, Vairupas, Navagvas, Atharvans, Bhrigus, Vasishthas, etc. (Muir, v. 310-311). They are mentioned in immediate connection with Indra. They seem also to have been a family of priests, and the ninth book of the Rig-Veda is attributed to members of it. Mr. Macdonell thinks that they were originally higher beings intermediary between god and men, and that their priestly character was a later development.

Anher (Anhur). An Egyptian sun-god and local god of Abydos. He is represented as a warrior and the Greeks associated him with Ares. Later he formed a dual god with Shu, and was worshipped at Sebennytus, where Hathor was regarded as his mother.

Anit. An Egyptian goddess, equated with Hathor, and the mother of one of the Horus gods. She was the wife of the Theban god Mentu.

Anqet. An Egyptian goddess, the third deity of the elephantine triad, called the Lady of Sati (Island of Sahal), where stood a temple to her honour. She was associated with the fertilising waters of the Nile. She is figured wearing a crown, or head-dress of upright feathers. In one representation (*see* Lanzoni) she is standing suckling a young king. She was, according to this authority, associated by the Greeks with Vesta.

Ansar. *See* under Cosmology, Babylonian.

Antu (Anatu). Wife of the Babylonian god Anu.

Anu. Chief of the Babylonian gods, whose cult is traced back to extreme antiquity. He was head of the great divine triad, composed of this god, Enlil, and Ea, and was the supreme king of heaven, the father of the gods, and the ruler of destiny. His name is found on the earliest known inscriptions, and even when Ashur had become the chief deity of Assyria, he still was given a high place in the Pantheon among the gods worshipped by Assyrians and Babylonians. His throne was said to be at the pole of the ecliptic. Anu's principal temple in the most remote days was at Uruk; another at Ashur was dedicated to him in conjunction with the storm-god Adad, and is recorded to have been embellished by Tiglath-Pileser I. (*see* under Cosmology, Flood, Legend of God Zu).

Anubis or Anpu. An ancient Egyptian god, son of Nephthys and of Osiris, Set, or Ra, with a cult as old, if not older, than that of Osiris. He was a god of the dead, and especially of embalming, and assisted at the embalming of Osiris. He received the body of the dead when placed in the tomb, and with another " opener of the way " led the deceased to the halls of Osiris, where he acted as guardian of the door of the judgment hall, and superintended the weighing of the heart. He is figured with the head of a jackal. His cult, which centred at Asyût, was widely spread in Egypt. The myth concerning him states that he swallowed his father Osiris, and seemingly alludes to the engulfing of the sun by the night.

Anunaki. In Babylonian mythology the spirits of the earth.

Apepi. The Egyptian impersonation of spiritual evil, and Lord of the Powers of Darkness daily warring against Horus, the sun-god. He is depicted as a great serpent, awaiting the sun in the west with his grisly band of Qettu or demons. All night the Sun fought with the monster, whom, as morning approached, he overcame. As enemy of the sun-god Ra, Osiris, or Horus, Apepi was enemy of the great host of the dead who might only win to life again through the ultimate victory of the luminary. Apepi is occasionally equated with Typhon, and later with Set. He is the night-dragon which appears in most mythologies who swallows the sun at evening, but some authorities feasibly compare him to the thunder-cloud which is driven back into its cavern by the golden sword of the sun-god, and the conception may be strengthened by applying to it one of his appellations " The Roarer." (Compare the name of the Central American thunder-deity Tohil, " The Rumbler.")

Apo. The Yazata (*q.v.*), who was regarded by the Persians as the genius of water.

Apocatequil. A deity of the ancient Peruvians, son of Guamansuri. He was the first mortal to descend to earth. Associating with certain dwellers of the dusk called Guachimines, he seduced their sister, for which they slew him. But his offspring by her, born from two eggs, survived although their mother was slain. These were the twin brothers Apocate-

Non-Classical Mythology 13

quil and Piguerao. The former recalled his mother to life, slew
the treacherous Guachimines, and under the guidance of the
god Ataguchu made an aperture in the earth with a golden
spade, through which the race of Peruvians emerged and took
possession of the land. Apocatequil (the name signifies " Chief
of the Followers of the Moon ") was regarded with great veneration by the Incan Peruvians, who also designated him " Prince
of Evil," possibly because of his connection with night. His
image was set up on many high places and mountain-tops in
all parts of the Incan empire. Because of their veneration for
these celestial twins all twins were regarded by the Peruvians
as sacred to the lightning wielded by Apocatequil. As he
represented night so did Piguerao (White Bird) represent day.
The Guachimines in this myth obviously represent the hosts
of night, while their sister may be regarded as the dawn, who
brings forth the white and black twins day and night.

Apochquiahuayan. Another name for Mictlan, the Aztec
hell (*q.v.*).

Apsarasas. These nymph-like beings of Hindu mythology
were associated with Gandharva (*q.v.*), and appear originally to
have been diaphanous atmospheric creatures, forms of mists or
clouds ; later they degenerated into more mundane nymphs,
who added to the delights of Indra's pleasure grounds, as
spouses of the Gandharvas, the god's musicians, and the rewards
of heroes. They even clamoured for mortal husbands, and
their fondness for dice is particularly mentioned. They were
able to change their forms, and various and somewhat contradictory ideas were associated with them. According to
accounts of their origin, they were created in the beginning by
Brahmā, or produced at the churning of the ocean, when as
neither the gods nor the Asuras (devils) would have them to
wife they became common to all. Fourteen classes of them are
enumerated in the Purānas, and they are further divided into
daivika, divine, and *laukika*, mundane. Beautiful and volup-
tuous, these fairy-like beings approximate closely to the nymphs
of Greek mythology.

Apuat. " The Opener of the Ways." A variant of Anubis
(*q.v.*). He guided the dead to the country of Osiris.

The association of the jackal with the guardian and leader
of the dead was owing to that animal haunting cemeteries and
making tracks in the desert. " The jackal paths are the best
guides to practical courses " (Petrie).

Aqas Xenas Xena (Aqas Xenas Xenas). An important myth of the Chinook Indians of North America. It recounts how a boy of that name who had slain his mother mounted to the celestial sphere by means of a chain secured to the end of an arrow. He had not proceeded far through the upper regions when he encountered the Evening Star, who asked him if he had seen his game, and told him that he was hunting men. He reached the abode of the Evening Star, and found his sons and daughters counting over the dead people in their father's game-bag. The daughter of the Evening Star is the Moon. Proceeding on his journey, he comes to the house of the Morning Star, whose daughter is the Sun. The sons of the one star are at war with those of the other. He marries the Moon, and they have children who are united in the middle. He returns to earth with his wife and family, and the children are separated by Blue-jay (*q.v.*). In this day and night myth we have a description of the geography of the celestial regions where men are not supposed to exist, as in the myth of Blue-jay and his sister. Such a conception is common to many American mythologies, which keep the paradise or other dwelling-place of the dead and the regions of the supernatural people strictly apart.

Aralu. The underworld of Babylonian mythology, "the land without return," described as a melancholy abode, devoid of all light, with dust on lock and door, while the dead, "clothed like a bird with wings," have only dust and clay to feed upon. It was ruled over by Nergal (*q.v.*) and the goddess Allatu. The Babylonians had, however, a more cheerful description of the next world in the Gilgamesh Epic (*q.v.*), for in that we hear of those who died in battle lying on couches and drinking pure water. Moreover, they knew of a Land of the Blest, an island somewhere in the sea, where the Noah of Babylonian myth (*see* epic quoted above) and his wife spend their immortal lives. The Babylonians provided food and drink for the dead, and decent burial was supposed to be necessary to prevent the deceased wandering about to pick up broken food or garbage. The idea of the restlessness of the dead who have not been buried according to prescribed rites has survived the long ages, and is found in many modern ghost stories.

Arawn. Lord of the Celtic Otherworld, the land of Annwyn. Little is known concerning him, but he appears in British semi-myth as having given battle to Amaethon at Cad Goddeu. (*See* Amaethon.) A province of his was usurped by a rival,

Havgan, and he sought the aid of Pwyll, Prince of Dyved, who took his shape, ruled his kingdom, and regained his province.

Arianrod. Daughter of Don, a British deity who, by her name, "Silver Wheel," represented the constellation of "Corona Borealis." She was the mother of that Lleu who with Gwydion and Amaethon carried on a strife with the powers of darkness. She had other sons by Lliaws ap Nwyvre, Gwenwynwyn and Gwanar, among them Dylan, the sun-god. Because of her great loveliness she was known as one of the three beauteous women of the isle of Britain.

Aricoute. A deity worshipped by the Tupi tribe of Brazil. He engaged in daily combat with his brother Timondonar, the fair, the god of light. Aricoute, the dark, represents night, and was daily vanquished by his brother the day. The myth is one of world-wide occurrence.

Arthur. In his mythical aspect a king of Britain. In reality there were probably several monarchs or reguli of the same name, and these may have become fused by later tradition into one outstanding figure, round whom a number of traditions clustered. It is again probable that a hero-god of the British Celts may have in later times become humanised into the Arthur of legend. Inscriptions have been found in France to a god of the continental Celts called Artaios, probably a deity of agriculture. Now it is well known that gods of agriculture often become in later times gods of war, and this may have occurred in the case of Artaios or Arthur. There was also a goddess of the continental Celts called Artio, who was probably originally a bear totem. The entire question is shrouded in the mists of time and philology, and its present condition by no means warrants the rather wild speculations which have been recently passed upon it. Like other hero-gods Arthur appears (according to Taliesin, poem xxx.) to have invaded the underworld, and to have braved its terrors, having returned with the magic cauldron of the gods of the Celtic Hades. Many of the knights of the Round Table are traceable to the figures of ancient Celtic deities.

Asgardh. In northern mythology the abode of the gods, where each had his or her separate dwelling. It was surrounded by a wall, the work of a giant builder, and the space between it and earth was spanned by the bridge Bifrost.

Asgaya Gigagei. A thunder-god of the Cherokee Indians. He is described as being of a red colour, and would appear to be of both sexes, as formulæ for the cure of rheumatism allude to him sometimes as "Red Man" and sometimes as "Red Woman."

Ashur (Assur, Asur). The local god of the city of that name (the present mound of Kalat Sherkāt), the metropolis of the first kingdom of Assyria. During the days of its splendour he rose to be the supreme deity of the Assyrian pantheon, the great national god, the people's friend and father, from whom the kings derived their power and by whom they were led to victory. Ashur was above all a god of war, and his symbol—the figure of a god in a horned cap, in the act of shooting an arrow from the bow, enclosed in a circle—was the ensign under which the Assyrians marched to battle. The same symbol is found decorating their palaces and engraved on the royal seals. The name most frequently associated with his is that of the goddess Ishtar.

Askr and Embla. *See* Woden.

Asuras. A name applied in early times to the deities of the Hindu pantheon, and in later days to those gods or demons inimical to good. "As the Suras were gods the A-Suras were not-gods, and therefore the enemies or opponents of the gods." "All the Vedic gods have shared the same title, not excepting even goddesses." (Banerjea, "Bengal Magazine," 1880.) The Vedic gods in general, Varuna, Agni, Mitra, etc., are styled Asuras; but the Asuras are also mentioned in the same category as Daityas, Danavas, Raxasas, as demons whom Indra destroyed. They had strong places in the mountains, in heaven, and under the earth; they could change their forms at pleasure and render themselves invisible. The name is derived from Asu = "breath, life," and according to one myth they were created from Prajapati's breath. Bergaigne considers that the dual use of the name is due to the equivocal character of the supreme gods, who always have a malevolent as well as beneficent side to their character. The following interesting passage from the Satapatha Brāhmana is given from Muir's text (iv. 52). "The gods and Asuras, both descendants of Prajapati, obtained their father Prajapati's inheritance, speech, true and false, both truth and falsehood. Speaking alike, they were alike. Then the gods, abandoning falsehood, adopted truth; where the Asuras abandoning truth, adopted falsehood." Dr. Banerjea has put forward the theory that the term "Asura" is a translation of the Persian Ahura Mazda or Assur, borrowed by the Indo-Aryans before their arrival in India from the Persians who adopted it from the Assyrians. At the present day the term is used only to designate the enemies of the gods with whose sacrifices they are regarded as interfering. Some of them are by no means inferior to the gods in power and reason, and several, for example, Bali Jalandhara and Rāhu, are regarded with deep veneration. In the Asuras we observe the result of a late conception of dualism breaking up a pantheon of deities probably neither "good" nor "evil" into opposing forces labelled with these qualities. Early gods or earlier conceptions of them frequently become opposed to later deities or their more advanced conceptions as "evil" deities. The Irish Fomorians (*q.v.*) are a good example of this mythological process.

Asvins. Twin Vedic deities, sons of Dyaus, or of Surya (Savitri, Sun). The interpretation of these gods has been a puzzle to the commentators, the older of whom spoke of them as Heaven and Earth, Day and Night, or Sun and Moon, and one has described them as pervading the earth with moisture and light. Modern scholars have identified them with the morning star, or with the constellation Gemini, and it seems generally thought that they are associated with dawn or morning twilight. They were wise and beneficent gods, possessed of mysterious power to deliver from material and spiritual evil, and were known as the divine physicians. Myths relate miraculous cures achieved by them, and of youth restored to age. The twins were known in later mythology as Nasatya and Dasra, having by this time lost their position as cosmic deities. Goldstücker thinks that they were originally renowned mortals, and that the cosmical and the human and historical elements in their myth have become blended, the link connecting them being the mysteriousness which in a remote antiquity was associated both with the nature and effects of light—for their luminous character as gods is beyond question—and of the healing art.

The Asvins drove in a three-wheeled chariot sometimes drawn by birds; they are also described as traversing the celestial waters in a boat, for they dwelt in all parts of the universe. They were born of the Sun and his wife after these two had assumed their equine form (*see* Saranyu). A drink called "Mádhu" (honey) is associated from early times with their cult (" Sacred Books of the East," 42, p. 58). The connection of the Asvins with the Greek Dioscuri " is possible but very uncertain " (Barnett, " Heart of India ").

Atago. A Shinto god of Japan, believed to have power against the destructive force of fire.

Ataguchu. The creative deity of the Peruvians.

Atar. A chief of the Yazatas (*q.v.*), worshipped by the Persians as the genius of fire, a powerful ally against all evil powers. With the Persians fire was an object of almost supreme reverence, and was secondary to their conception of the highest deity alone.

The ninth month and the ninth day of the month were named after him.

Atatarho. A mythical monarch of the Iroquois Indians. He robed himself in a garment of black snakes, symbolical of his prowess in war and magic, the snake or serpent being the symbol of the lightning or divine spear or arrow in many American tribes, as well as " great physic " in time of war. When he wished to don a new robe he simply dismissed the snakes he wore, and summoned another set in their places.

Aten. The solar disk, the cult of which was introduced by Amenhotep IV. (King of Egypt, *circa* 1383-1365 B.C.) in opposition to the worship of Amen. He erected temples to the new god at Memphis and Thebes, and changed his own name to that of Khu-en-aten, " the splendour of the solar disk." Finally he left Thebes because of the opposition of the Theban priesthood and retired to a spot now known as Tel-el-Amarna, and there set up a temple to this one god, who is always symbolised by the solar disk whence rays fall, each ending in a hand. No image was permitted to be raised to this deity, in whom, and from whom, were all things, and who in the beautiful hymns addressed to him appears as a creator and lord of love, a friend and comforter to the afflicted, and a source of delight. He is further symbolised by the ankh, the emblem of life. The god Aten fell with the royal family that supported him, and his worship was never revived. According to some authorities Khu-en-aten was a genuine reformer who endeavoured to introduce a monotheistic form of worship; others see in the new cult merely a more developed form of the worship of the sun-god at Heliopolis, set up in opposition to the priests rather than to the god of Thebes, and for political rather than for religious purposes. (*See* A. G. P. Weigall, " The Life and Times of Akhnaton, Pharaoh of Egypt," 1910, and G. Naville, " The Old Egyptian Faith," trans. C. Campbell, 1909.)

Atharvan. A Rishi, the eldest son of Brahmā (*q.v.*), to whom the latter revealed the knowledge of god. He was said to be the first to open the ways by sacrifice, thereby causing the sun to appear ; in this priestly character he is identical with Agni. He is represented as the inspired author of the fourth Veda, and he and Angiras are closely associated.

Atharvans. *See* Angirases.

Atius Tirawa. The chief deity of the Pawnees. He is associated by the Indians with the creation, and is supposed by them to have ordered the heavenly bodies in their original courses. He dwells in the heavens, and is described as omnipotent and intangible. How far this conception of him has been sophisticated by Christian influence it would be difficult to say, but there is reason to believe that the original Indian conception of Atius Tirawa has been coloured by contact with the whites.

Avatâra. *See* Brahmā and Vishnu.

Avesta. The sacred writings of the Persians, also known as Zend-Avesta, *i.e.* the Avesta with Pahlavi translation and interpretation.

The original sacred writings embodying Zoroastrian doctrine were, from all accounts, very extensive ; the first copy of them is said to have been written in letters of gold and sacredly guarded. It is reported that Alexander destroyed the whole, or most of these, but under the Sassanian dynasty a collection was made of all that still existed of the sacred texts, preserved either verbally or in writing ; again they suffered more or less destruction under the Mahometans, and it is only copies of what was saved from this wreck that have come down to us. The Avesta proper consists of the Vendidad, Visparad, and Yasna ; the remaining books compose the Khorda Avesta, or small Avesta, and consist of the Yashts, or Yeshts, *i.e.* hymns, and short prayers. The second division of the Yasna, known as the Gāthās, is the most ancient ; it differs in style and language from the remainder of the Avesta, and like all the oldest parts of the sacred text is metrical. It is thought that the Gāthās may be more directly the work of Zarathustra himself. The doctrine in them includes none of the nature worship distinguished in later writings, and they know nothing of the god

Mithra, of the Haoma, or the Fravashis, and of other figures introduced afterwards into the Persian Pantheon. The Visparad and Yasna are more distinctly liturgical in character than the Vendidad; they contain invocations of nature, of duties connected with times and seasons, and speculative ideas concerning creation. The Vendidad is more concerned with matters of social and daily life. It is in twenty-two fargards or sections. It starts with an account of the creation by Ahura Mazda of sixteen countries, excellent and perfect of their kind, and of the antagonistic creation by the evil spirit of all the ills and terrors that spoil the beauty and peace of these regions. Then follows the tale of Yima (*q.v.*); then the enumeration of the five most agreeable, five most disagreeable, and five most satisfying things; fargard four is a kind of criminal code, then several fargards follow with injunctions as regards impurities caused by dead bodies; two fargards treat of the different kind of dogs, good and bad, the proper treatment of dogs and penalties for injuring them. Other offences are then dealt with, followed by further regulations concerning matters of defilement; details of certain ceremonies are succeeded by the relation of the evil spirit's attempt to destroy Zarathustra, who not succeeding in this, proceeds equally without success to tempt the latter, and the prophet then questions the supreme being concerning souls after death. There ensues a notice of the first man who knew how to heal diseases; the phenomena of the sky is described, with invocations to the heavenly bodies and clouds. Ahriman having produced 99,999 diseases, Ahura Mazda is concerned to find remedies, and finally sends a messenger to Airyama, the Yazata, who presides over the healing art, with command to create useful animals, and consequently nine kinds each of horses, camels, oxen, and small cattle are produced. So the Vendidad ends. The form of the fargards is mostly that of a dialogue, a form which also occurs in other parts of the Avesta.

Awonawilona. The creative deity of the Zuñi of New Mexico (*see* Cosmology, Zuñi).

Azhi-Dahaka. The arch-serpent of Persian mythology (*see* Zoroastrianism).

B

God B. This god appears more often in the Mayan Indian pinturas than any other of the Mayan deities. He has a long truncated nose, almost like that of a tapir, and a peculiar head-ornament. The numerous aspects in which this deity is represented prove him to be a being who has almost undisputed power over the elements. Thus we find him brandishing fiery torches, walking the waters, paddling in a canoe, and sitting on the cruciform tree which symbolises the four cardinal points. Other circumstances in which he is found denote beyond all doubt that he is a culture-god or hero, for we behold him planting maize, carrying weapons and tools, and equipped for a journey. In short there can be no doubt that God B is no other than Kukulcan, who is identical in almost every respect with the Nahua deity Quetzalcoatl (*q.v.*). He is connected with the colours of the four cardinal points (yellow, air; red, fire; white, water; black, earth), which are subject to him, and his name is a literal translation of that of Quetzalcoatl (feathered serpent).

Ba (the Soul). Man, according to Egyptian belief, was a being composed of many parts. He possessed a corruptible and a spiritual body; a heart, the centre of will and feelings (Ab); a soul (Ba) which was capable of a second death ; a spirit, or " intelligence," something " shining, impalpable, and immortal " (Khu) ; a shadow (Khaibit) ; a double (Ka) (*q.v.*) ; and Sekhem, interpreted as " vital power." He had also a name, which was not the least vital part of his composition.[1] The elaborate funerary rites of the Egyptians were for the preservation of the body,[2] the Ba, and the Ka, to ensure which the living were

---

[1] The Egyptians set a superstitious value on a name. Nothing could exist without one, and the obliteration of a name meant annihilation for its owner.   The conferring of a name could give life to an inanimate object. To know the secret name of a god was to become his equal (*see* the tale of Isis and Ra).

[2] The careful mummifying of the body became customary only in the third and fourth dynasties (Petrie).   An elaborate ritual developed with the custom, with especial chapters for the opening of the mouth and eyes, the moving of the legs, etc., in order to secure the perfect reconstitution of the body.

constantly engaged in exhausting duties on behalf of the dead. The destiny of the soul varied according to different systems of theology or local belief. The primitive idea that it haunted the places of burial was co-existent with a belief in its after life in one of the distant realms of the dead. The association of the dead with the stars belongs to very ancient times. Later theology imagined the soul travelling after death to the kingdom of Seker (q.v.) or of Osiris, or the more spiritual destiny was assigned to it of remaining in company with the god Ra in his daily and nightly progress across the heavens and through the underworld. In all cases the soul needed assistance after leaving the body. There were different beliefs as regards its passage to the after world. According to one the soul shortly after starting on its terror-fraught journey came across one of the sycamore-trees with its presiding goddess (Hathor, Nut, or Neith), who refreshed it with cakes and water; then it continued on its way over a desert land peopled with wild beasts and serpents, and diversified with marshes and boiling torrents; it arrived at last, if it survived these horrors, on the borders of a lake, and now could see the blessed isles beyond, whither it was borne by the ferryman, or on the wings of the Ibis-god, Thoth. The account of the journey as given in the Books of the Dead associates the soul with the god Ra. Now the soul had to make its way to the west, to a spot near Abydos, where it reached the first division of the Tuat, and here waited in hopes of obtaining a place in Ra's " boat of a million of years." Having once started in this, it thereafter shared the fate of the god, and was menaced by the same enemies; but armed, as was Ra himself, with names and magic formulæ, it arrived in safety at the realm of Osiris. The living knew about the difficulties that the soul had to encounter, and in order to give it every chance of success, the text or part of the text of the Book of the Dead was inscribed on the walls of the sepulchral chamber, or on the inner side of the sarcophagus, or a copy on a papyrus roll was placed in the coffin. This served as a guide through the dark region, for the deceased must know the name of every god and demon and of every division of a gate that he encountered on his way through the Tuat, and further knowledge was required of certain words of power and magic texts, which had moreover to be pronounced in a particular way. Any ignorance on these matters was fatal and debarred his progress. Arrived at the realm of Osiris, the deceased had first to pass through the hall of the Maati goddesses (see Maat), which was guarded by Anubis, and there make his "negative confession" to the forty-two judges assembled. Having shown that he knew the names of the two sides of the intervening door and that of the presiding deity, he was allowed to enter the second hall, and now came the moment when his fate was actually in the balance, for here were the scales in which his heart was weighed. Anubis superintended this ceremony, and the reading of the pointer was communicated by an ape to the god Thoth, and all being well the deceased was then led by Horus into the presence of Osiris and his future happiness was assured. Should the heart have failed to balance Maat's feather, the deceased became the prey of Ammit, "the Eater of the Dead."

The more especial worshippers of Ra looked forward to a different future after death. The mundane delights of the fields of Osiris were no attraction to them, for their idea of spiritual bliss was to remain with Ra, rising afresh with him each morning as he emerged from the Tuat.

The soul is figured as a bird with a human face. It was believed to be able to take what form it chose, and to come and go as it liked. The Ba required to be fed, and like the Ka was thought liable to perish if proper food was not provided for it; the sycamore goddesses gave it food and drink as is stated above.

Bacabs. The Maya Indians of Yucatan supposed the firmament to be upheld by four beings whom they designated Bacabs, each of whom stood at one corner of the earth. The names of these were Kan, Muluc, Ix, and Cauac, representing the east, north, west, and south. Their symbolic colours were yellow, white, black, and red. They corresponded in some degree to the four variants of the Mexican rain-god Tlaloc (*q.v.*), for the races of Central America supposed that rain, the fertiliser of the soil, emanated from the four points of the compass, and may find a parallel in the Egyptian canopic deities. (*See* Horus, Children of.)

Bakha (Gr. Bacis). The sacred bull of Hermonthis, supposed to be an incarnation of Menthu (*q.v.*).

Bala-Rama. Brother of Krishna. The two boys were brought up together by the herdsman Nanda (*see* Krishna), and shared several youthful adventures. Among Bala-Rama's individual exploits was the frequent slaughter of an Asura, the demon assuming sometimes the form of an ass, sometimes that of an ape. On another occasion he forced the River Jamuna to leave its bed and follow him. Bala-Rama was fair-complexioned, as Krishna was dark ; legend relates that Vishnu plucked out two of his own hairs, one white and one black, which became severally these two gods. Bala-Rama was also the incarnation of the serpent Sesha, which issued from his mouth as he died, only a few minutes before his brother. At times he takes Krishna's place as the eighth avatara of Vishnu. His myth exhibits a resemblance to those which recount the adventures of celestial twins, one dark, the other fair, representing day and night.

Balder. Son of Odhin and Frigg, a god of light, beautiful as the shining white flower Baldrsbrá (Balder's Brae), who had his fair and pure abode in Breidhablik. He was a god of Denmark, Norway, and Iceland ; how far his cult spread beyond the northern regions is uncertain. In the Eddic poems his death is the prelude to the final overthrow of the gods. The two chief versions of his legend differ in facts and tone. The prose Edda gives the god's myth as follows: The gods take counsel how to ward off evil from Balder, who has had an ominous dream. Then Frigg lays all things, animate and inanimate, under oath not to harm him, only a shoot of mistletoe is passed over as being too young. The gods amuse themselves with shooting and throwing at Balder, who is now invulnerable. Loki, with malicious intent, finds out from Frigg about the mistletoe shoot, and immediately fetches it and puts it into the hand of Balder's blind brother Hodhr, who flings it, and the beautiful young god is slain. It was " the greatest sorrow that ever befell gods and men." The gods stand speechless with anguish, then they weep. Frigg asks who will go to Hel to ransom Balder, and Odhin's son Hermodhr rides off on the god's horse. But Hel refuses to give Balder up unless all things living and dead will weep for him. Loki, in the form of a giantess, exclaims, " Let Hel keep what she has," so Balder does not return. Balder's body is placed on a ship, which is pushed into the sea by the giantess Hyrrokin ; the funeral pyre is lighted, Nanna's body being burnt with that of her husband, for her heart had broken with anguish. The chief gods and Frigg, Valkyries and giants were present, and as a last gift to his son Odhin placed his magic ring Draupnir on the pyre, and whispered a mysterious word in the dead god's ear (*see* Vafthrudnismál, under Eddas). The tale as told by Saxo Grammaticus is divergent in many points. Here Balder is only a half-god, and he fights with his rival Hodhr for Nanna, who had set her affections on the latter. There is hard fighting ; the gods take part with Balder, but

Hodhr causes them to flee, for he has gained possession of the irresistible Miming sword, and is further protected by an impenetrable coat of mail. In another encounter Balder is victor, and fighting continues, Balder being daily renewed by a food prepared by three wise women, whom Hodhr visits in order to obtain some for himself, but they give him instead a magic belt of power. Returning that night he meets his enemy and thrusts him through, and next day Balder is with the dead. In both versions, Bous or Both, Ali or Vali, Balder's brother, avenges his death. In this form the tale is more closely related to the old pagan story, which was a hero saga, changed later into a god saga, and in the prose Eddic legend mingled with incidents of Christian origin. Mistelteinn was originally the name of Hodhr's magic sword, afterwards literally interpreted as the mistletoe (Kauffmann). Elsewhere, however, it is pointed out that as the mistletoe is not known in Iceland, it must have been an essential of the old tale, preserved by Icelandic writers. The story of the fatal mistletoe is Celtic or British, so Reinach states, as it is hardly known, if at all, in Norway. According to Mogk, Balder was a sun-god, somewhat similarly developed from Tiwaz as Apollo from Zeus. The whole myth has been interpreted as a solar or year myth. Kauffmann traces Christian influences in the Eddic version of the legend, and others (Bugge, Meyer, Golther) see in it the incidents of Christ's death transferred to Balder. Fraser (" Golden Bough ") explains the myth to be of ritual origin. Its two main features—the pulling of the mistletoe and the burning of the god—were, he says, reproduced in the old fire-festivals held at Easter and midsummer, in various places, as rites to make the sun shine and the crops grow. The mid-summer fires were formerly known in Sweden as Balder's bale-fires. The same authority thinks the Balder myth may be a relic of tree-worship. The circumstances of Balder's body being placed on a ship and pushed into the sea would seem to point to the myth being classified as a solar one like that of Osiris or Ra.

Balor. One of the gods of the Irish Celts of the Fomorian cult. He is perhaps a personification of the evil eye, as his glance withered the person or thing upon which it fell. His eyelid required four men to raise it.

Bast. An Egyptian goddess, " Lady of the East," sister goddess to Sekhet. The centre of her worship was at Bubastis, where, as we learn from Herodotus, an annual festival was held in her honour, on which occasion more wine was drunk than during the whole of the remaining year. She was representative of the kindlier solar heat that gives and supports life. Bast is figured with the head of a cat; she holds in one hand a sistrum, in the other a shield, and a basket hangs on one arm. She was identified with other goddesses. Her mate was Herhekennu, a variant of Horus. She is probably represented as a cat because of the penchant of that animal for basking in the solar rays.

Bau. The wife of Ninib (*q.v.*), and as such the counterpart of Gula (*q.v.*). This ancient Babylonian goddess was the daughter of Anu, and is thought to have personified some power of nature. She is found addressed by one as the " daughter of pure heaven," giving counsel and granting life, who adds, " I will seek refuge from my anxiety in thy shadow, under my mother's care" (Rogers, "Rel. Bab. and Ass.," 1908).

Inscriptions show that bridal gifts were made her at the New Year's feast (*see* Marduk).

Bêl. An appellative originally used by the Babylonians for " lord " or " master," and subsequently applied as a title to their chief gods, and one or two of these, as En-lil and Marduk, are sometimes referred to simply as Bêl. The last named of these gods was the Bêl of the Old Testament.

Bêlet. An appellative signifying " mistress," and used by the Babylonians as a designation for the chief goddess.

Beli. British Celtic god of the Otherworld or abode of the dead. The myth concerning him recounts that Ith, Beli, and Mile, his son, descried Ireland from a far watch-tower in Phœnicia which overlooked the whole earth, and decided to visit it. This lends some colour to the hypothesis that this deity was of Phœnician origin. It is certain that the Phœnicians visited Britain and that their influence was considerable in Ireland, and the fact that Beli is found in company with a god who possesses the Semitic appellation of Ith would seem to strengthen the theory. But its strongest prop, the likeness of the name Beli to that of the Palestinian god Bel or Baal, is too obviously fortuitous. Beli is undoubtedly the deity connected with the festival of Beltane or Bel's fire in Scotland.

Belisama, or " The most warlike goddess," was the tutelar deity of the River Ribble among the British Celts. Some authorities connect her with the Mersey.

Bennu. A sacred bird of the Egyptians which, according to the old legend, rose singing from the flames of a tree at Heliopolis. As an emblem of the resurrection it was sacred to Osiris, the soul of the dead being sometimes compared to it. The Phœnix legend is apparently a development of this of the Bennu.

Benten. *See* Luck, Gods of.

Berecyntia. A goddess of the continental Celts. She was a patroness of agriculture, especially of the vine. There is reason to believe that she was one and the same as the goddess Brigit of the Irish Celts (*q.v.*).

Bes. An ancient god of the Egyptians, whose cult was introduced from the hand of Punt. He had apparently a twofold character, for he was associated on the one hand with the lighter pleasures of dance and music, and was looked upon as a friend of children, and in some way helpful to women in childbirth. Objects in use in daily life are found adorned with his figure. But he had a fiercer aspect as an avenging deity, when he is seen armed with warlike implements. He was associated with the solar deities and became identified with certain forms of Horus, Sopt, and Harpocrates, and even with Set. Bes is figured with a dwarfish body, huge head and short legs, flat nose and protruding tongue (*see* Egyptian Gallery, British Museum). The hawk is associated with him as a solar deity. In a representation of him in the Metternich stele he is accompanied by every symbol of dignity and power. The British Museum has a bronze which shows him carrying the child Horus. The association of the old and young god in another figure of the above-mentioned stele is interpreted as signifying the varying phases of the sun. He is also depicted as a war-god. It has been advanced with some show of reason that he typified the grosser side of humanity, the "natural man."

Bhairava. There were eight Bhairavas, all manifestations of the more hideous characteristics of the Indian god Siva.

Bhrigu. One of the Rishis (*q.v.*).

Bhrigus, the "calm-souled." *See* Angirases.

Bimbo-Gami. A Japanese god of poverty ; a deity of later development (Aston).

Binzuru. A Japanese god of healing (Murray).

Bishamon (Tamonten). *See* Luck, Gods of.

Blue-Jay. An important zoomorphic or animal-like deity of
the Chinooks of Colombia River, who figures in nearly every
myth of Chinook origin. His character is that of a mischief-
maker, braggart, and schemer, not unlike that of Loki in the
mythology of Scandinavia. He was originally turned into a
blue-jay bird by the " supernatural people " because he lost
to them in an archery contest, and they placed a ban upon him,
telling him that the note he used as a bird would be a bad omen.
There is a trilogy of myths concerning Blue-jay and his sister
Ioi, which recounts their adventures among the Supernatural
People. It is indeed a myth typical of the " harrying of Hell,"
such as we meet with in the Kiche Popol Vuh (q.v.). Blue-jay
has an elder brother the Robin, whose duty appears to be to
point the moral to his relative's adventures. The trilogy recounts how Ioi, Blue-jay's sister, begs him to take a wife to
share her labour. He takes the corpse of a chief's daughter
from her grave, and carries her to the land of the Supernatural
People, who restore her to life. The chief her father finds this
out, and demands Blue-jay's hair as a recompense, but Blue-jay
changes himself into his bird-shape and flies away. His wife
dies again. The dead in the Land of the Supernatural Folk then
purchase Ioi his sister for a wife, and he sets off in search of
her. He finds her surrounded by heaps of bones, to whom she
alludes as her relations by marriage. The ghosts resume their
human shape, but on being addressed by Blue-jay become heaps
of bones once more, and he takes a mischievous delight in
reducing them to this condition and in mixing up the various
heaps of bones, so that the ghosts do not know their own heads,
legs, and arms when they materialise again. Such myths were
probably invented for the purpose of reassuring the savage
regarding the terrors of the next world, and to instruct him in
the methods and manners of its inhabitants. The hero who
overcomes supernatural terrors always possesses a high place in
the esteem of savages and children.

Bochica. A deity of the Muyscas of Bogota, symbolical of
the dawn. He is, like most dawn-gods, also a culture-god, and
was said to have instructed the Muyscas in the arts of building,
agriculture, and rudimentary science, as well as introducing
among them the use of the calendar. He also instituted a
legal code, and upon his disappearance from the earthly sphere
he deputed the surveillance of the people to four chiefs, who
scrupulously obeyed his injunctions. This myth bears a strong

resemblance to that of the Peruvian hero-god Viracocha, to which it is probably a parallel.

Books of the Dead. A collection of texts belonging to different periods and dealing with the life after death according to Egyptian belief. No two copies are exactly alike, as alterations of various kinds took place in the course of time, and many represent those portions of text which were chosen by survivors to inscribe on the walls of the chamber of the dead, on the tombs, or on the papyrus rolls which at a later period were buried with the corpse. The body of matter that exists contains endless instructions concerning all that it was necessary for the deceased to know in the way of charms, magic formulæ, etc., to enable him to travel in safety through the perilous regions of the Tuat (*q.v.*). The Egyptian name for Book of the Dead is Per-em-hru, which has been translated " Coming, or going forth, by Day." The texts are classified into four periods, beginning with those of the Pyramid age. The two chief versions belong to the Theban texts, namely, Am Tuat (of that which is in the underworld) and another known as the Book of Gates. They represent divergent theological views, Ra in one, and Osiris in the other, being the god to whom prominence is given. (*See* Naville for details of texts.) The British Museum has published a facsimile of the Papyrus of Ani. Many copies have been found, chiefly in mummy wrappings. The chapters are totally independent of each other, and of various dates. The longest known copy is in a Turin papyrus, which contains 165 chapters. "The beatification of the dead is the main subject of every chapter."

Borvo. A deity of the continental Celts, the tutelar god of hot springs. The Roman authors identified him with their Apollo. It is alleged that the name of the Bourbon dynasty originated in his.

Bragi. Son of Odhin, a hero and chief of the Scalds, god of eloquence and poetry. His mother was seemingly Gunnlodh (*see* under Odhroerir). Bragi is a god of later creation. He is described as aged, with flowing beard, armed and mounted. As wife he had Idhunn, the goddess of eternal youth. It is he who greets the slain heroes as they enter Valhalla, and he who objects to Loki's presence at Aegir's feast (*see* Loki). Poetry was called Bragr after him; he did not however supplant Odhin, who was the original source of poetic inspiration, the archetype of the Scald.

Bragi Boddason, who stands at the head of the long list of Norwegian and Icelandic Scalds, flourished in the ninth century, and between him and the god there seems to be a connection, but it is a question whether he was named after the god, whether the name was used independently to signify high proficiency in poetic faculty, or whether this historic Scald was raised to the rank of the Aesir (*see* Golther).

Brahmā. First god of the Hindu triad, the creator, as Vishnu was the preserver and Siva the destroyer (or regenerator). Also known as Pitamaha (Great Father), Sahampati, Svayambhu, Hiranyagarbha (or Prajapati), and Visvakarman. Brahmā's origin is associated with the legends of the Creation (*see* Cosmology). He was born from the golden mundane egg which floated on the waters at the beginning, and called Nārāyana (Nara=waters); or as Hiranyagarbha, the primeval germ itself, he sprang into being before all living creatures; in the Ramayana, after stating that Brahmā in the form of a boar lifted the earth from out the waters, the text adds, " Brahmā, eternal and perpetually undecaying, sprang from the ether "; epic myth also describes him as springing from the lotus that rose from Vishnu's navel. The avataras or conditions of boar, fish (connected with the flood), and tortoise are ascribed both to Brahmā and Vishnu. Brahmā was the father of Daksha (*q.v.*) and of other " mind-born sons " (*see* Rishi, Prajapati). He is represented as of a red colour, and with four arms and four heads; a fifth head was destroyed by Siva who was angered by Brahmā's presumption. He holds a drinking-vessel, a bow, a string of beads, a sceptre or spoon, and the Veda. He rides on a goose or a swan. Brahmā is the active manifestation of the first cause, the absolute, incorporeal, and infinite soul of the universe. " This triad (Brahmā, Vishnu, Siva)," writes Barth, " differing from the earlier one (Agni, Vayu, Surya), was not a cosmographic distribution of the deified forces of nature, but a threefold evolution of the divine unity. The Brahman, the absolute, manifests himself in three persons." There is not much information about these three gods in the Vedas, and it is considered doubtful whether in the ancient days represented by these writings there was any worship accorded them (*see* Wilson). Brahmā is not in modern times such a prominent god as Vishnu and Siva.

Brahmā's life consists of a hundred of his own years, and his year consists of days each of which (known as a kalpa) is equal to 4,320,000,000 of our years, followed by a night of equal duration. At the close of each kalpa the universe is destroyed to be re-created after Brahmā has rested through his prolonged night (*see* Kalpa and Yuga).

Brahmanaspati, or Brihaspati. A Vedic god, the Lord of Prayer, heavenly prototype of the earthly Brāhman. In certain texts he is identical with Agni, or with Soma, all three being associated with the rite of sacrifice. " The creation of this divinity is the most striking witness to the belief in the peculiar and, in some way, intrinsic efficacy of prayer " (Bergaigne). Roth (*see* Muir, v. 272) points out that the older divinities of the Veda are personifications of various departments of nature or of physical forces, but this god is the product of moral ideas and an impersonation of the power of devotion. He adds in a note, " All the gods whose names are compounded with *pati* (lord of) must be reckoned among the more recent . . . they were the products of reflection."

In later myth Brihaspati appears only as a divine sage. In the Mahābhārata he is the progenitor of the family of Agnis.

Bran. Son of Llyr and a lord of the Welsh Celtic under-world. He presided over poetry and bardic music, and was usually represented as being of gigantic height. On the sons of Don (*q.v.*) attempting to purloin the treasures of his realm he stoutly guarded them. In later mediæval legend he was metamorphosed into " Bran the Blessed " who first brought the cross to the isle of Britain from Rome, where he had dwelt for seven years as a hostage for his son Caradoc. An ancient British triad states that his head was buried under the White Tower of London, the eyes looking towards France, as a spell against foreign aggression, but Arthur, says tradition, disdaining to hold his realm by magic art, unearthed it, stating that Britain must remain a power by virtue of her own strength.

Bres. Son of Elatha and brother of Ogma, king of the Tuatha de Danaan (*q.v.*). His wife was Brig, or Brigit, the Celtic goddess of knowledge. He is also alluded to as a king of the Fomorians.

Brian, Iuchair, and Iucharbar. " The three sons of Danaan " in Irish myth. They were probably gods of knowledge or of the subtleties of bardic science, but their real significance is not known.

Brigit. A goddess of the Irish Celts and patroness of know-ledge. She presided over poetry, and was said to have had two sisters of the same name who were goddesses of smith-work and medicine. Brigit is a culture-goddess, and in some ways approximates to the Greek Athene. Inscriptions bearing her name in varying forms are found all over Britain, and as the goddess Brigantia she may have been tutelar of the tribe of Brigantes. On the assumption of Christianity by the Irish Celts she was metamorphosed into Saint Brigit, whose sacred shrine at Kildare no man was permitted to enter, and whose fire was guarded by nineteen nuns. Some authorities see in this aspect of the goddess signs that she was a deity of fire, or of the domestic hearth. In the Western Isles Brigit is regarded as a being who gives prophecies concerning the harvest, and this may go to prove that she was a goddess of fertility, as, curiously enough, a number of virgin goddesses were. That she was so, and that she was worshipped exclusively by women, is almost proved by the circumstance that her shrine at Kildare was guarded by a fence which no male dare break through.

Brisingamen. The resplendent necklace of the goddess Freyja. When the goddess was roused to great fury it broke asunder. According to later myth the goddess cast envious eyes upon the necklace, and only by surrendering herself in turns to each of the four dwarfs who had fashioned it did she obtain possession of the coveted treasure. At Odhin's command Loki contrived to steal it, and it was only given back to Freyja on condition that she stirred up irreconcilable enmity between two equally powerful kings. After the theft of the ornament by Loki, Heimdallr fought daily with the latter for its recovery. Brisingamen has been interpreted as the rainbow (Meyer), as the morning and evening red, daily overcome by darkness and daily renewed (Uhland and others).

Buddha. "The Enlightened." The last, the historic Buddha, one of many Buddhas who are believed to appear from time to time for the regeneration of the world, was born about 560 B.C. near the ancient town of Kapilavastu (a kingdom of Nepal, north of the present state of Oude), and according to tradition in the grove of a certain goddess, a tradition which is thought to be verified by the discovery of a pillar set up on the supposed spot by the Emperor Asoka. His family name was Gautama, and he was known as Prince Siddartha in his youth, being the son of Saddhodana, chief of one of the Sakya tribes. His mother was Mahāmāyā, to whom the birth of her son was foretold in a dream, in which he appeared in the form of an elephant, hence the sacredness of this animal in the eyes of the Buddhist. Signs and wonders gave notice of the approaching advent of the Buddha, and he himself showed marks upon his person when born which indicated his high destiny. He was surrounded in his youth by the luxuries of a rich home, but he had been manifested for a holy purpose, in which he was confirmed by four sights which were brought before him in spite of his father's precautions. These were an aged and a diseased man, a corpse, and a monk. Buddha is said to have made the great renunciation, and to have left home, wife, and child, when he was twenty-nine. For six years he led a life of austere privation, but finding that physical mortifications did not bring him the desired light, he gave himself up to meditation. From one long night vigil under the Bo tree he emerged a perfect Buddha. He delayed awhile before starting on the active propaganda of his doctrine, sitting deep in contemplation under one or other tree, during which time he was miraculously fed. He began his preaching at Benares, and there gathered round him his first disciples. From that time until his death he devoted himself to his teaching. He was over eighty when he lay dying under the trees of the grove of Kusinagara, delivering last words of exhortation to his disciples. Miraculous signs accompanied his death as they had his birth, and it is reported that the fire of his funeral pile ignited of itself. In 5000 years from the death of this Buddha the next one is expected to appear. This one is said to have been preceded by twenty-four others.

The religio-philosophic system taught by Buddha instructs mankind in that path which, leading through many other existences, brings the weary traveller at length to Nirvāna, the place of absorption into the mighty original soul-source. Such a result can only be attained by rigid self-abnegation, contemplation, and neglect of worldly affairs. A vast mass of mythical matter has grown up around the name of Buddha, and, like Confucius, he has attracted to himself a complete pantheon of gods and lesser deities. In many parts of India and the east a Buddhism debased by the addition of this mythology exists, but the higher Buddhistic castes resolutely shun contact with it. The system has lost hold somewhat in India, the place of its origin, and flourishes more strongly at the present day in Burma and Japan.

Bussumarus. A god of the continental Celts, whom the Romans identified with Jupiter. The name signifies " The Large-lipped."

C

God C. This deity is very frequently represented in the Mayan Indian pinturas, but his description tallies with none of those gods of whom the writings of Spanish colonial authors have informed us. He is supposed to have an astronomic significance, and may perhaps represent the Polar Star, as in the Codex Tro-cortesianus he is surrounded by planetary signs, and in another place his head is represented as surrounded by a nimbus of rays, and other circumstances in which he is found confirm his stellar character.

Camaxtli. Was the war-god of the Tlascaltecs, or Tlascalans, of Mexico, the tribe from whom the Aztecs captured most of their war-sacrifices. He was closely associated with the god of the morning star, wearing the same colours on the body and face. Thus it follows he was also nearly related to Mixcoatl. With Huitzilopochtli he has much in common, although their origins are strikingly different. Huitzilopochtli was a god who had taken his rank as war-god through a variety of causes, chief among which was his possession of the lightning-spear; Camaxtli was a god of the chase in all probability ere he adopted his martial robe. Yet he too wielded the lightning, as we know gods of the chase were able to do, notably Mixcoatl.

Camazotz. "Ruler of Bats." A bat or vampire god of the Kiches of Guatemala, alluded to in the Popol Vuh (*q.v.*). When the hero-gods Hun-Ahpu and Xbalanque endeavoured to pass the night in his "House of Bats," he cut off the former's head, which was, however, replaced by his brother.

Camulos. A god of the continental Celts, who was also worshipped in Britain. The town of Colchester, anciently Camoludunum, was originally called after him.

Caswallawn. A war-god of the British Celts. The name means "War-king," and probably the British chief Cassivel-launus was called after him. The personality of the deity has, however, become so merged in the myths surrounding the figure of the famous captive of the Romans, that it is difficult to disentangle one from the other.

Cessair. One of the tribal goddesses or tutelar deities of the peoples who preceded the Celts in Ireland. In later mediæval times, however, she was regarded as a daughter of Noah and the first person to set foot in the island. This tradition shows that she was regarded as a deity of the aboriginal population.

Chac. The Mayan Indian rain-deities. The name signifies "the Red Ones." They are analogous to the Tlaloc deities of Mexico (*q.v.*).

Chalchihuitlicue. This goddess was the wife of Tlaloc, the god of rain and water. Her name signifies "Lady of the Emerald Robe," in allusion to the green colour of water. Sahagun says that she was worshipped with the conviction that she was able to bring peril upon seafarers, but as the Mexicans were not a seafaring people this description of her appears inexact. There is no reason to doubt that she was the spouse of Tlaloc, the feminine counterpart of the rain-god pure and simple. The people who specially worshipped her were those persons who sold water, and whose employments brought them into connection with that element. She was decorated with a marvellous collar of precious stones, from which depended a gold medal or pendant. On her head she wore a coronet of blue paper, surmounted by green feathers. Her eyebrows were of turquoises set in as mosaic, and her robe was of the green-blue tint of water edged with sea-flowers or water-plants. She carried in her left hand a large water-plant, and in her right a vase surmounted by a cross—a symbol emblematic of the four points of the compass, whence the rains come.

Chin. Moon-goddess of the Muysca Indians of Bogota. She well illustrates the connection with moisture and water that the moon has in all barbarian mythological systems. In her insensate spleen she was supposed to have at one time flooded the entire world. If a Muysca believed himself to be under her displeasure he dressed himself as a woman and undertook feminine tasks in order that he might lead her to believe that he was a female, and thus escape her wrath. This was of course because of the supposed feminine influence wielded by the moon.

Chun Chin, or Book of Spring and Autumn, a book of the annals of the Chinese state of Lu, extending from 722 B.C. to 484 B.C. It consists merely of bald entries of fact, and may be classed with the Pictish Chronicle, the Katuns of the Mayas of

Central America, or any other early chronicle. Lu was the state in which Confucius was born, and its annals were either compiled or edited by him. It contains but little information about mythological matter.

Churning of the Ocean. A myth of the Hindu epic period, described in the Ramayana and several of the Puranas. Durvāras, a saint and a portion of Siva (*q.v.*), was given a sweet-smelling garland by a celestial nymph, which so delighted him that he exhibited his pleasure in dancing. Indra, who happened to pass, asked the reason of his joy, and Durvāras handed him the flowers, which the god placed on his elephant's head. The beast manifested joy similar to that of the saint, and cast the garland upon the ground, but this displeased the holy man, who cursed the god, and prophesied ruin to his kingdom. The curse appeared to spread to the entire pantheon of deities, and, fearing that they would be overcome by the Asuras or demons, they asked help from Brahmā, who advised them to seek aid from Vishnu. Vishnu told them to join with the Asuras, collect all the various plants and herbs, cast them into the sea of milk, and, taking the mountain Mandara for a churning-stick and the serpent Vāsuki for a rope, to churn the ocean, which would produce a beverage the source of strength and immortality. The mountain required a pivot, and Vishnu took upon himself the form of a tortoise and acted as this. From the brew there emerged the sacred cow Surabhi, the goddess of wine, Vāruni, the tree of Paradise, Pārijāta (*q.v.*), the heavenly nymphs called Apsarasas, the moon, the poison, which was seized by the snake-gods, the peerless goddess Lakshmi, and Dhanvantari, the gods' physician, who bore the immortal nectar, which was drunk by the gods, who subsequently overcame the Asuras.

Ciuapipiltin. The goddesses called by this name, which signifies "venerated or honoured women," were supposed to be the spirits of those women who had died in childbed, for it was thought by the Mexicans to be as honourable for a woman to die under these conditions as for a warrior to expire on the field of battle. They descend when they so desire to the earth, where they afflict infants with divers maladies and enter human bodies. They were said to lurk at cross-roads for the purpose of working their will on the passers-by. Parents in Mexico took peculiar care that their infants were not permitted out of doors on the days that these spirits were supposed to visit the

earth. When they were smitten with paralysis or troubled with
a demon, says Sahagun, it was thought that these spirits had
invaded their bodies. For the purpose of placating these beings,
temples were built in their honour at the cross-roads, and loaves
of bread were made in various shapes, some in that of butter-
flies, called tlauitequiliztli and tamalli xocuichtlamatzoalli, or
cakes made in earthenware dishes were offered up to the shades
of the Ciuapipiltin. The images of these goddesses had blanched
white faces, and the hands, arms, and limbs were whitened
with a powder known as tisatl. Their eyebrows were set in
gold, and their tresses were dressed as those of the great ladies
of Mexico. The peplum which some of these figures wore was
coloured in black, the jupon of divers colours, and other parts
of the costume were white.

Coatlicue, or Coatlantona (Female Serpent, or Robe of
Serpents). The mother of Huitzilopochtli, the Aztec god of
war (*q.v.*).

Cocidius. A war-god of the British Celts. The Romans
equated him with Mars. His name is found on no less than
thirteen inscriptions of the date of the Roman occupation in
Britain, and it is certain that the invaders regarded him as one
of the principal deities of the island whom it was probably
necessary to placate.

Confucianism. Confucius (551-479 B.C.) was a Chinese
philosopher whose attitude of agnosticism towards the form
of Chinese religion which he found existing in his day profoundly
influenced Chinese thought, and, indeed, paved the way for a
system more or less philosophical which has been designated
by the name of its originator. He recognised the existence of
supernatural beings, but would not admit that he or any one
else had any knowledge concerning them. He says that
although they are everywhere, and disseminated throughout
the cosmos, yet they are neither to be seen nor heard, but in
some degree he appeared to regard himself as a heaven-sent
prophet, as he looked to God to preserve the wisdom he incul-
cated into the Chinese mind to future generations. He even
sacrificed to the spirits like the rest of Chinamen. He was a
pronounced fatalist. Yet with all these evidences of his belief
in supernatural beings he would not discourse concerning them,
believing that human existence and its aspects were quite
sufficient for the mental energies of man to be concerned with.
Man's duty towards God was with him inferior to man's duty

towards his fellows. For many centuries the personality of
Confucius has been the central object of a worship which has
little to do with his philosophy. It is, indeed, a good instance
of how a great culture-hero may be transformed into a deity
by the admiring generation which succeeds him. In 195 B.C.
his worship was revived by the first emperor of the Han dynasty,
who sacrificed to his spirit a pig, sheep, and ox. In A.D. 72 his
seventy-two disciples were also deified, and in a short time the
mass of the Chinese people came to regard Confucius as a god.
Later, idols of Confucius were introduced into the temples.
The deities associated with the Confucian religion are innumerable. Beginning with the basic deities of heaven and earth, a
long list of imperial ancestors who have achieved godhead follow.
The sun, the moon, the ancestors of the illustrious sage, his
disciples, and those connected with him in many ways all swell
the train of divine beings who cluster round him as a pantheon.
The Tien-Shen are the Confucian deities of the visible sky, who
display their powers in rain, wind, and thunder. The Ti-ki are
animistic deities of mountain, river, and ocean ; whilst T'ai-sui
is the Confucian Jupiter or demiurgic orderer of the universe
and of men. A multitude of animistic conceptions crowds upon
the heels of these more exalted divine beings, and we conclude
a very complete and embracive pantheon by mention of deified
physicians, the god of fire, gods of the ancient walls of Peking,
of the porcelain stones, of the treasury of the national and
traditional canons—indeed, on descending to the lower strata
of the Confucian faith, the student discovers a myriad lesser
gods. Each mountain, stream, and grove has its own particular
deity, and it would seem as if popular imagination has enriched
the Confucian religion or embarrassed it by the addition of a
myriad conceptions, the fruit of local or national superstition.
The emperor was at the head of the Confucian religion, and, as it
stands to-day, it may rightly be classified an ancestor-worship
pure and simple. The memorabilia of Confucius are contained
in the Confucian Analects and the Li-Chi, or "Record of
Rites." The first-named work with the Ta Hsio, the Chung-
Lung, or "Doctrine of the Mean" or equilibrium, and the
works of Mencius, compose the Shu, or Four Books, the principal
collection of Chinese classics.

Cosmology. The world-wide similarity of the creation-myths
of barbarous or semi-barbarous peoples is remarkable in that it
cannot be accounted for by any theory of circulated or borrowed

conceptions. This is demonstrated by the similarity between European, Asiatic, and American creation-stories, which by reason of geographical and other considerations could not possibly have influenced each other, especially in the case of those myths of the Western Hemisphere, which, in many instances, bear a close resemblance to those of Europe and the East. We find in general the conception of a vast world of waters over which broods the creative agency, who, by force of thought or dint of physical labour, raises from the flood beneath him the solid earth. The advent of man is rarely so simple a process as described in the Book of Genesis, and often many evolutionary processes have to be passed through ere he emerges in his present state. Often, too, the gods try their 'prentice hands upon unsatisfactory types of humanity which they afterwards destroy and supersede, or else they themselves descend to earth and become the ancestors of the human race. The conception of the cosmic egg from which the universe is hatched, the heaven-born twins, the fecund mother of humanity who falls from heaven, are found not only in the older mythologies of India and China, Egypt and Babylon, but also in Scandinavian creation-story, Persian cosmogony, and the many world-legends of North and South America—a striking testimony to the world-wide similarity of the workings of the barbarian human mind.

INDIA.—Numerous ideas concerning the origin of the universe and man are found in Hindu mythology. A hymn of the Rig-Veda describes a time when there was neither non-entity nor entity, when the universe was undistinguishable water enveloped in darkness. " Then desire (Karma) arose in It, which was the primal germ of mind . . . the bond between non-entity and entity." So the universe was developed, the gods being a subsequent creation. According to another Rig-Vedic idea it was through sacrifice that the gods delivered the world from chaos and brought life into being; the giant Purusha (q.v.) was the sacrificial victim, and all existing creatures issued from his limbs (cf. the Teutonic Ymir). The work of creation is associated with the names of Brahmā, Visvakarma, Manu, and Prajapati (see under these names), and with a further conception of a golden mundane egg, from which sprang the first man, whose word became the universe, and by whom the gods were created. The origin of being has the additional legends attached to it of Brahmā dividing into a dual being, male and female (see Purusha and Viraj), and of the primeval twins, Yama and

Yami (*q.v.*). (*See* also the Boar and Tortoise avatara of Vishnu, and Dyaus and Prithivi.)

EGYPT.—*See* Nu, Khepera, Ptah, Khnemu, Tem.

BABYLONIAN ACCOUNT.—Remains of different versions of this are extant. In an incantation tablet, said to date at the earliest from 600 B.C., it is stated that " a movement in the waters" preceded creation. Then Marduk (Merodach) (originally Ea: *see* " Ency. Rel. and Eth.," article "Cosmogony") makes man of dust and reeds, and continues his creative work with animals, rivers, and green things of the earth, etc. The chief epic version is preserved in what are known as the Seven Tablets of Creation, brought from the library of Ashurbanipal at Nineveh, and now in the British Museum. Here there are the two primeval beings Apsu and Tiamat, embodiments of the great deep, and their son Mummu. There is an account of the creation of gods, including the great triad, Anu, En-lil, and Ea, whose "way" is not pleasing to Apsu and Tiamat, and they rebel. Apsu and Mummu do not long resist the power of the gods, but Tiamat carries on warfare aided by monsters of her creation. The crisis of the myth is the combat between Tiamat and Marduk. The great god arms for the encounter (*see* Slabs 28 and 29, Nineveh Gall., B.M.) and Tiamat is annihilated. Marduk cuts her body in two, and with one half forms the heavens, and it is expressly stated that he divides the upper from the lower waters. He proceeds to make dwellings for gods, and the lights of heaven, for which he ordains the regular courses. A great part of Tablet 5 is missing. In Tablet 6 comes the crowning act, when he has his head cut off, and with his own blood and bone (or clay, Jeremias) makes man. The last tablet is a hymn in honour of Marduk.

Berosus, a priest of Marduk who flourished in the third century B.C., wrote a Greek history of Babylonia, unfortunately lost, but known in part by quotations from it by later writers, and introduced into it the history of creation, which appears to be nearly similar to the above, with variation in the names, and the additional statement that half of Tiamat went to form the earth. (For full details, *see* King, " Seven Tablets of Creation," 1902, and " Bab. Rel. and Myth." 1899.)

CHINA.—Chinese philosophy is quite definite concerning the beginning of things. During countless ages nothing condensed into unity, and the Mighty Atom was formed—no inapt description of the present scientific theory of the formation of matter. In the course of ages the original atom split into the male and female principles in nature much as binomial fission takes place in the lowest known forms of animal life, and the universe came into being. Although this system was sufficiently comprehended by the initiated, a more simple one had to be framed for the people, who were instructed that the male and female principles were again divided into a great and a small. From the co-operation of these four elements came a demiurge called P'an Ku, whose function was to rightly order the universe. Upon his death the various parts of his body served to compose parts of the world, much in the same way as those of the giant Ymir did in the mythology of Scandinavia. His eyes became the sun and moon, his breath the wind, his hair trees and vegetation, his flesh the earth, his sweat rain, and the worms which sprang from his decomposing body were men. The sceptical philosopher Chucius, on being asked whether God existed before heaven and earth, replied that such was certainly the case, but although Tien or Shang-ti is called the " First Cause," it does not appear that he is in any way responsible for the direct creation of the universe, however he may have inspired it. (*See* Tien.)

EDDIC ACCOUNT.—According to this there was in the beginning neither earth nor heaven, nor sea, nor shore, nor any verdure, only a yawning abyss (or chaos), Ginnunagap. To the north of this gap was a realm of cold and mist, Niflheim, to the south a realm of fire, Muspelheim. Ymir (*q.v.*) was brought into being. The sons of Bor (Odin, Vili, and Ve), after killing Ymir, raised the disk of the earth out of the waters, and so formed Midhgardhr. Sun, moon, and stars — sparks from Muspelheim — wandered as yet in trackless ways; then the gods made a pathway for them, and the sun shone down on the earth and the first green appeared. The gods next assembled in the Idafield, and built temple-like dwellings with golden tools, and played with golden toys, and knew no care. This golden age continued till three giant women (Norns) came from the north, and the first world war was started (*see* Vanir). (For the creation of man, *see* Ymir, and Askr and Embla.)

IRANIAN ACCOUNT.—Ahura Mazda (*q.v.*), the creator of Avestan belief, fixed the number of years for the world's duration at 12,000. During the first 3000 he created the spiritual world. Ahriman (*q.v.*), his evil opponent, was not aware of his existence till light betrayed it to him ; then dazzled, or in some way spiritually controlled, he was prevented at first from beginning his counter-creation. He refused Mazda's offers of peace and retired to his own abode to prepare for mischief. During the next 3000 Mazda created the material world, heavenly bodies, water, earth, plants, animals, and man. Meanwhile, Ahriman had created evil spirits to help him in his work of destruction, which he now began. For every good and beautiful thing that the one god made, he produced a corresponding evil, and from him emanated all noxious plants and injurious animals and reptiles, diseases, death, etc. For another 3000 years the conflict between the two powers rages bitterly. With the birth of Zarathustra there are signs of the coming victory of the good which the close of the last 3000 years is to see accomplished. The first living things to be created were animals, and the first of these was an ox, which was assailed by so many and great evils by Ahriman that he died. From his members sprang every kind of grain and wholesome plants, and two creatures, male and female, of the same species were generated by him, from which were born many further kinds of useful animals. The world was now ready for man, and the great god took sweat, uttered a prayer, and produced the youthful figure of a man, who was called Gayomart. Him also Ahriman slew, but many years later, his seed having fertilised in the earth, there sprang up twins, at first combined in the form of a shrub. From these two, Mashya and Mashyāna, were born two other beings whom they devoured, and then seven other couples, the progenitors of the human race.

CREATION MYTHS OF THE WESTERN HEMISPHERE

ALGONQUIAN INDIANS.—The words for "light" and "rabbit" are identical in the tongue of the Algonquian Indians, so that Manibozho or Michabo, their creative agency, in reality the sun, has become confounded with the rabbit. On one occasion Manibozho was hunting, and the wolves which he employed as dogs entered a great lake and disappeared. He entered the waters for the purpose of effecting their rescue, but they suddenly overflowed, and submerged the entire habitable world. The god immediately sent off a raven to discover a piece of earth, but it returned. An otter had no better success, whereupon Manibozho despatched the musk-rat, which returned with sufficient to re-create the terrestrial sphere. The trees had become denuded of their branches, so he discharged arrows at them, which provided them with new boughs. Having executed summary vengeance upon the instigators of the catastrophe, Manibozho married the musk-rat, by whose aid he peopled the world.

ANTIS INDIANS (Bolivian Alps, North-Western Brazil, Ipurinas, Yurukares, etc.). — The Antis Indians, who are in all probability cognate with the Quichua-Aymara stock, possess creation, flood, and fire myths similar to those of the Tapuyas and other South American races. Among the Yurukare the subterranean cavern from which the human race emerged was suddenly closed up by supernatural agency, because some one emanated therefrom " who wished to be master." This is a striking variant of the Tapuya and Mandan ideas (q.v.). The Yurukare deluge myth differs only from the others in the circumstance that a rod is stretched from the cave where the refugees are imprisoned to discern whether or not the flood has subsided. Animals are considered as transformed men, who met with this fate at a period of fire or flood, and, as in the case of the Kiche Indians of Guatemala, those who sought refuge in trees became monkeys. When all men had been destroyed by fire the god Tiri opened a tree, from which he brought various tribes, until the earth was sufficiently peopled. But the men were weak and ignorant. Then a maiden prayed to Ule, the most beautiful tree of the forest, and he came forth at her prayer, and from their union arose a culture-hero who taught them the arts of life.

As regards the heavenly bodies, the Ipurinas believe the sun is a kettle of boiling water, which, falling over, once consumed the earth. The moon, they say, is a boy, who is fattened up by his grandmother, and who, as the month advances, becomes more and more corpulent. Another sun-myth of the Yurukare relates how the sun gave a man who had been saved by him from the universal fire a maiden to wife, who bears him a daughter as well as sons. A man is created for the daughter out of a ule tree, and is torn to pieces in the chase by a jaguar. The woman, the sun-daughter, gathers the pieces together, all but a portion of the face, but the resuscitated man is ashamed of this defect. He follows her to the house, but only upon condition that she does not turn round. But she breaks her promise and he disappears. The myth bears an almost exact likeness to that of Orpheus and Eurydice, and to some extent to that of Osiris and Isis, and possesses an undoubted resemblance to many other myths. Indeed the people sprung from this pair are born in quarters, to typify the early morn.

ARAWAKS.—The Arawakan family inhabiting the Guianas, Northern Brazil, and part of Colombia, believe that in the beginning of the world the animals were created by Makonaima, the great spirit whom no man has seen. (W. H. Brett, " Indian Tribes of Guiana," 1868, p. 378 *et seq.*) The beasts had at that time the power of speech, and Sigu, the son of Makonaima, was placed to rule over them. Makonaima created a marvellous tree, each branch of which produced a different kind of fruit. The acouri discovered it first, and, coming daily to the tree, ate his fill without apprising the other animals. Sigu, suspecting him, ordered the woodpecker to keep him in sight. The bird did so, but failed to detect him. But he was convicted by the rat, and the tree was thrown open to all. The animals were about to consume the fruits *in toto*, when Sigu determined to cut down the tree, and replenish the whole earth by planting every seed and slip which it would furnish. To this end he employed the birds and beasts, all of which assisted willingly, except Iwarrika, the monkey, which thwarted the labours of the others. The stump of the tree was discovered to be full of water containing the fry of every description of fresh-water fish. The water began to flow, but Sigu covered the tree-stump with a closely-woven basket. The monkey removed this, however, and precipitated a terrible flood. Sigu led the animals to an eminence where some high cocorite palms grew, and these he made the birds and climbing animals ascend. Those which could not climb and were not amphibious he placed in a cave, which he closed and sealed with wax. He then ascended the cocorite palm himself. A terrible period of darkness and storm ensued, during which Sigu dropped the seeds of the cocorite into the water beneath to judge by the sound of its elevation. At length he heard them strike the soft earth, and knew that the period of flood had passed. The Macusis believe that the only person who survived the deluge re-peopled the earth by converting stones into human beings, as did Deucalion and Pyrrha. The Tamanacs say that one man and one woman were saved by taking refuge on the lofty mountains of Tamanucu, and that they threw over their heads the fruits of the Mauritius palm, from the kernels of which sprang men and women. The Warrau tribe of the Arawaks possess the following legend of their own origin and that of the Caribs. The Warraus originally dwelt in a pleasant region above the sky, where there were neither wicked men nor noxious animals. Okonorote, a young hunter, having wandered far in pursuit of a beautiful bird, discharged an arrow at it which missed its mark and disappeared. While searching for it he found a hole through which it had fallen, and on looking through it, descried the lower world. He made a rope, down which he led the Warraus to the earth, but a corpulent woman, as in several of the North American myths, remained fixed in the aperture, and filled it up. In answer to the people's cries for water the Great Spirit created the Essiquibo River. Later, Korobona, a Warrau maiden, became pregnant to a water-demon, and produced the first Carib—a terrible warrior, who slew many Warraus. The Paressi tribe of the Arawaks had a belief that the neglect of the couvade brought misfortune upon the world. They also related that Maiso, a stone woman, produced all living beings and all rivers. Even the domestic animals and iron tools of the whites are borne by this original mother.

The Arawaks of Guiana had a myth to the effect that Aimon Kondi, the Great Spirit, scourged the world with fire, from which the survivors sought refuge in underground caverns. A great flood followed, in which Marerewana and his followers saved themselves in a canoe. Still another Arawak myth relates that the creator, having completed the cosmic scheme, seated himself in a great silk-cotton tree by a river side and cut off pieces of its bark, which he cast all around. Those which touched the water became fish, those which touched the air birds, and those which alighted upon the earth animals and men.

ATHAPASCAN INDIANS.—The Athapascan Indians of North-West America attribute the creation to the raven Yetl, a bird with fiery eyes, which produced thunder from its wings, a common enough conception among American tribes. On passing from heaven to the sea the plane of earth arose from the waters. From this being the Athapascans trace their descent, that is, they regard the raven as their totem, or eponymous ancestor. Yetl saved their ancestors from the flood and, like Prometheus, brought them fire from heaven. Those Athapascan tribes who live further east believe their common ancestor to have been a dog.

CADDOAN INDIANS (Pawnees, Wichita, Kichai, etc.).—The Caddo tribes believed that they came from the underworld, and said that the first persons to penetrate into the sphere of day were an old man who carried a pipe, fire, and a drum, and his wife, with corn and pumpkin-seed. Their creative agency they designated Atius Tirawa, who was omnipotent and invisible, who dwelt in the upper regions of air, and guided the heavenly bodies.

CALIFORNIAN INDIANS.—Although there are no less than twenty-one different linguistic families in California, the similarity of their mythological conceptions is remarkable. The Maidu have a most intricate creation myth, in which the principal figure is Kodoyanpe, the creator, and Coyote. They discovered the world and rendered it habitable for men. These were small wooden images like those in the " Popol Vuh," but the mannikins were no more tractable than were those of Guatemala, and were at last changed into animals. Kodoyanpe the beneficent perceived that Coyote was bent upon evil courses, and conceived the idea of his destruction. In this he was aided by a being called the Conqueror, who destroyed many monsters and evil things which would have menaced the life of man still unborn. But at length Kodoyanpe was defeated by Coyote, and fled eastwards, as did Quetzalcoatl in Mexican myth. The Indians then sprang from the places where the mannikins of the first creation had been buried. Other versions of the myth state that at first there was only the primeval waste of waters, upon which Kodoyanpe and Coyote dropped in a canoe. " Let this surf become sand," cried Coyote, and it became sand. The Achomawi, neighbours to the Maidu, state that the creator originally emerged from a small cloud, and that Coyote sprang from a fog. The Aschochimi of California had a flood myth which recounted the drowning of the world so that no man escaped. But by planting the feathers of divers birds the Coyote grew a crop of men of various tribes.

CARIBS.—The ancient Caribs of the Antilles, now extinct, regarded the earth, which they designated Mama Nono, as "the good mother, from which all things come." They believed that their original ancestor created the race by sowing the soil with stones, or with the fruit of the Mauritius palm, which sprouted forth into men and women. (Mueller, "Amerikanische Urreligionen.") The Bakairi Caribs possess a belief akin to that of the Zuñi Indians of New Mexico regarding the coming together of the " Sky-father " and the " Earth-mother," which, originally set in opposition to one another, touched and established direct communication, until at last moving away from one another they exchanged places. In the legends of the Bakairi the mystical twin-heroes, Keri and Kame, brought the original animals from the hollow trunk of a tree. This tree-stem the Bakairi connect with the Milky Way. The Caribs possess the same myth as the Arawaks regarding the efforts of the original culture-hero to gauge the depths of the volume of water which enshrouded the earth. Another Carib deluge myth related that excessive rains brought about a great flood, from which humanity was saved by the ibis, which had scooped up so much earth with its beak that hills could be formed from the heap. The Bakairi believe that the sun and moon were in the beginning aimlessly carried about by two birds, until at last Keri and Kame seized them by cunning, and made them proceed in a regular course. They aver that the luminaries are concealed by certain animals, lizards, birds, and spiders, which swallow the sun at night and the moon by day, disgorging them in the morning and evening respectively. Others believe that the moon is obscured at night by a shaman taking the form of a bird, and covering its disk with his wings. The Pleiades the Bakairi believe to be parakeets. In Orion they see a dried stick of manioc.

IROQUOIAN INDIANS.—The Iroquois tribes believe that their original female ancestress fell from heaven into the waste of primeval waters. But the dry land bubbled up under her feet, and quickly grew to the proportions of a continent. Several of the Iroquois tribes, however, are of opinion that some amphibious animals, such as the otter, beaver, and musk-rat, noticed the fall of the original female from heaven, and hastened to break it by shovelling up earth from the mud beneath the waters upon which she might stand. Indeed the Indians of this family were wont to point to a mountain near the falls of the Oswego river as the locality where this took place.

MEXICAN.—In the Mexico of the Aztecs the sun was held to be the cause of all material force, and the gods as the holders of the fluctuating fortunes of man. The sun, like man himself, was regarded as a being dependent upon food and drink, and, according to Aztec cosmology, several suns had perished through lack of provision, as had older races of men. The original sun had no other nourishment than the water it absorbed from the earth, and was thus nothing but a semi-liquid mass, which was designated Atonatiuh, or " The Water-Sun." It was supposed to have absorbed enormous quantities during the course of centuries, which it ultimately discharged over the whole earth, causing a complete destruction of animal and vegetable life. This water-sun was sometimes identified with Tlaloc, the god of moisture (*q.v.*), but this is a comparatively recent addition to the popular legend. The conception of a general destruction of terrestrial life by elementary physical forces was extended by the Mexicans to include catastrophes wrought by earthquake, wind-storms, fire, and the collapse of the vault of heaven itself. (Gomara, "Conquista de Mejico," Madrid, 1749, chap. 215.) These holocausts were traced to some defect in the sun. Other accounts relate that the gods Tezcatlipoca, Quetzalcoatl, and Xiuhtecutli (all of whom *see*) had each attempted the rôle of the God of Day without success. At length it became evident that a special god must be created for the express purpose of fulfilling the functions of the office, so the existing sun was brought into being. However the Mexican myths may vary according to the method by which the creation of the sun was achieved, authorities are at one as regards the Aztec belief that the luminary was an animal which was originally a man, but who, by the action of fire, had become transformed, and had received the intense vitality necessary for the performance of his functions from the blood of the gods, voluntarily shed for that purpose. The gods met at Teotihuacan in order to make a sun. They kindled a mighty fire, and signified to the worshippers that whosoever should first leap into it should become the new sun personified. The sun rose from the midst of the fire, but was unable to ascend into the sky for lack of strength. In order to give him the necessary motive force the gods resolved to sacrifice themselves in the usual Mexican manner, by having their hearts torn out. This was done by the god Xolotl, who had by their agency created man, and who lastly performed the act of sacrifice upon himself. The sun then ascended the sky. (Mendieta, "Hist. Eccl. Ind.," Mexico, 1870, lib. i., chap. 2.) According to another tradition the creation of man was subsequent to that of the sun. Men were in fact created to be the food of the luminary, and were ordered to fight and slay one another so that the sun might be supplied with food. The Mayas of Yucatan increased the previous number of suns by one. Two epochs had terminated by devastating plagues. These were known as the "Sudden Deaths," for so swift and mortal was the pest that the vultures dwelt in the houses of the cities, and devoured the bodies of their former owners. The third epoch closed with a hurricane or an inundation known as *hun yecil*, "the inundation of the trees," as all the forests were swept away. The Kiche of Guatemala had a very complete creation legend, which may be studied in the "Popol Vuh," their sacred book. To begin with, there only existed the vast waste of primeval waters, in which slept "the Old

Ones covered with Green Feathers," the father and mother deities, Xpiyacoc and Xmucane. Then came Hurakan the mighty, " he who hurls below," a Kiche variant of the Aztec deity Tezcatlipoca. He commanded light to be and the solid earth. The gods in council created animals. They carved mannikins out of wood, but these were intractable and disobedient, so the gods resolved to destroy them. They sent a deluge upon the world and the mannikins were drowned. The posterity of the few who were saved are the monkeys. After the catastrophe the earth-god Vukub-Kakix (Macaw) and his progeny gave more trouble to the gods, but were ultimately destroyed. Hurakan latterly created four perfect men from yellow and white maize, and supplied them with wives, after which the sun was created, and the cosmological scheme was complete. (Spence, " The Popol Vuh," London, 1908, pp. 9-26.)

MUSKHOGEAN INDIANS (Creeks, Choctaws, Seminoles, etc.).— In the Muskhogean conception of creation we find several original ideas embedded so far as America is concerned. In the beginning the primeval waste of waters alone was visible. Over the dreary waste two pigeons or doves flew hither and thither, and in course of time observed a single blade of grass spring above the surface. The solid earth followed gradually, and the terrestrial sphere took its present shape. A great hill, Nunne Chaha, rose in the midst, and in the centre of this was the house of the deity Esaugetuh Emissee, the " Master of Breath." He took the clay which surrounded his abode and from it moulded the first men, and as the waters still covered the earth he was compelled to build a great wall upon which to dry the folk he had made. Gradually the soft mud formed and dried into bone and flesh, and Esaugetuh was successful in directing the waters into their proper channels, reserving the dry land for the men he had made. There is a great resemblance in this myth to that in the Book of Genesis. The pigeons appear analogous to the brooding creative spirit, and the manufacture of the men out of mud is also striking. So far is the resemblance carried that we are almost forced to conclude that the entire myth is the result of Christian sophistication, and that Christian conceptions have been grafted on to a native legend.

MUYSCA-CHIBCHA FAMILY.—The Chibchas of Colombia were unique in believing that light existed as a species of original matter before the beginning of things, and was enclosed in a casket called Chimini-pagus, whence it was carried to the earth by blackbirds, who bore the shining air in their beaks. Their creation myth proper recounts how Bochica, a culture-hero, carried the globe upon his shoulders like another Atlas, and when fatigued changed his posture—hence the phenomena of earthquakes.

Another of their hero-gods, Nemquetcha, created four chieftains, from whom the four-fold divisions of the Muyscas of Bogota were traced. The deluge they attributed to the overflowing of a lake through the spite of Chia, the moon-goddess.

PERUVIANS.—The Incan Peruvians held that all things emanated from Pachacamac, the universal spirit, from whom proceeded the spirits of the animals or plants which are produced by the earth. The earth itself they designated Pachacamama, or " Earth-Mother." Thus we have a conception of a general spirit of living things coalesced with one totally different in its origin, that of a creator. The idea of a great spirit, a former and shaper, not necessarily a creator of substance, is almost universal throughout America. But it must sooner or later occur to the barbarian mind that the making of living beings postulates something more than giving shape to the matter of which they consist. They must have received the breath of life from some creator. Such a creator the Peruvians found in Pachacamac, an anthropomorphic deity representing the creative mind. The conception of Pachacamac as a ruler and director of the universe belongs to a later period of Incan rule, and we know that a shrine was built to him in the new aspect by Apu-Ccapac-Inca Pachacutic, at the north angle of Cuzco. The Peruvians declared that all things were made by the word of the spirit, by the mere exercise of will, or thought. In the prayers to the creator and in other fragments of aboriginal rite which have survived, we read, for example : " Let a man be : let a woman be," and such expressions as " the creative word." Occasionally the sun acts as a species of demiurge. For example, it is he who creates the city of Cuzco, and sends to earth the three eggs of gold, of silver, and of copper, from which issue the Curacos and their wives and the Mitayocs and their wives. Tiahuanaco is regarded as the theatre of the new creation of man which followed upon the deluge. In that district it was supposed the creator made man and separated him into nations, making one of each nation of clay, and painting the dresses that each was to wear, besides giving the people their national songs, languages, seeds to sow suitable to the environment of each, and food. Then he gave life and soul to each one, and ordered that they should pass under the earth. Thence each nation came up in the places to which he ordered them to go. This myth is obviously an attempt to harmonise two conflicting creation stories, the original one of the genesis of the people from caves, and the later one of the creation in Tiahuanaco. We also find local creation-myths in some of the Peruvian valleys. For example, Pachacamac was not considered to be the creator of the sun in the coast valley of Irma, but to be himself a descendant of it. Of the first human pair created by him the man perished of hunger, but the woman maintained herself upon roots. The sun took pity upon her, and gave her a son, whom Pachacamac slew and buried. But from his teeth there grew maize, from his ribs the long, white roots of the manioc, and from his flesh pumpkins and esculent plants.

PUEBLO INDIANS (Zuñis, etc., of New Mexico).—In the mythology of the Pueblo Indians we have an example of a very complete creation-myth. At first existed solely Awonawilona, the maker and container of all in the primal darkness. He projected his creative thoughts through the primeval gloom, and from them sprung fogs which bore within themselves the germs of growth and life. He then took shape as the sun, and playing upon the damp fogs evolved the sea. Then from his own flesh, " extended from the surface of his body," he made the seed of two worlds, and spread it upon the sea. Hatching this with his sun-heat, he formed green scums, which grew into the ·" Four-fold containing Mother Earth," and the " All-covering Father-sky." From the embraces of these elements sprang life, after which they separated. Then the wombs of the earth were heavy with life, and in the lowest of the four the seed of living men and animals stirred and grew until the lowest womb grew full to overflowing of living and embryonic beings. So great became the press that Poshaiyankya, the shrewdest of mankind, was forced to make his way out of it by a road difficult to follow. Working his solitary way through the lower caves and recesses, he came at last to the upper world, a great flat island of slippery land, where he found the Sun-father, whom he besought to save his creatures from the horror of the lower shades. This was safely accomplished, and the name of the wise pioneer is still held in reverence by the Zuñi tribes.

SHOSHONEAN INDIANS (Comanches, etc.).—The Shoshonean people appear to believe that the earth always existed as at present, and seem to know nothing of a first creator. The human race, as in so many American mythologies, emerged from the underworld through a hole called the Sipapu, probably the Grand Cañon of the Colorado. Their dead they believe return to this primal abode. The Sky-father and Earth-mother they believe uphold the universe, but they say nothing as regards their having a hand in its creation.

SIOUAN INDIANS.—The Mandan tribes of the Sioux possess a type of creation-myth which is common to several American peoples. They suppose that their nation lived in a subterranean village near a vast lake. Hard by the roots of a great grape-vine penetrated from above the earth, and clambering up this several of them got a sight of the upper world, which they found to be rich and well stocked with both animal and vegetable food. Those of them who had seen the new-found world above returned to their home bringing such glowing accounts of its wealth and pleasantness with them that the others resolved to forsake their dreary underground dwelling for the delights of the sunny sphere above them. The entire population set out, and climbed up the vine, but no more than half the tribe had ascended when their further progress was arrested by the breaking of the vine owing to the weight of a corpulent woman. To the underground world where they originally dwelt the Mandans believe they will return after death, the worthy reaching the village by way of the lake, the bad having to abandon this passage by reason of the weight of their sins. The Minnetarees believed that their original ancestor emerged from the waters of a lake bearing in his hand an ear of corn. The Mandans possessed a myth very similar to that of the Muskhogees concerning the creation of the world.

TUPI-GUARANI FAMILY OF BRAZIL.—A two-fold destruction befell the original Tupi-Guarani people of Brazil. According to the myth, Monan, the creator, vexed with mankind, resolved to destroy the world by fire. But one Irin Magé, a magician of might, extinguished the conflagration by a heavy rain-storm. This in turn caused the rivers and lakes to overflow. When the flood subsided, a quarrel between the hero-brothers Tawenduare and Arikute precipitated another deluge, for the former stamped his foot so deeply into the ground that a flood of water issued therefrom, from which the two brothers and their families were forced to take refuge in trees. The Mundruku tribe possesses a myth to the effect that a god Raini formed the world by placing it in the shape of a flat stone upon the head of another demiurge. Some other Tupi tribes believe in an interchange of heaven and earth, as do the Zuñi Indians, whilst the Mundruku hero, Karu, creates mountains by blowing feathers about. The River Chaco Indians, who are cognate to the Guarani, believe that the universe was created by a gigantic beetle. After having made the plains, mountains, and forests, it scraped a hole in the ground and entered the earth. From this hole numerous living beings issued, and covered the face of the earth. These beings after death became evil spirits, who constantly torment mankind. From the particles of soil thrown up by its excoriations the beetle constructed a man and woman, who became the progenitors of all human kind. Subsequently other evil spirits emanated from the hole, and attempted to overthrow the man and woman, but the beetle gave power to the humans to resist them, and then withdrew, taking no further interest in cosmological proceedings. An early traveller, Hans Staden, writing in 1550 of the Tupi-Guarani tribes, states their belief in the destruction of their ancestors by a powerful supernatural agency, Maire, who sent upon them an inundation from which but a few were saved by climbing trees and hiding in caves. The same authority gives the names of three brothers, Krimen, Hermitten, and Coem, from whom they claimed descent. The southern tribes speak of four brothers, and give two of them names as Tupi and Guarani respectively, parents of the racial divisions designated after them. Among the northern Tupi proper a very definite scheme of cosmogony is discovered. Toru-shom-pek, the sun, stands for their principle of good, and Toru-guenket, the moon, represents with them the power of evil. The latter is supposed to fall periodically and destroy the earth, and from her all baneful influences, such as thunderstorms and floods, emanate. Tupi cosmology appears to rest primarily upon the idea that all created things possess a mother or maker who is solely respon-sible for the scheme of creation, no male influence being trace-able. There are further three superior deities, to whom are apportioned the construction of the various natural families. These are known among the generality of Tupi tribes as Guaracy, the sun, creator of all animals, Jacy, the moon, creator of plant-life, and Peruda or Ruda, the god of generation, who promotes the reproduction of human beings. Each of these has a number of demiurges under him, and these again are served by numerous spirits who protect every individual animal, plant, and person. But Tupi cosmology varies with locality, and this fact will account for the seeming conflicting notices of its several investigators. Like the Arawak, the Tupi believe in Tupan, who alone of his four brothers survived the deluge. But he does not appear as a creative agency. The conception of natural phenomena among the Tupi-Guarani tribes is no less curious than their theories of creation. They believe the Pleiades to be a swarm of celestial bees. The Uapes possess a myth to the effect that a girl of the tribe, Temioua, fled her village in order to escape from the local marriage customs, and entered the house of a Yacami chief, who took her to wife. She brought forth two eggs, from which a boy and a girl were hatched, both covered with stars. The boy Pinon, girdled with a star-serpent, was Orion, the girl, semi-decked with seven stars, the Pleiades. The Borros Indians believe the Southern Cross to be the track of an ostrich, and the Milky Way an ash-track, as do other tribes.

TUPUYA OR GES INDIANS (Eastern Brazil and Bolivia).— These tribes believe the universe to be kept together or destined as the case may be by human or quasi-human agencies. The flood myth of the Karaya relates that the malevolent agency Anatiwa originated the deluge, and sent fish to pull down those who had taken flight to the hill Tupimare. The Ges attributed the rebuilding of the earth to the water-hen Saracura, which fetched earth to the hills where those saved from the flood congregated, so that the area of safety might be enlarged. The Karaya ancestral god, Kaboi, led his people from the under to the upper world by the call of a bird.

Credne. A deity of the Irish Celts, the patron or tutelar god of brasiers.

Creirwy. Daughter of Tegid and Keridwen (*q.v.*) in British Celtic myth. She was a fascinating goddess of love, a description of Celtic Venus.

D

God D. God D represents the moon-god of the Mayas of Central America. He is usually drawn as an aged man with sunken jaws and wrinkled brow. On his head he wears a pendant ornament which encloses the sign Akbal, night, and in his hieroglyph it appears before his head, surrounded by dots to indicate a starry sky. His first hieroglyph is nearly always followed by a second. This sign stands also for the number 20, to show the duration of the moon. In the full moon only once does this deity occur in feminine guise (Dresden Codex), so that we cannot compare him with the Metztli of the Aztecs (*q.v.*). He is, indeed, depicted elsewhere in the same codex with a short beard. He has a connection with the Water-goddess I, and both wear the serpent head-dress, in the case of God D to show the power of the moon over water (*see* remarks on Metztli). Like Metztli he is connected with birth, for in some passages he wears the snail, the symbol of parturition, on his head. Numerous authorities believe God D to be the great Mayan deity known as Itzamna, and make him a sun-god. But the symbols accompanying him seem to be altogether against such a conclusion. Other authorities appear to think that D was originally a sun-god, and that his character as a moon-deity was a later innovation, and this would square with calendric changes.

Dagan. A Babylonian and Assyrian god, whose name occurs in conjunction with that of Anu as one of the chief deities. His relation to the Dagon of the Philistines is a matter of discussion among scholars, depending mainly on the question whether the latter's name is derived from a root signifying fish or one signifying corn. The oldest and most probable derivation is that of Philo Byblius, who states that it means " corn." Dagan appears in Babylon, where he was introduced by the Amorite invaders, as early as 3150 B.C. (For different views on this subject, *see* Sayce, " Higher Crit. and Mon.," 1908; Hastings, " Dict. Bibl."; " Jewish Encyclopædia"; and H. Clay Trumbull, " Jonah in Nineveh," 1902.)

Dagda. An important god of the ancient Irish Celts, originally called Dagodevos, " the good." He was to some extent regarded as the beneficent god of the seasons, which he played into being with his harp. From the cauldron of his plenty, which was called Undry, he fed the whole earth. He belongs to the group of the Tuatha de Danann, and by some authorities he is described as fire in its genial sense. He is sometimes alluded to as " The Lord of Great Knowledge," for he was possessed of the perfection of human science, and Cera, perhaps meaning creator. He was ousted from his reign by his son Oengus, who probably belonged to the pantheon of a later tribe or people; or Oengus, although Dagda's son, may have become more popular in the general imagination. His agricultural or seasonal significance is seen in the circumstances that he has power over the growth of corn and the supply of milk, and he is frequently called the " God of the Earth." He dwelt in an underworld which has something in common with the realm of Pluto in Latin myth, in that it is the laboratory of growth and fertility. He was usually represented as wielding a large club or fork, symbol of his dominion over the food supply.

Daikoku. A Japanese god of wealth, figured seated on bags of rice. (*See* Luck, Gods of.)

Dainichi A Japanese god, the personification of wisdom. One of the Buddhist trinity, or Triratna.

Daityas. Giants or demons. Enemies of the gods in post-Vedic times (*see* Indra). Legend relates that they endeavoured to seize the Amrita (or immortal nectar of the gods) at the Churning of the Ocean, but Vishnu beguiled them, and rescued the precious draught, and the Daityas were driven down to Patala (*q.v.*); we also hear of their succeeding in obtaining sovereignty over the earth, but Vishnu again sent a deceptive vision to entice them from the path of the Vedas and so cause them to perish.

Daksha. One of the mind-born sons of Brahmā ; a chief Prajapati (*q.v.*) ; also an Aditya (*q.v.*) ; a later account relates that he was born from the right thumb of Brahmā. In a second birth he was son of the ten Prāchetasus, who had religiously performed penance in their devotion to Nārāyana (*see* Brahmā and Vishnu) by remaining immersed in the sea for ten thousand years. Daksha's daughter Sati (*q.v.*), or Uma, was married to Siva ; on account of the quarrel between her father and husband she voluntarily abandoned herself to death. The story of Daksha's sacrifice is told variously in the epics and Puranas. On one occasion Daksha was enraged that his son-in-law did not rise to greet him when he entered the assembly of gods, and hurled insults at him; accordingly, when Daksha had prepared a great sacrifice he invited neither Siva nor his wife. Siva rushes in with his followers, tears out Bhaga's eyes, knocks out Pushan's teeth, and cuts off Daksha's head; an addition to the tale in another account is the creation by Siva of a terrible being, Vira-bhadra, who with others created for the purpose commit these acts of violence. A reconciliation was effected, and Daksha's head being irrecoverable, Siva replaces it with that of a goat, with which Daksha is seen represented. (*See* Rudra for version of tale under this god's name.) Daksha also appears as an incarnation of Vishnu.

Damkina. A Babylonian goddess, the wife of Ea.

Dānavas. Similar to the Daityas, with whom they are associated (*see* Indra).

Danu. Mother of the gods of the Irish Celts, and daughter of Dagda (*q.v.*) (*see* also Tuatha de Danann). The name may be derived from " ana," plenty, and she is obviously an earth-mother, or goddess of fertility, associated like all earth-mothers with the underworld, or place of the dead and of growth. It is probable that human victims were sacrificed to her as to other earth-deities, and it is notable that in Leicestershire they still recount the deeds of a terrible " Black Annis " who dwelt in a cave in the Dane Hills and devoured folk. (*See* also Brigit.)

Dasyus. Enemies of the gods, destroyed by Indra, originally, it is thought, the dark aborigines of India. In the Vedic hymns they are distinguished from the Aryas. The title of Dasyus was given later to the fourth caste, composed of non-Aryans, whose duty it was to serve the Aryans (Bergaigne). (*See* Indra.)

Dea Domnann. A goddess of the Irish Celts, or more probably of the Irish aboriginal population, connected with the worship of the lower regions, and, therefore, with the cult of growth and fertility. Some authorities connect her with the sea, but this is scarcely likely.

Deva (*f.* Devi). In Hindu mythology, a divine being or god.

Devaki. Wife of Vasudeva and mother of Krishna (*q.v.*).

Devi. Designation of Siva's wife (Sati, or Uma); she is also referred to as Mahā-devi, great goddess.

Diancecht. The Irish Celtic god of medicine. The name signifies " Swift in Power." At the battle of Magtured he sat by a stream which possessed magic healing properties, in which he bathed the mortally wounded. He must therefore be equated with such gods of the continental Celts as presided over healing wells. In Christian times his memory survived as an enchanter, as ancient Irish manuscripts show.

Dirona. A goddess of the continental Celts, mated by the Roman writers with Mercury, probably because she was regarded as the consort of some deity who bore a resemblance to the Roman god.

Diti. A name which occurs in the Vedas in association with and in contrast to that of Aditi, and variously interpreted. One, the illimitable space, abode of mystery (Aditi); the other, space enclosed within the visible boundaries of the world, that is, between the disk of the earth and the vault of heaven (Bergaigne). " At all events the two together appear to be put by the poet for the entire aggregate of visible nature " (Muir). In later mythology Diti is the daughter of Daksha, wife of Kasyapa, and mother of the Daityas. She desired to have a son who would have power to slay Indra; certain conditions of piety and purity were imposed upon her in order that her wish might be fulfilled; she failed in one item of ceremonial purity, whereupon Indra divided the embryo in her womb, and created the Maruts from the several portions (*see* under Maruts).

Don. The sister of Math in British Celtic myth. She is probably the same with the Irish Danu (*q.v.*), as her offspring are equivalent to those of the Irish goddess in many cases. She was a goddess of fertility and culture, and was identified with the constellation Cassiopeia.

Durga. A warlike goddess of destruction ; a terrifying form of the wife of the Hindu god Siva. She is also known as Kali (*q.v.*), the name of Durga being that of a giant whom the goddess slew. Accounts of her origin vary, but in some way she was formed from the glory that issued from the faces of the gods, or from that of Vishnu alone. In a hymn addressed to her she is spoken of as " of the colour of fire, burning with austerity (or heat)." She was a resplendent being, armed with resistless weapons supplied by the gods ; she is represented with ten arms, but in countenance and general appearance she is not so hideous as Kali. "If at a later period Durga decidedly appears to have taken the place of the evil goddess Nirriti,[1] this is no proof that the case was so from the beginning, but only shows that the original signification had been lost" (Muir, v. 363). Durga is known under other forms besides that of Kali.

Dwarfs. (*See* Alfar.) Northern mythology would be incomplete without its dwarfs. According to the Eddic account of their origin, they were engendered in the giant Ymir's flesh, and at first were only maggots. Some dwelt underground, some in rocks. They were skilled artificers, and several magic and beautiful treasures were the work of their hands: Thor's hammer, the ring Draupnir, the ship Skidhbladhnir (*see* Freyr), Odhin's spear Gungnir, Sif's golden hair, Freyja's necklace, and Freyr's boar. They also fashioned human forms (*see* Askr and Embla). (Cf. Ribhus, "Indian Mythology.")

Dwyn. The British Celtic Venus. Subsequent to the introduction of Christianity she was regarded as a saint, being alluded to as "The Saint of Love."

Dyaus (from Div=to shine; Gr. Zeus). An ancient Indo-European divinity. The sky, or heaven; an abstract deity, without the exact personality of the supreme Greek god. He is invoked at times as "Dyaus Pitar," Father Heaven, and is generally referred to as the universal father, in association with Prithivi (earth), the two being the primeval parents of the gods and the human race. Both, however, are also in places spoken of as being themselves created, and to have been fashioned by one or other of the deities. Indra absorbed most of the attributes of Dyaus. (*See* the Teutonic god Tyr.)

Dylan. "Son of the Wave," made for the sea as soon as he was born, says British Celtic myth, he at once partook of the nature of that element. He was slain by his uncle Govannon (*q.v.*), and loud lament was made for him by the waves, his burial-place being where their murmur sounds sullenly along the sea-coast. However, instead of being an entity apart from the waves, his history and many circumstances in connection with his myth make it plain that he is the waves themselves, or a personification of them. The noise of the waves at the bar of the Conway River was regarded as his dying groans.

[1] Destruction personified (Bergaigne).
Note.—The Saktas are worshippers of divine energy personified in a female deity, especially in one of the forms of Siva's wife. The Tantras are the sacred books of the various sects of Saktas.

E

God E. The leafed ear of maize is the head-ornament of this deity of the Maya Indians, so that we have but little difficulty in recognising him as a maize-god. His head has been " evolved out of the conventional drawings of the ear of maize, and what was originally a head-ornament finally passed into the form of the head itself, so that the latter appears now as an ear of maize surrounded by leaves " (Schellhas, " Die Göttergestalten der Mayahandschriften "). That God E is a god of agriculture is seen from the Madrid Codex (Tro-cortesianus), which might almost be described as the Maya Georgics. E must therefore be parallel with the Aztec maize-god Centeotl. Brinton calls this god Ghanan, and Schellhas thinks he may be " identical with a deity Yum Kaax, who has been handed down to us, and whose name means ' lord of the harvest fields.' "

Ea, or Enki. The third of the great Babylonian triad of gods (*see* Anu and En-lil). He was a god of the waters, of the primeval deep, " his is the bed of the primeval mother," runs an old hymn (*see* Sayce). He was naturally associated with the idea of creation and fructifying power, and was believed to have much hidden knowledge and occult power, and to be the giver of wisdom as well as of life. In the tale of the flood it is written, " Who but Ea created things. And Ea knoweth everything " (Rogers, " Bab. and Ass. Rel."). According to the old historian Berosus, culture was brought to mankind by Oannes (Ea), who rose from the sea and was part man, part fish. Ea's dwelling was supposed to be at an opposite point of the heavens to Anu's high abode at the pole of the ecliptic. The site of his chief temple was at Eridu, which stood, before the waters receded, on the shore of the Persian Gulf. It was a home of the exorcist cult associated with the god. Marduk, the Bêl of Babylon, was Ea's son; the latter's wife was Nin-Ki, lady of the waters. (*See* Cosmology, Flood, and Adapa legend.) The conception of a fish-god as creator is comparatively rare. The Peruvians of the coast in Incan times worshipped the whale, which they designated Mamacocha or " Mother Sea," and a Mexican creative deity is alluded to as " Old Fish-god of our Flesh."

Ebisu. *See* Luck, Gods of.

Eddas, The. The chief vernacular source, exclusive of the songs of Scalds or Norse bards, whence we draw our knowledge of Norse mythology.

The Elder or poetic Edda was brought to light by the Icelandic Bishop Brynjulf Sveinsson about 1643, and at first attributed to the historian Saemund, who was born towards the middle of the eleventh century, and hence known as the Saemundar Edda. It is a collection of about thirty-five songs, partly dealing with gods, partly with heroes. Of the mythic poems the first is *Voluspá*, the prophecy of Volva, the sybil or prophetess, whom Odhin rides down to Hel-gate to visit, and who tells him the ancient history of the creation of the world and man, of the coming of the Aesir (or gods), and other matters, and ends by prophesying the final doom of the gods (*see* Ragnarok). *Havamál* is a collection of proverbs; *Vafthrudnismál* tells how Odhin in disguise visits the giant Vafthrudni; they test each other with questions; at last Odhin asks, " What did Odhin whisper in his son's ear before he mounted the pyre? " and as no one but Odhin himself knows the answer the giant loses his head, the forfeit agreed upon between them. *Grimnismál* relates another of Odhin's visits in disguise, this time to his foster-son, Geirrodhr, who, not knowing who he is, ill-treats him, and kills himself when he finds out the truth; *Skirnisför* is the journey of Skirnis (*see* Freyr and Gerdhr); *Harbardhsljodh*, the dialogue at the ferry between Odhin and Thor (*see* Thonaraz, note); *Thrymskvida* (*see* Thrymr); *Aegisdrekka* (*see* Aegir); *Hymiskvida* (*see* Hymir); *Alvissmál* (*see* Alviss); *Vegtamskvida*, or Balder's dream (Odhin questions a wise woman as to Balder's evil dreams); *Rigsthula* (*see* Heimdallr and the begetting of the three classes); *Hyndluljódh*, the giantess Hyndla instructs Ottar, Freyja's favourite, as to his ancestry and that of other noble houses; *Lokasenna* (*see* Loki and Aegir's feast). Among the heroic poems is the *Volundarkvida*, the song of the famous smith of old saga, Volund (German, Wieland).

The poems of the Edda are anonymous, and older than the manuscript which contains them. They are thought to date principally from the tenth century. Jönsson, the historian of Norse literature, assigns only a portion of one poem to as early a date as the end of the ninth century. Bugge does not credit Eddic mythology as a genuine body of traditional belief, but thinks it is merely a fictitious compilation imitated from Christian,

Jewish, and classical models. To him are opposed scholars who see in it a development on Norse soil of ancient Teutonic myths, to which a powerful impetus was given during the viking period, which was the age also of Scaldic poetry (*see* Saussaye). The land of origin of these poems is also a matter of various opinions, Norway or Iceland, the British Isles and Greenland, having the honour conferred on them in turn. Jönsson assigns them mostly to Norway; Bugge states that they were composed by Norwegian poets in Britain, whence they travelled through Scotland to Iceland, where additions were made to them. The manuscript of the Elder Edda is known as the Codex Regius, is housed in the Royal Library, Copenhagen, and belongs to the thirteenth century.

The Younger or prose Edda was compiled by the historian Snorri Sturluson (1178-1241). In the mythological part he borrows largely from the old poems. After an introduction (Formáli), we have the *Gylfaginning*, Delusion of Gylfi; it gives the cosmogony, the myths of Loki and Thor, and among other tales an account of the ploughing of the land, which became the island of Zealand, by the giantess Gefjon (*see* Frigg); in *Bragaraedhur*, Bragi's sayings or narratives, we have legends of the gods; *Skaldskaparmál* is a treatise on the art of poetry; *Háttatal*, a poem in honour of King Hakon, giving examples of the chief forms of Norse metre. The Younger Edda was first discovered in manuscript in 1625; it is preserved in three manuscripts, one a fine copy at Upsala (*see* Dr. Wilken's " Die Prosaische Edda," Paderborn, 1878).

Emma-ō. A Japanese Buddhist god looked upon as the lord of the regions of hell and the judge of the lower world. He is figured holding a large mace, with a cap on his head in the shape of a biretta.

Enigorio and Enigohatgea. Twin brothers who in the mythology of the Iroquois Indians symbolised the good and evil principles, the names signifying " Good Mind " and " Bad Mind " respectively. The good creative offices in the building up of the cosmic scheme of Enigorio were neutralised by his evil brother, who wandered over the earth transforming the beneficent creations of Enigorio into the things that have proved harmful to mankind. Thus if the kindly deity created rivers, plains that blossomed with fertility, and trees that bore delightful fruits, Enigohatgea strove to nullify these benefits by the creation of floods, lonely deserts, and thorny bushes. Exasperated at the evil wrought by his wicked brother, Enigorio fell upon him, and with a mighty blow sent him through the earth's crust, where he became ruler of the dark underworld. This myth was originally a typical " light and darkness " tale, and is a good example of the manner in which native legend may become sophisticated and radically altered by Christian influence. As told by a French missionary of the seventeenth century, it is the struggle of Iosheka, the white one, and his brother Tawiscara, the dark one. The spirit of dualism or the conception of good and evil is altogether absent, and we have to do no longer with a good and a bad mind, but merely with the powers of nature.

En-lil. (*See* Bêl.) An ancient Babylonian god, second of the great cosmic triad of which Anu was chief. As the latter was lord of heaven, so this deity reigned over earth as " lord of lands " and of all the spirits of the earth. The tablets of destiny are said to be in his possession. He had his abode on the great " earth mountain," and a chief temple at Nippur. Excavations here have given evidence of the great antiquity and importance of his worship. The kings of old Babylonia traced their descent from him, and considered the beautifying of his temple an addition to their other achievements. His name is literally translated En=lord, lil=demon, and this is thought alone sufficient to testify to his early origin. He became later more or less absorbed in Marduk (*q.v.*). (*See* Flood.) From these considerations it is clear that En-lil was originally an animistic nature- or earth-spirit, who later achieved the rank of godhead.

Ennead. A cycle of nine or more Egyptian gods. The theological system of Heliopolis, a chief school of religious thought in Egypt, embraced three companies of gods, of which the two first were known as the great and the little. The gods composing the former were Tum-Ra, Shu, Tefnut, Seb, Nut, Osiris, Isis, Set, Nephthys, with addition occasionally of other gods. When the doctrine of Heliopolis was adopted at another centre, the chief local god became merged with the leading Heliopolitan deity, and this composite god became head of a new Ennead.

Epona. A British and continental Celtic goddess, the tutelar deity of horses, and probably originally a horse totem. At Mayence a bas-relief exists which depicts her riding upon horseback.

Epunamun. The war-god of the Araucanian Indians of Chili. He is probably of Peruvian origin, as his name is Peruvian in its origin, and he seems to possess attributes in common with the sun-idol Punchau Inca, depicted as a warrior armed with darts.

Esaugetuh Emissee. The chief god of the Creek Indians. The name signifies " Master of Breath." He was the deity of wind, and his name is eloquent of that element. (*See* Tezcatlipoca for remarks upon American wind-gods in general.)

Etana. The hero of a Babylonian myth of which a copy was preserved in Ashurbanipal's library, an older fragment having also been discovered.

It relates how Etana is borne aloft on the back of an eagle, with the hope of obtaining a particular herb that would ensure the safe birth of his son. The eagle and his burden arrive safely at Anu's dwelling, but Ishtar, who has care of the herb, has a still loftier abode. Etana is not able to bear a giddier height, and he falls to earth, dragging the eagle with him. What happens after is not known as the end of the tale is missing. In the course of it there is a description of how the earth looked to Etana as it gradually fell away from his feet. Etana reappears in the Gilgamesh epic. He was credited with being the founder of the kingly state on earth. The myth bears a close resemblance to that of Icarus in Greek legend.

F

God F. A marked likeness exists between this deity of the Maya Indians and the Death-god A, and Schellhas thinks he resembles the Aztec Xipe, the god of human sacrifice, or a god of death by violence. He is unfailingly recognised by the presence of a black line usually running down the face and passing over or round the eye, in the possession of which characteristic he resembles Xipe. In the Codex Tro-cortesianus God F is represented with similar black lines on his body. The Death-god A has also the black lines on his body, and we will perhaps recall that Huitzilopochtli, the war-god of the Aztecs, was lined with stripes of blue. Schellhas thinks that "these lines probably signify gaping death wounds, and the accompanying rows of dots are intended to represent the blood."

God F is often represented along with the death-god when human sacrifice is the subject, and in some passages they are pictured as exactly similar in every detail. In other passages he is to be observed with the death-god, setting houses on fire and hacking them to pieces with his spear. The early Spanish authors make no mention of this god, although from the frequency with which he appears in the codices he must have been one of the most important of the Maya divinities.

It is by no means difficult to explain why the gods of war and of human sacrifice should be combined in one individual. The war-captive in Central America or Mexico was almost certainly immolated on the stone of sacrifice, with or without having a chance for his life afforded him, so that the conception of death by war or by sacrifice became merged in one. In Mexico, again, the conceptions of the gods of war and human sacrifice, Huitzilopochtli and Xipe, were maintained as strictly separate entities.

Fenrir (Fenris-wolf). One of the monsters brought forth by Loki (*q.v.*). The gods failing to find any fetter that would bind him securely, sent to the dwarfs, who fashioned the fetter Gleipnir, which was made, among other curious things, of the noise of the footfall of a cat, the breath of fish, and the spittle of birds; it was as soft as a silken string, but it effectually accomplished its purpose. The gods bound the monster with it, who struggled in vain to free himself; he bit off Tyr's hand, but was finally left a captive in a dark, deep place of the earth, his jaws fixed open with a spear, there to remain till Ragnarok, the last day of the gods. When once more free he was to help to vanquish the gods and himself be slain by Vidharr. Fenrir in reality depicts the death which springs from sin (Loki), to which even the gods are at last subject.

Fjorgyn. Mother of the god Thor, and identical with Frigg (*q.v.*), with Jord (earth), and Hlodyn (*see* Thor).

Fjorgynn. Father of the above, or rather, according to Kauffmann, to be considered her husband, who as Fjorgynn exactly corresponds to the Lithuanian god Perkunas. The etymological association between these two, however, is not definitely established (Saussaye).

Flood. There are two Babylonian accounts extant, one from Berosus and the other in the Gilgamesh epic. Berosus states that it took place in the reign of Xisuthros, the tenth Babylonian king, who was warned of what was coming. The tale he gives is the usual one of the ship with its freight of men and all kinds of creatures, and birds sent out, followed by the translation of the king and those belonging to him. In the epic the flood is said to be sent by the gods on account of the sinfulness of the people of Suruppak. Ea warns Utnapishtim (or Sit-napishtim), and directs him to build a ship. There is a terrible description of the breaking of the flood, and the work of the gods of thunder and storm; even the gods themselves are alarmed, and Ishtar feels remorse at having given her consent to it. Utnapishtim is saved with his family and the creatures he had taken with him in his ship. The flood lasts seven days before it subsides; then he sends out three birds, and the last does not return. Divinity is conferred on Utnapishtim and his wife, and they are borne to a far region " at the mouth of the rivers." (*See* Rogers, " Rel. Bab. and Ass."; King, " Bab. Rel. and Myth.")

For version of flood tale in Egyptian myth, *see* Tem; in Indian myth under Manu; *see* also under Yima (Persian) and various American legends under Creation Myths.

Fo or Fo-Hi is the Chinese Buddhist conception of deity. His aim is to save mankind by a process of instruction, but he is to be regarded as nothing but exalted humanity. Fo dwells always upon the verge of Nirvana, and may be taken as having a merely academic interest in human destiny. An ancient account of him states that he was the first Chinese emperor, a manifest anachronism, and relates that as his mother was walking on the banks of a lake she was enfolded by a rainbow, conceived, and brought forth Fo-hi, who as a child was brought up by some poor fishermen. He discovered his heavenly origin by means of the miracles he wrought. These legends have doubtless been superimposed upon the original myth. Shin-men is the son of Fo-hi, and is identical with the Hindoo Ganesa.

Fomorians. The Fomorians were the deities of an aboriginal population in Ireland, perhaps of the tribe known to mythology as Fir-bolgs. They were regarded by the later Celtic inhabitants of Ireland as hurtful, but it is a recognised phenomenon of mythology that the gods of an older people are invariably looked upon by newcomers as spiteful and vindictive. As a matter of fact, the Fomorians appear (when the veil of Celtic prejudice is lifted) as peaceful deities of the soil, gods of fertility, who ensured good harvests and kept the kine in milk. The Celts transformed this aboriginal pantheon into a veritable hell of evil deities, making the Fomorians the gods of storm, death, night, and winter. They were, naturally, in opposition to the Celtic gods, and by an allied train of ideas furnished the darker side of Irish Celtic dualism, illustrating the perpetual strife between good and bad, light and darkness, summer and winter, growth and decay. Thus the drama of chance and change and seasonal development had as its actors the bright Celtic deities and the dark aboriginal ones. But although the camps of light and darkness are opposed, their members are all of divine origin, and have relationship with one another in marriage and affinity. The more prominent of the Fomorians were Balor of the evil eye; Elatha, a god of knowledge; Indech, an earth-god; Tethra, god of the underworld of the dead; Net, a war-god; and Bres, who was a king of the Tuatha de Danann, or Celtic gods, for a space, probably to illustrate the occasional defeat of light by darkness. Most of these are mentioned under their several names.

Forseti (Vorsitzer=president). A god worshipped by the Frisians as a god of justice, who had a shining palace, Glitnir, where he sat at his tribunal. A temple and a spring on Heli-goland—formerly known as Forsitesland—were sacred to him, and human sacrifices are said to have been part of his worship. No one might touch the flocks that fed on the sacred island, or speak a word as they drew water from the spring. Forseti, it is thought, may perhaps have been identical with Wodan, or with Tyr (cf. Mars Thingsus). The sheep that might not be touched remind us of the sacred flocks of the Greek Apollo.

Fravashis.   In Persian mythology guardian spirits whose worship is traced back to an ancient ancestor cult.   They have been compared to the manes of classical mythology, but there was something apparently more personal and intimate about them.   They were part of the spiritual creation which took place during the first 3000 years of the world, and legend relates that they voluntarily took mortal shape, in order to further Ahura Mazda's cause on earth.   Anyhow, the Fravashi was one of the spiritual components of man, and seems to have become united with the soul after death.   The Fravashis are believed to watch over the earth, protecting home and land, as well as to be helpful agents of the supreme being.   The first month of the year is dedicated to them (the year beginning on the 21st March), and they are specially honoured during the closing days of the year, food being spread for their reception.   First days and months of the year are often dedicated to creative or assistant-creative deities, and this would appear to be a case in point.

Freyja (=Lady). A Scandinavian goddess, at one time identical with Frigg (q.v.), a sister of Freyr and daughter of Njordhr. She was a favourite of the Icelandic poets ; " an invention of the Scalds " (Saussaye).   Freyja was a beautiful and beneficent goddess of love, of marriage, of fecundity, and of the dead. Her dwelling was Folkvangr (Folk Meadow), and in Sessymir, her " hall of many seats," preparation was made for the dead who there congregated, for half the slain in battle were allotted to Freyja.   Freyja, like Frigg, was the wife of Odhin (who appears in some sources as Odhr), and their matrimonial relations with the god were similar.   She, too, had golden tears, which she shed when Odhr left her.   Freyja had two children whose names signified " ornaments " or " jewels."   Among her own was the poetic one of Mardoll, " Shining over the Sea." The chariot of the goddess was drawn by cats, for the same reason as Venus's was drawn by sparrows—that both were symbols of fecundity—and her special robe was one of feathers, in which she could fly far and wide.   Noted above all her possessions was the famous necklace (see Brisingamen), whence she was named Menglodh, " ornament loving " or " necklace glad."   Freyja has been identified with Menglad, the heroine of the poem of Svipdag and Menglad, in which the hero has to penetrate a wall of fire to reach his destined bride (see also under Gerdhr).   The myth is derived from the ritual marriage of human sacrifices to the goddess of fertility in agricultural

rite, and is similar to that of Sigurd and Byrnhild in the Volsunga Saga. She was associated with the return of spring as
was her brother Freyr. "The Icelandic Freyja is resolvable
into her three primary components—Freyr, Frigg, Venus"
(Golther). Freyja was demanded as part of his wage by the
giant who built the gods' citadel, and also by the giant who
stole Thor's hammer as the price for its return; in each case
she was saved (*see* Loki and Thrymr).

Freyr (OHG., frô; Anglo-Saxon, freá=lord). Called Frikko,
the lover, or wooer (Meyer), by Adam of Bremen, a chief
representative of the Vanir, worshipped in the north, Sweden
and Iceland being the chief centres of his cult; he was one of
the three great deities to whom was dedicated the splendid
temple at Upsala. Freyr was an agricultural deity, especially
associated with the idea of fertilising sunshine and rain, and of
general prosperity; sacrifice was offered to him for the crops,
and his image was yearly borne in a car round the country at
the approach of spring to insure a blessing on the fields (*see* in
this connection under Njordhr and Nerthus). Freyr's name is
often found joined with that of Ingr, the progenitor of the
Ingvæones (*see* Mannus), which appears to identify them, and
the kingly race of the Ynglingar traced its descent from Ingvis
(=Frey). Yngir in the Ynglingasaga is described as a mild
ruler under whom peace and prosperity reigned.

Freyr had Njordhr and the giantess Skadhi for parents; his
abode was Alfheim; his horse, Bloodyhoof, made the earth
tremble as it coursed over the rocks; his ship Skidhbladhnir,
built by the dwarfs, was able to contain all the gods, but could
be folded up like a cloth. The god sometimes rode on a golden-
bristled boar, fleeter than a horse, this animal being consecrated
to him. His sword had the same magic property as Thor's
hammer; he parted with it to Skirnir when he sent the latter
to woo the giant maiden Gerdhr for him, and so, being unarmed,
fell a victim in the last great conflict to the fire-demon Surtr.
The chief myth connected with Freyr is his wooing of Gerdhr
(*q.v.*), interpreted as the conquest of spring over dark powers
of winter (Meyer).

The whole character of Freyr, according to Mogk, is that of
a god of light; he sees in him the old sky-god, and with his
cult as a god of fertility shows the connection with the legend
of Sceaf, the wonderful babe who arrived on the coast of Schles-
wig, in a rudderless boat that came sailing out of the west, his
head resting on a sheaf of grain (*see* also Heimdallr). Golther

sees in Freyr all the essential characteristics of Tiwaz, although the warlike qualities are not so prominent as the sunnier and more peaceful ones. "The northern Freyr has more of the Apollo than Mars about him." Meyer describes him as a milder and more modern Thor, and in another place as an idealised elf of thunder. A good definition of Freyr would be a deity of the fecund spring-time. Like Apollo and the Irish Dermot he is associated with the boar—an animal with which several love-gods are brought into connection. The difference of opinion concerning him in the minds of the above-mentioned authorities is due to the circumstance that gods of fertility are very often thunder and rain gods as well.

Frigg. A chief goddess of the Teutons (OG., Frija; Anglo-Saxon, Frig; Langobardic Saga, Frea)=the beloved, the friend, the wife. Frigg was wife of Odhin and sharer of his throne, a mother of the gods and mistress of heaven. Through Odhin she knew the secrets of men's fates, but was unable to reveal them. Frigg was goddess of love and of the household; she conferred blessings of all kinds on marriage, and was pictured with a spinning-wheel—in Sweden and some parts of Germany the constellation of Orion is known as her distaff or spindle. Frigg was lavish in the distribution of gifts from her magic casket, of which Fulla, sometimes referred to as Frigg's sister (*see* old Merseburg charm), had the care, as also of the goddess's slippers. Fulla was one of a train of sixteen goddesses attendant on Frigg, who in the duties attached to their offices more or less personified different attributes of the chief goddess. One was skilled in healing, another had the gift of removing every obstacle that stands in the way of the union of lovers, another punished those who broke their troth, another had special care of those whom Frigg wished to preserve from harm, another performed Frigg's errands on a horse that could ride through air and water. Freyja was also among Frigg's following, and ranked next the latter, whose place she afterwards occupied. Gefjon was another of the attendant goddesses; she claimed as her handmaidens all those who died unmarried. Both her name (one of Freyja's surnames was Gefn), and the reference in the Eddic book of Lokasenna to her knowledge of the world's fate, and to the surrender of herself in order to obtain an ornament, seem to make her one with Freyja; it is uncertain if she is identical with the giantess Gefjon, of whom a tale of ploughing is told similar to that associated with Dido. Frigg was chief of the warrior maidens in Valhalla; she had also an especial abode of her own, called Fensalir, " the halls of the sea " or " halls of the clouds," where she wept golden tears for her son Balder. A less pleasant view of Fensalir associates it with mists and darkness, and makes it a place in the depths of the earth where the dead who died other than in battle and were in part Frigg's booty " breathe the damp vapours from the rotting bogs " (Kauffmann). In this connection Frigg appears to have relation with Hel (*q.v.*). Frigg was probably identical at one time with Freyja; she was so with Fjorgyn, or Jordh, the mother of Thor. Possibly also, as some think, with the goddess whom Tacitus likened to Isis, whose symbol was a ship, and who was worshipped by the Suevi.

From this goddess we get our Friday (Frjadagr, Friâtag, the Latin Dies Veneris). Her responsibility for the name of Langobard rests on a tale told by P. Diaconus : The Vinili asked her help against the Vandals ; Odhin had promised victory to whichever of the opponents he saw first on awaking in the morning ; Frea advised the Vinili to bring their wives with them with their hair tied round their faces like beards, and she then introduced them into her husband's room. When the god awoke he asked who were these long-bearded men, whereupon Frea exclaimed, " As you have given them their name, give them also the victory ; " and so the Langobards got the name by which for ever after they were known.

The popular figures of Fru Freke, Gôde, Perchta (Bertha), Holda or Holle, etc., who ride through the air, and are surrounded with legendary fancies, belong, according to Saussaye, entirely to mediæval folk-lore and are not to be connected with this goddess ; Meyer, however, thinks their relationship with the goddess Frija-Frigg unmistakable. " Jordh, Frigg, Freyja, Nerthus, Fulla, Nanna, and others are all essentially the same, personifying life, producing nature " (Much). (*See* for necklace, under Freyja.)

Fudo. A Japanese Buddhist deity, worshipped as a god of fire. He sits, stern and "immovable," surrounded with flames, and holding a two-edged sword and a rope ; the latter he uses like some of the Indian gods to restrain the wicked. The flames are interpreted as symbols of wisdom, of which he is also said to be a god (Murray).

Fukurokuju. *See* Luck, Gods of.

G

God G. The chief portion of the hieroglyph of this deity of the Maya Indians of Yucatan is the sun-sign, *Kin*. There is very little doubt that the god is a sun-god pure and simple, not a culture-hero who comes from the sun like Kukulcan, but the veritable luminary himself—and for this reason we may take it he is a god of very considerable antiquity and of prime importance, yet strangely enough he seldom appears in the codices. Although the conception of the sun in most mythologies is generally that of a life-giving sustaining deity, this is not always so in the Central American system, where we must sharply differentiate between the sun and the man of the sun—the last a benign being who instructs mankind in the arts and crafts of civilisation, and cultivates the desert until it blossoms as a garden; the first a deity whose sole sustenance is human blood, and who must be well supplied with this gruesome pabulum or perish, plunging the world into a dark and desert abyss of gloom and famine. We must, therefore, not be surprised to see God G accompanied at intervals by the symbol of death. He is generally represented wearing an elaborate nose-peg, and occasionally as having a serpent-like tongue.

Gandharva. This Hindu god was a dweller in the upper spaces of air, was connected with light or fire, a guardian of the sacred Soma plant, and associated with the waters by his connection with the Apsarasas (*q.v.*). He is described as beautiful, clothed in sweet-smelling garments, and armed with bright weapons.

Gandharvas. One of the bands of semi-divine beings created in the beginning by Brahmā. They were 6333 in number, and were born " imbibing melody." There are different accounts of their origin. In later myth they are met with as the musicians of Indra's heaven, espoused to the Apsarasas. They have been identified with the Centaurs. Prof. Macdonell, after throwing doubts on the etymology, adds, " the two conceptions appear to have nothing in common." (*See* Soma.)

Ganesa (Gana-pati). The Hindu god of wisdom, or of good luck, worshipped especially as a remover of obstacles. He is invoked at the beginning of any undertaking, when starting on

a journey, etc. Being also a patron of learning, his name is
found at the beginning of literary works, as one able to ensure
their success. In one Purāna only is it stated that he was the
son of Siva and Parvati, or, according to legend, either of one
or the other parent singly. He was the leader of Siva's hosts.
There are variants of the myth accounting for the loss of his
head. His mother, in her pride, showed her child to Saturn,
and his glance destroyed it; or it was cut off in anger by Siva;
in either case reparation as far as possible was made by one or
other of the gods, by substituting the head of an elephant.
Ganesa also lost a tusk, this in a struggle with Rama of the
axe, when barring the latter's passage to Siva's room, while
the god was sleeping. Figures represent Ganesa as corpulent,
with elephant head, and four or more hands, and riding on or
attended by a rat, this animal as well as the elephant being
symbolical of wisdom. He strongly resembles the Egyptian
Thoth.

Gangā (Ganges). The sacred river said to flow from Vishnu's
toe. The name of Bhagirathi is also given it, as by his prayers
it was brought down to earth. The myth of the descent of the
Ganges is told in both epics ; in the Rāmāyana it runs as follows : Sagara, King of Ayodha, was at last promised offspring,
after he had long done penance in order to have his prayer for
them granted. One of his wives, he is told, will have one child,
the other sixty thousand sons, who are accordingly born. The
next incident is the king's preparation for a horse sacrifice, but
Indra, fearful of the power this will confer on him, steals the
horse, and the sixty thousand then go in search of it. They find
it grazing quietly somewhere far down in the depths of earth.
They see the sage Kapila seated near and rush towards him,
and are immediately consumed, only their ashes remaining, for
Kapila was an incarnation of Vishnu. Their father is told that
if the water of the Ganges could reach his sons' ashes it would
wash away all sin and enable his sons to mount to heaven.
Thousands and thousands of years go by, until at last a grandson, Bhagirath, obtains Brahmā's promise that the Ganges shall
flow down, he having won this favour by his austerities. Siva
undertakes to receive the falling waters on his head. Gangā
was highly incensed at having to comply with this promise,
and so Siva to punish her kept her flowing through his hair for
a long period, until at last he allowed her to descend to earth,
where the waters separated into seven streams. The waters

in time reached the hidden regions where the ashes of the sixty thousand were lying, and accomplished the deliverance of Sagara's sons.

Garuda. The king of birds, half man, half eagle, the swift vehicle of the Hindu god Vishnu. Legend relates that he stole the Amrita or nectar, and only after a fierce struggle did Indra recover possession of it. He was the son of Kasyapa and Vinata, the latter sister to the queen of the serpents, the animosity between the sisters being alleged as the reason that Garuda was an enemy of the serpent race.

Gāyatri. An address to the sun (Savitri). The most sacred verse of the Vedas. It is held to have a deep mystical signification. Some transcribers are said to hold it in too great reverence even to copy.

Gayomart. The first created man, according to Persian mythology (*see* Cosmology).

Gefjon. *See* Frigg, and Gylfaginning, a part of the prose Edda.

Geirrödhr. A Norse giant associated with a tale of Thor. Loki having clothed himself in Freyja's feathered robe, goes and spies at Geirrödhr's dwelling, is caught, and only released on condition that he will persuade Thor to visit the giant without his usual armour of defence. On the way a friendly giantess, Gridh, warns Thor, and gives him her own staff, iron gloves, and belt of strength. Before he reaches the giant's dwelling Thor is nearly drowned in a river, in spite of his belt, for its waters continue to rise, owing to one of the giant's daughters standing astride it; Thor throws a stone at her, and reaches the bank with the help of an ash. Arrived at the giant's home, he feels the iron chair on which he is seated rising to the ceiling; pushing his staff against the beams he forces the chair down, and the giant's two daughters being underneath it, both their necks are broken. The giant endeavours to kill Thor with a red-hot iron wedge, which the god catches with his iron gloves and therewith puts an end to the giant. The tale has been interpreted as the victory of the god over powers of the nether world, the description of the place in the version of Saxo Grammaticus lending colour to this idea, which is however combated by some scholars. Saussaye gives preferable adherence to the possible mythical kernel of the tale consisting in the meeting of two mountain thunderstorms, but the former is almost certainly the correct interpretation, and bears a close resemblance to many other tales of " The Harrying of Hades " (*see* Popol Vuh and Blue-Jay).

Gerdhr. One day the god Freyr looked down from Hlidhskjalf, Odhin's throne, whence the whole world could be seen, and his eyes lighted on a giant maiden, who, as she moved, set air and sea and all the worlds quivering with light from the glitter of her arms.   He desired to gain possession of this most beautiful of women, and providing his messenger Skirnir with his own horse and sword, he sent the latter to win her.   The task was not without difficulty; Skirnir had first to make his way on Freyr's horse through the circle of fire which surrounded Gerdhr (cf. the myth of Siegfried and Brunhild, and the tale of Svipdag and Menglad (*see* Freyja)), and he then met with further opposition from the desired bride herself; gifts of golden apples and of the magic ring Draupnir proved of no avail, and Skirnir had to resort to more forcible persuasions before Gerdhr consented at last to meet Freyr nine days later in the forest of Barri.   The attempt to reach Gerdhr through the fire alludes to the ancient agricultural rite (*see* Freyja).   Gerdhr is the stern, unyielding, but beautiful winter moved by the spring and sun god Freyr, who in the end employs force to complete her conquest.

Gilgamesh Epic.   The remains of a copy of this old Babylonian poem were found inscribed on twelve tablets in Ashurbanipal's library at Nineveh, and are among the most interesting literary relics of antiquity.   It begins with an account of two men—Gilgamesh, an oppressive ruler of Erech, but gifted with a knowledge of hidden things, and Eabani, a hairy, savage creature, who lives like the beasts, and who is allured into more civilised ways by a woman, who tells him he will " become like a god."   These two having been brought together, start on an expedition against Humbaba, an Elamite ruler, under whose watch is Ishtar, whom he keeps at the " Cedar Mountain in the East." [1]   In the fight that ensues Humbaba is killed.   There are incidents in connection with Ishtar, and then we hear of Eabani also dying.   This leads to the great episode of Gilgamesh in his grief seeking his ancestor Sit-napishtim (or Khasīsatra), who has been granted immortality (*see* Flood).   He has a difficult passage till, having passed the Dark Mountain, he reaches the " Park of the Gods," where the trees are hung with

[1] " Recent discovery confirms the existence of a sacred cedar forest in Elam " (*see* art. Paradise, " Jewish Ency.").

precious stones. (This passage is compared with a similar one
in Ezek. xxviii.) Then he crosses the waters of death to the
fields of the blest. The interview with his ancestor follows, in
the course of which the latter relates the tale of the flood (q.v.).
A further episode is the finding of the plant of immortality and
its subsequent loss. On his return to Erech, Gilgamesh tries to
get into communication with his friend Eabani, who at last is
allowed to visit him, and gives him details of the underworld
(see Aralu). Within this framework of general incident are a
diversity of details, concerning the way to paradise, the fountain
of cleansing, of dreams, and of the early life of Eabani, etc.
Gilgamesh has been identified by some scholars with Nimrod.

Girru (Gibil). Babylonian god of light and fire, addressed as
the first-born of heaven. He was associated with the three
primeval cosmic deities, as the son of Anu, and of Ea, and the
messenger of Bêl, for Girru personified the fire of heaven, the
fire at the heart of the earth, and the fire of the altar. He
was the god of smith-craft, and, as identified with the sacrificial
fire, the intermediary between god and men. (See Nusku.) He
may be equated with Vulcan and Thor.

Gobniu. See Govannon.

Govannon. A deity of the British Celts, equivalent to the
Irish Gobniu. He was the god of smith-craft and workmanship,
who made the weapons of the gods, and brewed their mighty
ale. He may well be equated with the Roman Vulcan in many
respects. In later myth he appears as Gobhan Saer, an architect
of magic power, who was responsible for the much-disputed
round towers of Ireland and many of her early churches. He
was the brother of Amaethon (q.v.).

Grannos. A deity of the continental Celts, equated with
Æsculapius by the Romans because of his patronage of healing
springs. Several localities in France are named after him,
notably Aix-la-Chapelle (Aqui Granni), Graux, and Eaux
Graunnes. An inscription to Grannos has been found at
Musselburgh, near Edinburgh.

Gucumatz. The Kiche (Guatemala) name for the god
Quetzalcoatl (q.v.).

Guecubu. Guecubu, or Aka-kanet, was a mischievous or evil
agency believed in by the Araucanian Indians of Chili. The
name means " The Wanderer without," an evil demon hostile
to humanity, who ever lurks in the confines of camps or other

places where men do congregate with the intention of tormenting or destroying them. All the misfortunes which occur to the tribesman he attributes to the Guecubu. If an earthquake happens the Guecubu has caused it. If a horse tires the Guecubu has ridden him, and so forth.

Gula. Wife of Ninib (*q.v.*). A Babylonian goddess of healing, referred to as the " Great Physician." Death and disease were subject to her power; she had power to restore life, but, like her husband, she is represented at times as a destroyer, slaying with the diseases she had under her control.

Gwion Bach. Son of Gwareang. (*See* Keridwen.)

Gwydion. The ideal bard of the British Celts, and the patron of those who practised the arts of poetry, divination, and prophecy. By the theft of the swine from Pryderi which is recounted in the Mabinogion, in which connection Pryderi must be regarded as a divine being, Gwydion poses as a culture-hero who, by the " harrying of Hell," or the underworld, has brought gifts to mankind from the domain of the earth-gods. In another version of the story, however, he is caught and confined. He is found so much in connection with swine that the theory has been hazarded that he was perhaps a swine-god or pig totem in still more ancient times. But it is hard to reconcile such a shape with the deity who became the beau-ideal of bardic art. The very fact that he was transformed into a pig by Math would almost serve to show that he could not originally have been one.

Gwynn. A British Celtic deity and a god of the underworld. He was the son of Nudd (*q.v.*), and in post-mythical times was regarded as monarch of the Welsh fairies or Tylwyth Teg, and chief of the Ellyllon, a band of puckish elves, not unlike brownies or goblins. He was usually described as being accompanied by an owl, probably to indicate the nocturnal character of his revels and adventures.

H

God H. A Maya god. The hieroglyph of the day Chiccan (Great Serpent) in the Maya calendar includes a sign or quantity like the scale or skin-spot of a serpent, and this occurs on the forehead or temple of God H, therefore Schellhas combats Seler's opinion that in some of the figures represented under this hieroglyph a " young god " may be observed, and in this contention he appears to be correct. That God H has some relation to the serpent appears possible, but the significance of the relationship is vague.

Hachiman. The deified Japanese Emperor Ojin of the third century A.D., who is worshipped as a Shinto god of war.

Hanuman. The monkey chief of whose deeds we hear in the Mahābhārata and Rāmāyana (*q.v.*). His father was said to be the god of the wind, so Hanuman was partly divine. Legend states that his mother had been a nymph transformed into a monkey, which accounted for Hanuman having this form. The hideousness of his jaw was said to be due to Indra, who had broken it in trying to kill him. His monkey hosts built a bridge for Rama between India and Ceylon.

Haokah. A thunder-god of the Sioux Indians. He was equipped with horns to typify his connection with the lightning, or else with the chase, with which nearly every thunder-god is in some manner associated. The two halves of his countenance displayed varying expressions and colours, and when cheerful he wept copiously, when downcast laughed uproariously. Heat affected him as cold, and cold was to him as heat. The wind was the stick which he employed to beat the thunder-drum. Like Zeus he hurled the lightning in the shape of thunder-bolts or meteors.

Haoma. In Persian mythology the personified sacred plant and the drink produced from it (*see* Soma). Its worship is believed to have been common to the Indians and Iranians before the races separated.

Hāp, Hāpi. God of the Nile. As god of the North River he is figured red, with a bunch of papyrus on his head ; as god of

the South, blue, with lotus plants. The river was held in
mysterious reverence, and the god was looked on in the same
way, "there was that in him which no imagination could
fathom, no sculptured stone represent." Like all gods associated with life-giving waters, he was connected with ideas of
productiveness and resurrection. He is usually figured as a man
with the breasts of a woman ; lotus or papyrus plants, and a
vase or vases, are his symbols. There is an emblematic representation of the union of the North and South in a scene of the
two Nile gods tying stems of lotus and papyrus round a symbol
of union (*see* Lanzoni). Hāpi was early identified with Osiris,
and with Herschef the ram-headed god of Herakleopolis.

Hap (Gr., Apis). Sacred bull of Memphis, in whom Ptah-
Osiris was believed to be incarnate. The dead Apis was the
Serapis (Osiris-Apis) of the Greeks. Sixty-four mummied bulls
were found in the Serapeum discovered at Memphis by Mariette
in 1851.

Hara. A name of Siva or Rudra.

Hari. Name of Vishnu or Krishna. These two names are
sometimes found combined to represent the union of the two gods.

Hathor (Het-Heru). "House of Horus," so called because
Horus, the sun, rose and set in her. An ancient Egyptian
goddess, the chief centre of whose cult was at Dendera, where
she was worshipped under seven forms. Hathor was a cosmic
deity, goddess of the sky, mother of Shu and Tefnut, mother and
daughter of Ra, queen of heaven, creatress of all existing things,
resplendent mother of light, eye of Ra, armed with punitive
fires for the wicked. When Ra desired to destroy mankind, he
sent Hathor to carry out his decree (*see* Ra). She was the
personification of the sky, figured in the form of a cow, the
nourishing mother. She was also a goddess of the dead, for
like Nut she was the "Lady of the Sycamore," and provided
refreshment for the soul (*see* Ba). All other native goddesses
were forms of Hathor. The Greeks saw in her their Aphrodite,
and she was further identified with the Astarte of Byblos.
Similarly with Isis she was astrally identified with the star Sept.
She is figured as a woman, with head surmounted by horns and
solar disk, the feather of Maat, and a head-covering of vulture's
wings. She was furthermore the goddess of beauty, love, and
joy, and in this respect may be equated with Venus or Aphrodite,
with whom the Greeks identified her. When other goddesses

were identified with her it was as a compliment to their beauty and feminine virtues.

Heimdallr. A Scandinavian god, known only to Norway and Iceland, " a poetical hypostasis of the old sky-god " (Mogk), and in connection with whom no trace of cult is found. Heimdallr was a god of light, of the early sun, " the dawn and the beginning of all things " (Uhland), akin to the Greek Helios. He was born on the far horizon, of nine giant sisters, " suggestively typical of waves," and nourished by the strength of the earth, the sea waves, and the blood of sacrifices. He kept watch on the frontiers of highest heaven (Himinbjorg), guarding the rainbow bridge (Bifrost) against the assaults of the giants. His sight and hearing are said to have been of such matchless keenness that either by night or day things a hundred leagues off were visible to him, and his ear could detect the sound of the grass growing on the earth and the wool on the sheep's back. Descriptions of Heimdallr speak of his golden teeth, of his horse with golden mane (Gulltoppr), on which he rode to Balder's funeral, of his wonderful sword, Hofud (head), of his horn (Gjallarhorn), that like Roland's awakened echoes afar, and with which the gods were summoned to the last great battle. He had deadly feud with Loki, with whom he fought daily, the combatants taking the form of seals, for the recovery of Freyja's stolen necklace. At the end of all things they slay one another. This incident possesses all the necessary elements of a light and darkness myth.

A further account of this god in the Rigsthula relates that he wandered on earth as a king, and engendered three classes of men: serfs, freemen, and nobles. All, rich and poor, the Voluspa tells us, are his sons. That is, all alike share in the sun's light. " The distinguishing traits of Heimdallr are those of Tiw (Tyr), with whom he was identified in pagan times " (Kauffmann). Rydberg shows how he is associated with the religion of Sceaf (see also under Freyr). Much does not agree with his identification with Tiwaz; he compares Heimdallr with Freyr; " these two and Njordhr," he writes, " are essentially one with Balder, only more developed as gods of the seasons."

Hel (Old Teutonic, Halja; literally " the coverer up, or hider," " Oxford Dictionary "). In early Scandinavian mythology the general abode of the dead, and the name of its presiding goddess, the Proserpina of the north. Hel was not originally associated with the idea of punishment, but rather with Elysian delights ;

Balder, the god and warrior, went there when killed, and he was longingly awaited in the underworld, where Hel's high hall, Eljudnir, was decorated and mead prepared for his reception. Later, when slain warriors were believed to enter on another warlike existence in Odhin's Valhalla, Hel became the home after death of those who had not fallen by the sword, men, women, and children ; manner of death, not manner of life, then divided the souls of the departed, as in Mexico, where we find the dead warriors join the sun, and the drowned or dropsical go to the paradise of Tlaloc, god of rain. It remained for a later development of myth, influenced by Christian dogma, to confer on Hel and her realm the most repellent attributes of death and the underworld. Hel's habitation is now described as, hunger her table, starvation her knife, delay and slowness her servants, precipice her threshold, care her bed. Hel herself was always a vague personality belonging later to " the higher demonic beings rather than to the goddesses " (Meyer, Mogk). She was the offspring of Loki (q.v.), and All-Father, fearing her evil power, cast her into Niflheim and gave her power over nine worlds, among which she distributed the dead. Niflheim was a place of fog and darkness, and distinguished from Hel (see Cosmology). Within the domain of Hel was Mimir's well of immortal mead, his grove of sinless beings destined to repeople the world, and Urdhr's fountain.

NOTE.—Old Teutonic ideas concerning the dead were not very defined. Souls were conceived as in the air, sweeping past on the winds; they formed the phantom host accompanying the wild huntsman of popular tradition.[1] Or they might be dwelling in the hills, perhaps feasting there with Odhin, before Valhalla was known, many hills being sacred to him, whence may have arisen the legends of sleeping heroes—as Charles in the Odenberg and Barbarossa in the Kyffhäuser. The soul was also believed to haunt places of burial and cross-roads. It might return and visit the living, which was not always a pleasant experience for the latter, as it produced on a sleeper the sensation of oppression as of nightmare (Alp-druck). The departed, however, occasionally returned with kindly purposes of warning, but on the whole the general desire was to keep them away, to which end many curious customs were in vogue. The soul could assume

---

[1] Autumn was the time when the dead were thought more especially to revisit the earth; it was therefore necessary to propitiate them by rites, which, as Reinach puts it, the church has christianised in the observance of All Souls' Day.

what shape it liked of bird or beast. A land of the dead was not, however, unknown to our forefathers. It lay out in the west beyond the sea, and in one source Britain is spoken of as this blest abode. That the departed were further believed to lead a life after death similar to the one on earth is proved by the various arms, ornaments, and useful articles buried with men and women, or burnt with the body on the funeral pyre, although this prehistoric custom according to Aston (*see* Shintoism) is not necessarily associated with a fixed belief in a future existence. Offerings were also made to the dead, and other ceremonies were associated with soul-cult, of which ancestor-worship was a particular form (Saussaye).

Heliopolis. The On of the Scriptures. The centre of the worship of the sun-god in Egypt (*see* Ennead).

Heqet. An Egyptian frog-headed goddess, mother of one of the forms of Horus. Birth and resurrection were ideas associated with her by her worshippers. She is sometimes referred to as the consort of Khnemu. The frog-symbol is sometimes associated with idea of water, and deities of water are often those of birth also, as in the case of Chalchihuitlicue, Mexican goddess of water.

Hermopolis. There were two cities of this name in ancient Egypt. The first (Pa-Tehuti—city of Thoth) was the capital of the fifteenth nome or division of Lower Egypt, the modern El Bakalîyeh. Its tutelar deity was Thoth, God of Wisdom. The second (Khemennu) was the capital of the fifteenth nome of Upper Egypt, the modern Eshmunnên. Of this city also Thoth was the principal god. Hermopolis (city of Hermes) was the Greek name of these cities, Hermes Trismegistos (Thrice-great Hermes) being the Hellenic name of Thoth.

Hiranyagarbha. *See* Brahmā.

Hoenir. A lesser god of northern mythology, found in constant companionship with Odhin and Loki. He plays no prominent part as one of the triad, though fair in face, tall in stature, and fleet-footed, and spoken of by the Vanir, to whom he was given as hostage by the Aesir, as a mighty prince. But he was failing in higher mental qualities, and when any one consulted him he had no reply to make but " let others advise." So Mimir (*q.v.*) had to be sent with him to the Vanir, and the gods lost their chief counsellor. Hoenir, with Odhin and Lodhurr, gave life to the first pair of human beings (*see* under Odhin). Kauffmann identifies him with Tyr. This god so incapable of speech, " dark in person as in name," who takes his place between the other two gods, has been interpreted as a sun, forest, or cloud god, as the first passing of winter into spring, or twilight between night and morning. Uhland calls him the singer. Hoenir, although dull and incomprehensible during this earlier period of his existence, played an important part when, after the last great battle and destruction of the world, it rose afresh from its ashes. (*See* Ragnarok.)

Horus (Heru). " He who is above." There were two deities of this name who in course of time became blended. Horus the Elder (Gr., Aroëris), the sun-god, the Egyptian Apollo, was the hawk-god of Upper Egypt, chief of the triad at Ombos, the most ancient god of the pantheon. He is figured as a man with a hawk's head, or simply as a hawk. Among several names under which he was worshipped at different centres were Heru-Khuti (Gr., Harmakhis), " Horus on the two horizons," to whom the great sphinx at Ghizeh was dedicated; Horus of the two eyes (sun and moon); golden Horus, etc. The sun-god at Edfu, where his temple stands, was figured as a sun with wings of many colours; and his emblem was placed over the entrance to temples to ward off evil powers.

Distinct from this Elder Horus was Horus the Child (Heru-P-Khart, Harpocrates), son of Osiris and Isis, who avenged on Set the murder of his father, and performed with filial care all the obsequies due to the dead Osiris. Horus the Child is figured with the curl of youth at the side of his head, and with one finger pointing to his mouth, sometimes seated on a lotus leaf. The young sun-god, according to one legend, rose from the primeval waters seated on a lotus flower. The hostility between Horus and Set, though it symbolised the conflict of powers of light and darkness, and became intimately enwoven with the Osiris myth, is thought to have a foundation in some far away historical fact, some old tribal feud between worshippers of the hawk and worshippers of the Set animal (?), in which the hawk-tribe, which became the dynastic tribe, was victorious. Hence the Pharaohs always had a Horus name.

Horus, Children of = Amset (Mestha), Hapi (Hāp), Tuamutef, and Gebhsennuf. These four assisted Horus in his offices for the dead. The intestines of the deceased were placed in canopic jars under their care, each jar being surmounted by the head of one of the four. A primitive belief pictured the heaven supported by these sons of the sun-god. These four genii of the dead represented severally the south, north, east, and west. They find a parallel in the Bacabs of Mayan Indian myth, who supported the heavens, standing one at each corner of the world. These were called Kan, Muluc, Ix, and Cauac, and jars containing their effigies held the entrails of the dead in vessels similar to those of the funerary genii of Egypt.

Hotei. *See* Luck, Gods of.

Hou Chi. A Chinese divine personage, stated to be the founder of the house of Chou, and often alluded to as " The Associate of God." He was the son of the lady Chiang Yuan, who, in order not to be childless, trod in a footprint of God, and conceiving, brought forth Hou Chi. It is curious to read in the ancient odes of China that on his birth " sheep and oxen suckled him." The entire myth is undoubtedly connected with parthenogenesis, or virgin birth. Hou Chi was exposed in a wide forest, but was discovered by wood-cutters. He lay on cold ice, but the birds covered him with their wings. When he became a man he taught the Chinese the art of agriculture, for which service he was deified, and during the existence of the Chou dynasty was worshipped in association with God himself. He may be regarded as a description of " culture-hero " like the Mexican Quetzalcoatl.

How-Too. The Chinese god of earth, to whom the emperor sacrificed annually. In connection with his worship the great objects of nature are adored, mountains, rivers, and hills being worshipped by their names, and on account of their size and sacredness. In the sacrifice of How-Too silk and prayers written upon parchment are buried before his temple, as well as the chief domestic animals used for food. The Spirit of Earth is the only spirit beside that of Heaven to whom the emperor believed himself subject. This conception appears to apply to earth itself in its terrestrial aspect, and not to any personification of it such as the Titans of Greek mythology or the Jotunn of Scandinavian myth.

Hrungnir. A Norse giant whom Odhin challenges to a race ; the giant springs on his horse Golden Mane, and rides after Odhin over sea and through the air to the gods' abode. Then he grows arrogant and boasts of transporting Valhalla to Jotunheimr, and finally in single combat with Thor is killed, although it is told that his head, heart, and shield are of stone. He falls with his foot on Thor's neck; the gods are unable to remove it, but the feat was accomplished by Thor's three-year-old son Magni. A piece of the weapon Hrungnir had hurled at Thor, and which had been broken in pieces by the god's hammer, remains lodged in the latter's forehead. Groa, a wise woman, succeeds in loosing it by her magic chanting, during which Thor tells her that he has brought her husband, Orvandill,[1] safely back from the giant's home in a basket, with the loss of a toe only, this having been exposed and frostbitten, but Thor had thrown it up to the skies and turned it into a star. Such good news is distracting to Groa, who forgets her singing and leaves Thor with the stone fragment remaining in his forehead. All Thor's encounters with giants have been interpreted as nature myths, as victories over the demoniac powers of winter. Hrungnir has been thought a giant of the wind; Meyer sees in the encounter between him and Thor the clash of storms, which occurs on the Norwegian coast at the sudden onrush of the east wind; but such "nature-myth" interpretations are somewhat discredited nowadays, and if we regard Hrungnir as a wind-demon who had not achieved godhead, or the wind-god of an older strata of the population—therefore inimical to the Æsir or later Scandinavian deities—we will probably be nearer the truth.

Huitzilopochtli was the war-god of the Aztecs of ancient Mexico. His myth of origin relates that his mother Coatlicue, a devout widow, picked up a ball of bright feathers on her way to the temple of the sun-god and placed them in her bosom. She soon became pregnant, and her family, conscious of the disgrace, threatened her life. Huitzilopochtli, however, was born fully armed, and fell upon them, slaying them. The name signifies "Humming-bird to the Left," from the circumstance that the deity was represented as having the feathers of the humming-bird on the left leg. From this it has been surmised by some that he was a humming-bird totem. But that is not an explanation which will altogether appeal to the serious student of mythology. It is seen that Huitzilopochtli is closely connected with the serpent. The name of his mother signifies "Female Serpent," and he is represented as being circled round with serpents. His great drum is a serpent-skin, and the caryatids of his image are serpents. His sceptre is a serpent.

---

[1] Anglo-Saxon, Earendel, the morning star.

In aboriginal America the serpent was highly honoured as the symbol of warlike might, as it typifies the lightning, the divine spear. Fragments of serpents were eaten as powerful warphysic. It is further closely associated with the bird. Thus the name of the god Quetzalcoatl (q.v.) signifies "Feathered Serpent," and many other examples could be adduced. We may thus regard Huitzilopochtli as a god, the primary conception of whom arose from the idea of the serpent, the symbol of warlike might and of the divine war-spear, and the humming-bird, the harbinger of summer, the season when the serpent or lightning-god has power over the crops. For he was not a war-god alone. As the serpent-god of lightning he had a connection with summer, and therefore had some dominion over the crops of the earth. We must, in considering the nature of war-gods, recollect the connection in savage consciousness between war and the food supply. If war was not waged at least annually the gods would be deprived of the blood of the war-captives, and would perish, and if the gods succumbed the crops would fail, and the race would die out. His principal festival was the Toxcatl, celebrated immediately after that of Tezcatlipoca. Huitzilopochtli was usually represented as being crowned with a panache or plume of humming-birds' feathers. His face and limbs were striped with blue, and in his right hand he carried four spears. He bore a shield in the left hand. He was war-god of the Aztecs *par excellence*, and was believed to have brought them from the fabled Aztlan to the site of Mexico, which was called after one of his names, Mexitli, " Hare of the Aloes." The high priest of Huitzilopochtli, the Mexicatl Teohuatzin, was the religious head or pontiff of the Aztec priesthood, and held office by right of descent. He was regarded as being next to the monarch himself in power and dominion.

Hun-Ahpu. A hero-god of the Kiches of Guatemala, and a figure in the " Popol Vuh," or sacred book of that people (q.v.). He was the son of Hunhun-Ahpu and Xquiq, and together with his brother made a marvellous progress through the Kiche Hades.

Hurakan. The " Heart of Heaven," a deity of the Kiche Indians of Central America. He was in all probability identical with the Mexican Tezcatlipoca (q.v.). He was undoubtedly a wind-god, as he is also designated " He who hurls below." For further particulars concerning him the reader is referred to the article " Popol Vuh," of which he is one of the central figures.

The assertion that the word " hurricane " was derived from his name may be accepted with some reserve.

Hymir. A Norse giant, father of Tyr. He owned a large cauldron, and the gods being in need of one of the kind, Tyr and Thor start off to fetch it from the ice-bound palace in the far east where the giant lived with his mother and his beloved. The latter warns the strangers of danger, and the gods hide under the pots. Hymir comes striding into the hall, with frozen beard, the ice groaning under him, the beams giving way, and the pots rolling down. So Hymir sees the god Thor—a sight boding no good. He prepares a feast of three oxen, of which Thor eats two. The next day the giant and Thor go out fishing together, taking an ox-head for bait. Thor drags the Midhgardh worm up to the side of the vessel and strikes it on the head with his hammer, but Hymir in fear cuts the line so the monster sinks back into the water. On their return Thor carries the ship and two or three whales that had been caught up to the giant's house ; he gives other proof of strength, and finally takes up a cauldron which Tyr could not move, puts it over his head, and goes off, Hymir following in pursuit ; the god turns and slays the latter, and so secures the cauldron for the gods, who use it every year at the flax-harvest feast in Aegir's hall. Another version of the tale makes Thor knock the giant overboard, and wade to land himself, the ship being shattered.

I

Goddess I : The Water-goddess. From the representations of her in the Dresden MS. the Mayan Indians of Central America evidently regarded the water-goddess as an old woman with wrinkled brown body and claw-shaped feet, wearing on her head a serpent twisted into a knot—symbolical of the sinuous flow of water—and holding in her hands an inverted earthenware vessel from which water flows. She is obviously no water-deity like the Mexican Chalchihuitlicue, spouse of Tlaloc, but a personification of water in its devastating aspect—a bringer of floods and waterspouts, dreaded of the folk of Central America, and in this character it is not surprising to see that in places, especially in the Dresden MS., she wears the cross-bones of the death-god. No fixed hieroglyph of this goddess can be proved with certainty.

Idhunn. In Norse mythology the goddess of eternal youth and wife of Bragi. In her keeping were the golden apples, tasting which the gods for ever renew their youth. She was the chief figure in one of the many tales with which Loki was associated. He, Odhin, and Hoenir were one day preparing an ox for their meal, but could not get it to cook properly. An eagle perched overhead on a tree called out to them : " If you will let me have my share of the flesh it will soon be cooked." The gods consenting to the bargain, the eagle flew down and seized such an immense portion that Loki, incensed, thrust at him with his staff ; the eagle flew off both with staff and Loki, who was unable to leave go of it, and the eagle, who was the giant Thjazi in bird form, would not let him loose till Loki had promised to bring Idhunn to him. Loki, to entice Idhunn from Asgardhr, pretended he knew of better apples than hers, and Idhunn fell into the trap ; no sooner was she in the forest than the eagle flew down and carried her off. The gods, missing their apples, which Idhunn had taken with her, grew old and grey, and insisted on Loki recovering the lost goddess. So Loki put on Freyja's falcon robe, flew to Thjazi's dwelling, changed Idhunn into a nut, and bore her away in his claws ;

the eagle pursued him, flew into a fire the gods had lighted on the outskirts of their dwelling, and so perished. Idhunn is the goddess of immortality, and she is therefore the wife of the poet or Scald Bragi. The idea that the immortal gods require nourishment at set intervals is widely disseminated, and is at the root of all conceptions of sacrifice (*see* Huitzilopochtli). Thjazi who seizes such a large piece of flesh and proves too much even for Loki, the father of evil, may be an elder interpretation of death, who seems for a space to have overcome immortality, but who in the event is vanquished.

I-em-Hetep (Gr., Imouthis). "He who comes in peace." A third deity of the Memphian triad, a son of Ptah and Nut. He was a god of learning and healing, a friend to the living and the dead. He is figured seated with an open scroll on his knees, and is thought to be a deified physician. In later Greek times his cult waxed strong, and he was credited with great powers of exorcism.

Igigi. In Babylonian mythology the spirits of heaven.

Ikto. A deity of the Sioux Indians, the inventor of human speech, and a being whose craft makes him a parallel with the Scandinavian Loki.

Inari (Uga-no-Mitana). A Japanese goddess (sometimes a bearded god) of rice. The fox was originally sacred to her (Florenz), and figures of foxes are always found beside the entrance to her temples. The cult of the fox now overshadows that of the rice-god. The animal is held in dread by the Japanese owing to their belief in its superhuman power of assuming whatever form it chooses, even entering as a spirit into man. (*See* Chamberlain, "Things Japanese.")

Indra. A Hindu god of the firmament, and in a lesser sense a god of rain and battle. He is the king of the gods, and the twin-brother of Agni (*q.v.*), but post-Vedic literature teaches that his reign extends for a hundred divine years only, at the end of which time he may be superseded by another deity, or by a human hero of especial attributes. A martial atmosphere often surrounds the rain-god (*see* Huitzilopochtli), especially in torrid climates where the crops depend on rain, as it is believed that if the gods languish for lack of war-captives the crops will fail. Indra is not an uncreated deity, but the son of Heaven and Earth; and he is rarely regarded as creative. Like the Aztec war-god who had power over the crops, and to the entry on whom the reader has been referred, Indra immediately after birth commenced his strife with the demons of drought, headed by Vritra, thus probably symbolising the suddenness of the cloud-burst or the rain-storm. He quarrels and fights with Krishna, whose wife desires the Pārijātā tree which grew in Indra's heaven, and is worsted. The virtuous on earth are accepted in Swarga, his heaven, until the time for their next incarnation arrives. His home is on the fabulous Mount Meru, supposed to be to the north of the Himalayas, and in the centre of the earth—perhaps the land whence the Indo-Aryans originally migrated—and here dwelt the Apsaras or nymphs in everlasting sensual delight (q.v.). In Bengal he is worshipped one day in each year, and in seasons of drought special offerings are made to him. To this unequalled warrior mankind owed some of their most precious gifts, for the sun and dawn were of his begetting, and it was he who overcame the demon Vritra (Ahi, or otherwise named), the dragon that encompassed and held the waters in thrall, till Indra by his victory loosed the rains and streams. He vanquished the Asuras, other opponents of deity, and clove the mountains, the " cloud fortresses," so that the torrents, or as it is symbolically expressed, the cows (used to signify both waters and dawns), were released. He also captured the cows (for sacrifice, Macdonell) from the Panis (q.v.). Other enemies over whom he was victorious were the Dānavas, Daityas, and Dasyus, thought to personify dark-skinned aborigines of India, with whom the Aryans came into conflict. The myth of his attack on Ushas and the destruction of her chariot is interpreted by Bergaigne as the sunrise scattering the tardy dawn. Indra was usually accompanied by his allies the Maruts, by Vishnu and Agni. He was said to have found the latter god when hidden in the waters, and the two gods were mystically blended in a dual personality. Vayu was also frequently found with him in his chariot. A dog also figures as Indra's companion, and on one occasion helped to recover stolen cows. Indra (or Vayu) formed with Agni and Surya a triad of deities (see under Agni).

Indra is represented with four arms and hands, holding lance and thunderbolt; he is covered with a thousand eyes, into which were changed marks impressed on him by Gautama for dis-honourable conduct. He has other weapons—bow and arrows, a hook, and a net which was of service in the overthrow of his enemies, and he could assume what shape he chose. His chariot was golden, harnessed with ruddy " sun-eyed " steeds, numbering at times over a thousand or thousands. When he rode he was mounted on a white elephant (Airavata) or horse. Indra's "figure has become very anthropomorphic, and surrounded by mythological imagery more than that of any other god in the Veda" (Macdonell).

As one of the guardians of the world, Indra was regent of the eastern sky.

Innana (Ninni). Title conferred on an ancient and supreme Babylonian goddess, afterwards merged in Ishtar. According to Jastrow, Innana or Ninni was a general appellative for a chief goddess.

Ioskeha and Tawiscara. These deities, whose names signify the "White and Dark Ones," were among the principal gods of the Hurons, who say that their mother, a virgin, died in giving them birth. In a quarrel which arose between them Ioskeha used the horns of a stag as a weapon, whilst Tawiscara brandished a trailer from a wild rose-bush, and was vanquished. He sought safety in flight, and the blood which fell from him turned into flint stones. Ioskeha, freed from his evil influence, founded the human race, and commenced a crusade against the great frog which had swallowed all the waters of the earth. This monster he slew, and directed the waters he had swallowed into rivers. He then received from the great tortoise which supports the earth the secret of making fire, and this art he communicated to men. He was in fact the universal culture-hero who, in his character of light-bringer, scatters the powers of darkness and sows the seeds of civilisation. The allusion to the blood of Tawiscara turning into flints is, of course, due to the fact that all night-deities were wielders of the lightning, as when the sky grows dark before a thunder-storm night, according to the savage, temporarily returns. The flint is the symbol of thunder and lightning in nearly all American mythologies.

Ishtar. A goddess worshipped by the Semitic peoples under different names (Astarte, Ashtart, Ashtereth, etc.), and known to the Babylonians and Assyrians as Ishtar. Other goddesses were of slight importance in comparison with this great "Queen of Heaven" and chief of the Igigi (*q.v.*). She had two sides to her character; in one, as a "mother of mankind," she was full of pity for the afflictions of her offspring on earth, and we are told that she wept at the destruction caused by the plague-god, and that she repented of the consent she had given to the flood. It is in this light that she is figured suckling a child, and that she is appealed to in a prayer found in Ashurbanipal's library as "the merciful goddess." But she had a fiercer aspect. She was goddess of sexual love, and very indifferent to her suitors or husband, and licentious rites were a feature of her cult, such as those described by Herodotus (bk. i. 199). Of war, too, she was a great deity "clad in terror," and causing trembling to the very gods. The martial Assyrians delighted in her as their great ally in battle, as did the Philistines, who hung up Saul's armour as a trophy in her temple.

Ishtar is spoken of as daughter both of Anu and of the moon-god, and she appears as wife of one or other of the chief gods. Her name and Ashur's are often found linked together, invoked on the eve of battle, and any one who should presume to carry off one of the tablets in Ashurbanipal's library had their combined wrath called down upon him. Ishtar's oldest temple was at Erech (Uruk) in Babylonia ; here she was also worshipped as Nana ; while at Agade and Sippar of Aminita she was known by this latter name ; she was worshipped at Nineveh and Arbela, each place having its Ishtar, and there was a temple to her at Ashur (see Anahita).

Ishtar was identified with the planet Venus among many other astral associations. Her cult was connected with that of Tammuz (q.v.), the lover or husband for whose death she was responsible, but for whom she afterwards made her descent into Hades to seek for the water of life. To reach the throne of Allatu (q.v.) she has to pass through seven barriers, and at each of these a portion of her raiment, beginning with her crown, is taken from her, and she arrives nude at her destination. During her absence in the nether regions the earth ceases to bring forth. Ishtar is subject to much affliction, due to Allatu's anger at being disturbed in her regions. At last a messenger from Ea arrives, who secures the water of life, and releases Ishtar from the dark goddess's power by sprinkling some of it over the former, who is thus delivered from the shades. Her connection with Tammuz and her descent into Hades identify her as a "corn-mother" like the Greek Demeter, whose reappearance clothes the earth with fertility. In the primitive mind agriculture and the cult of sex are often connected, and joined in the person of a single deity.

Isis (Ast, or Hest). The great Egyptian goddess, daughter of Seb and Nut. She is the mother of Horus and the archetype of motherhood and all the wifely virtues. For the myth of how she sought her husband, *see* Osiris. Additional tales attached to her name occur in connection with the main Osiris theme, and are chiefly concerned with her powers of magic. One relates that a child who had died from the bite of a scorpion was resuscitated by the magic spells that Isis uttered over him. A more important legend tells how Isis desired to be equal to the great god Ra, which was only possible by gaining knowledge of his secret name. This Ra was not willing to divulge, but he was old at this time, and Isis got him into her power, for she formed a serpent from his slaverings and the earth and set it in the path of the god, who was bitten and brought near death; then Isis undertakes to heal him by her magic powers if he will tell her that which she desires to know, and after putting her off with his other names, Khepera, Ra, and Tem, he finally consents that " it shall pass from his bosom to hers." So Isis became endowed with supreme godhead. We hear further of how her head was cut off by her son because she interfered in the fight between him and Set, and how Thoth, who often intervened at critical moments, replaced it with that of a cow.

The chief shrines of Isis were at Abydos and Busiris, and later there was a famous one at Philæ. She is figured as a woman, and represented in the costume of an Egyptian queen, with the head-dress of the queen-mother; her head at times is surmounted by horns and the solar disk or the double crown. On her head is also seen a throne, the ideogram of her name. The cow was sacred to her. The Greeks identified her with Athene and Demeter. She was astrally associated with the star Sept. The greater number of nature-goddesses were more or less forms of Isis. Her worship spread from Greece to Rome, and was finally carried to nearly all parts of the world.

Italapas, the Coyote, is one of the most important of the deities of the Chinook Indians. He assisted Ikanam the creator in the making of men, and taught them various arts. He framed the first prairie by willing the sea to become land, and afterwards fixed the various taboos or forbidden things regarding hunting. He does not in this way resemble the Coyote of the Californian myths (*see* Cosmology, Californian tribes), who was a mischievous being, and who attempted to thwart the creative agency in every way.

Itzamna. A sun and culture god of the Maya Indians of

Yucatan. He has several other names of merely tribal significance, such as Votan, Kab-ul (The Red Hand), all local variants
of one great sun-myth in which is pictured the " Master of the
Dawn " or " Man of the Sun " as the leader and founder of
culture and civilisation. He was perhaps a relatively aboriginal
sun-god to Kukulcan, to whom he was evidently a powerful
rival.

Ixtlilton, or " The Little Black One," was the brother of
Macuil Xochitl (*q.v.*), and was the Mexican god of medicinal
virtue, the being who kept men in good health or who assisted
their recovery from sickness, therefore the brother of the god
of good luck. His temple was composed of painted boards,
which sounds as if it still retained the characteristics of the tent
of the tribal medicine man or shaman, and inside this oratory
were kept little jars of water known as tlilatl, or " black water,"
which children afflicted with any malady were wont to partake
of. If any parent whose child had benefited from this treatment desired to show his gratitude by offering a feast to the god,
he had his image conveyed to his private dwelling, where odorous
gums and incense were burned before it, and solemn dances
performed in its honour. The celebrants formed round it in
groups, waving flowers and plumes, dancing gracefully to the
sound of the native drum, their bodies swaying in a combined
and rhythmical motion, "very graceful to be seen," says Sahagun.
The deity was then supposed to descend and to open fresh jars
of pulque liquor. He next examined the jars dedicated to him
which stood in the courtyard of the house, and if any unclean-
ness was found therein, the master of the house was proclaimed
as a wicked man, an adulterer or an evil liver. The officiating
priest presented to the miscreant a mask to cover his shame,
called ixque.

Izanagi and Izanami. The creative pair of Japanese mythology. The full myth connected with them is given in Koji-Ki
(Records of Ancient Matters), a Japanese history written in
the early eighth century which starts with the creation and is
carried down to the earlier part of the seventh century. The
following account is an extract from the translation of Koji-Ki,
by B. H. Chamberlain (" Transactions of the Asiatic Society
of Japan," vol. x., 1882). " The names of the deities that were
born in the Plain of the High when the heaven and earth began
were the Deity Master-of-the-August-Centre-of-Heaven ; next
the High-August-Producing-Wondrous-Deity ; next the Divine-

Producing-Wondrous-Deity. These three Deities were all born alone, and hid their persons." Two other deities were then born " from a thing that sprouted up like unto a reed-shoot when the earth, young and like unto floating oil, drifted about Medusa-like." They also were born alone and hid themselves (*i.e.* died, *see* Chamberlain, note). After this start follow the names of succeeding divine generations, till the seventh, Izanagi and Izanami, is reached. These two were commanded by the other deities to begin the work of creation. Accordingly they took their stand on the floating bridge of heaven, and with a jewelled spear they stirred up the brine ; the drops that fell from its point became the island of Onogoro. On this the two deities erected a dwelling-place, and from their union issued in turns more islands, and numerous gods of the elements. Izanami died giving birth to the god of fire. Her husband in his affliction cut off the head of his fire son, from whose blood sprang other deities. Then Izanagi descended into Hades in search of his wife. He lit a tooth of the comb that held his hair to illuminate his passage, but finding only the decaying corpse of his wife, he fled away in horror. Reaching earth again he hastened to bathe and purify himself in the river. From every garment he threw off, and from every part of his body to his " august nose," was born a fresh deity, certain evil powers also coming into being. (*See* Ama-Terasu and Susa-no-o.)

It is noticeable that there is no account here of the creation of human beings.

J

Jagganath (Juggernaut). "Lord of the World," a Hindu deity, dubiously connected with Vishnu. Probably of local origin, he is worshipped at Puri in Orissa, his devotees believing that the sight of his image is more essential to their welfare than any actual worship. He is regarded as the great dispeller and remover of sin. In the Ain-i-Akbari the myth relating to him is as follows: A certain Rajah who had raised a temple by the sea-shore dreamed that a log of wood which would be drifted up by the ocean must be treated with great reverence. The log duly appeared, and was called Jagganath. Another myth states that Visvakarma fashioned a shrine to hold the bones of Krishna, killed accidentally by the hunter Jara. However, a mortal king, Indradhumna, spied the god at work, who left the image handless and footless. The monarch's distress was so great, however, that Brahmā endowed the image with hands, feet, and a soul. Three days in each year the image of Jagganath is on view. On the first of these days —the Bathing Festival—the image is bathed by the priests. Ten days elapse, during which the god is supposed to suffer from a cold. On the tenth day the Car Festival is held, when the deity is supposed to be taken for a change of air to the nearest temple. After remaining a week the car is pulled back among shouting thousands, the recovery of the god being thought complete. Formerly it was the custom of fanatics to cast themselves beneath the car containing the deity in the belief that immediate entrance to paradise would be their reward.

Jimmu Tennō. The first Japanese emperor of human origin, who is said to have succeeded the dynasty of the gods in the seventh century B.C.

Jingo Kōgō. The great Empress of Japan, the date of whose reign is given as the first half of the third century A.D. She is noted for her warlike deeds, a chief of these being the conquest of Korea. She was mother of Hachiman (*q.v.*).

Jizō. A Buddhist god of Japan, looked upon as the helper and protector of women, children, and travellers. He is very kindly in aspect, is figured as a shaven priest, and carries a pilgrim staff. A jewel he holds in one hand is said to symbolise wisdom. He has besides a heap of small stones in his lap, and this is out of pity for hapless dead children, whom a cruel hag forces to pile up stones beside the Buddhist river that corresponds with the Styx. As travellers are also under his care, his image is frequently placed where there are cross-roads (Murray and Papinot).

Jord (Earth). *See* under Frigg and Nerthus.

Jorōjin. *See* Luck, Gods of.

Jötunn. The giants or evilly disposed nature-powers of Scandinavian mythology. These may be classed with the Titans or earth-giants possessed by so many mythological systems, but in the religion of the North they typified the rigours of winter, snow, frost, ice. When they are conquered by the hammer of Thor, the rain-god, the hard, frost-bound earth is broken up. In such a climate as that of Scandinavia heat and cold were often regarded as good and evil by early man, and take the place of the perpetual struggle in more genial climes between light and darkness.

Jurupari. The principal deity of the Uapes Indians of Brazil and of other Brazilian tribes. His cult is invested with the utmost secrecy. The myth of his birth states that he was born of a virgin who conceived after drinking a draught of cachari, or native beer. She possessed no sexual parts, and could not give birth to the god until bitten by a fish whilst bathing. When arrived at man's estate, Jurupari invited the men of the tribe to a drinking-bout, but the women refused to provide the liquor, and thus gained his ill-will. He devoured the children of the tribe because they had eaten of the uacu tree which was sacred to him. The men, enraged at the loss of their offspring, fell upon him, and cast him into a fire, from the ashes of which grew the paxiuba tree, which the Uapes say is the bones of Jurupari. Whilst it was night the men cut down the tree and fashioned it into sacred instruments which must never be seen by the women, on account of the dislike Jurupari had conceived for them. Should a woman chance to see the sacred symbols pertaining to the worship of Jurupari, she is at once poisoned. On hearing the " Jurupari music " of the priests on the occasion of one of his festivals the women of the tribe at once rush into concealment, nor dare to emerge from it until all chance of danger is past. In all probability this custom proceeds from the ancient usage common to most American tribes that the rites of initiation of the men of the tribe must not be witnessed by the women thereof, probably on account of some more or less obscure totemic reason or sex-jealousy analagous to the exclusion of women from the rites of freemasonry, to which, strange to say, the worship of Jurupari bears a strong resemblance.

K

God K. This god of the Mayans of Central America is probably closely related to B (*q.v.*) and is described by Schellhas as the " god with the ornamented nose." Seler sees in him a benevolent deity as the sign for good days is frequently depicted with him, and his obvious connection with B would bear out this assumption. In the Paris MS. B is represented as holding K's head in his hand, and elsewhere he is depicted as carrying it in different positions. Brinton considers K as a variant of B, and Forstemann regards him as a storm-deity, his ornamental proboscis, like that of Quetzalcoatl, being intended to represent the blast of the storm. We shall see that in " The Popol Vuh " the gods Gucumatz (the Kiche name for Kukulcan or Quetzalcoatl) and Hurakan, " he who hurls below," are separate entities, and that no attempt is made to confound them. At the same time their attributes are not dissimilar. Hurakan is a wind-god *par excellence*, and if Gucumatz has shed some of the boreal qualities of Quetzalcoatl in his removal to a southern clime it is not likely that he would lose them altogether. In God K, moreover, we observe certain stellar signs which go to show that he is a deity of the Quetzalcoatl class or group. If, according to Forstemann, K were a storm-god, he would probably be identical with Hurakan. But his astronomic significance makes it almost certain that he is, as Schellhas suggests, merely a variant of God B, that is, Kukulcan. It is the features of this deity which are so frequently to be met with on the corners and copings of the ruined structures of Central America, and whose trunk-like proboscis has led so many superficial " antiquarians " to write of " an elephant-headed god," " an elephant-headed Buddha," and suchlike monstrosities. As has been indicated, the trunk-like snout is merely a funnel through which such gods were supposed to emit the gales over which they had dominion, as can be seen from a careful study of the pinturas, where the wind is usually depicted as issuing from the snout in question. Whether or not the snout was evolved from that of the tapir is another question. " If the rain-god Chac is distinguished in the Maya MS. by a peculiarly long nose curving **over** the mouth, and if in the other forms of the rain-god, to which, as it seems, the name Balon Zacab belongs, the nose widens out and sends out shoots," says Dr. Seler, "I believe that the tapir, which was employed identically with Chac, the rain-god, furnished the model" (Bulletin 28, "Bur. Am. Ethnol.," p. 45). Is God K identical with Chac the rain-god of the Mayas? Forstemann places God H as the deity of the day Cauac, the rainy season, and K under Muluc, the glyph of which shows a flood or rainy clouds. He mentions, however, regarding H's connection with the day Cauac, that "a proof of positive correspondence does not appear." One would expect to find the god Chac corresponding with the day which is practically identical in Mayan with his name. H possesses serpentine characteristics which might lead to the assumption that he was Chac, only these do not appear to be sufficiently definite. Again, K is so closely related to B, that is Kukulcan, that it would be unwise to surmise without much stronger proof than we possess that he was Chac, or rather the original figure from which the several Chac gods proceeded. Chac bears every sign of affinity with the Mexican Tlaloc, the Nahuan rain-and-water god, whose face was evolved from the coils of two snakes, and bears some remote resemblance to the snout of B and K. But again the Mexican pictures of Quetzalcoatl are not at all like those of Tlaloc, so that there can be no affinity between Tlaloc and K. Therefore since Tlaloc and Chac may be regarded as identical, and Tlaloc differs from Quetzalcoatl, who in turn is identical with B and K, it is clear that Chac has nothing to do with K.

Ka. The "double," which, according to Egyptian belief, was born with every man. It survived after death, but its immortality depended on the care of the living, for it perished unless it had a figure to which it could attach itself. To secure it a dwelling therefore, in case the mummy was destroyed, statues of the dead were placed in a chamber by the tomb, so that the Ka might not wander homeless. It also required to be fed, and to this end daily offerings of food and drink were placed in or near the tomb; failing these the Ka might exist for a while on whatever it could pick up, but was finally doomed to die of starvation. The Egyptians believing that every inanimate object also possessed a Ka, drawings or sculptures of articles of food, etc., came in time to replace the actual things, as by virtue of their doubles they could thus vicariously nourish the dead. Not wholly for the sake of the dead were all these rites performed; the living had a selfish interest in them also, for the neglected Ka might become a very unpleasant and ghostly visitant to the scenes of its former life. The offering of food developed later still into a mere ceremonial rite, a formula being pronounced over it by the priest whereby it was converted into a spiritual aliment for the soul. (*See* Budge, "The Liturgy of Funerary Offerings.") The Ka is undoubtedly a survival of pre-historic belief, stone-age burials yielding good proof that its existence was credited throughout long ages. We find its parallel in the "shell" of modern theosophy, which is supposed to survive the parent body for a short space only.

Kaboi. A deity of the Karaya Indians of Brazil, who led the ancestors of that tribe from the lower regions of the earth to its surface. (*See* Cosmology, art. Tapuya.)

Kala (Time). A form of Vishnu, described in the Rig-Veda as "the source or creator and lord of all things." Kala is also a name given to Yama.

Kāli. "The Black One." A hideous goddess, one of the repulsive and terrifying forms of Siva's wife (*see* Durga). Her necklace is of skulls, her other ornaments dead men's hands and bodies; in one of her four hands she holds a sword, in another a decapitated head; she is besmeared with blood, and has her tongue out of her mouth, which, according to one account, represents her grimace at finding that during one of her frenzied dances of triumph she had trampled her husband under foot. The worship of this impure goddess was accompanied by sanguinary rites. From the ritual in the Kālika Purāna it is clear that Kāli is a goddess of thunder who is also a war deity. One account of her origin states that she sprang from the eye of the war-bred goddess Durgā, as Athene sprang from the head of Zeus. She is the special tutelar deity of the Thugs, who sacrifice to her before setting out on an expedition.

Kalpa. A day of Brahmā, the length of time from a creation to the destruction of the world; divided into fourteen periods, Manvantaras, over each of which reigns a Manu. (*See* Manu and Yuga.)

Kama. Hindu god of love. Son of Vishnu and Lakshmi under the forms of Krishna and Rukmini, or perhaps of Brahmā. As desire he was associated with creation (*see* Cosmology); this mere abstract Kama developed into the "inspirer, or fulfiller of desire," and finally was looked upon as the god of sexual love.

Among myths associated with him is one in connection with Siva, who is reported to have mourned long over the death of his wife Sita, desiring no woman to take her place. But the gods wish for a son of his to fight a certain demon, and send Kama to try and induce the great god to come out of his seclusion and take another wife, in which mission Kama is successful, but at a sacrifice. Siva, angry at being thus interfered with, slew the god of love on the spot with the rays from his third eye. Kama has much in common with the Greek Eros, who was also associated with the creation of the universe. He is usually personified as a handsome youth, equipped with a bow and arrow, and carrying wreaths of flowers. He is accompanied in his journeys by the cuckoo, the bee, the personification of spring and the breezes. He is worshipped in Bengal at the time of marriage.

Kartikeya (or Skanda, Kumara, etc.). A Hindu post-Vedic god of war. According to different versions of his origin he was son of Siva, or of Agni and the Ganges. He was nursed by the Pleiades (with these were identified the wives of the Rishis), hence his six heads. Another myth makes him the offspring of Agni and a female who took in turns the form of the wives of the Rishis, with whom the god of fire had become enamoured ; and yet another describes that sparks from Siva's eyes became six infants, whom Parvati embraced with such rapture that their bodies became one, though their six heads remained. Kartikeya was leader of the hosts of heaven, and the destroyer of the demon Tārika, whose austerities had made him formidable and feared by the gods. This deity is represented riding on a peacock, armed with bow and arrow.

Keridwen. A nature-goddess of the British Celts. She was a divinity of the under-water Elysium. She possessed a mystic cauldron called Amen, from which proceeded a draught which conferred the gift of inspiration upon whomsoever drank of it. Keridwen's son by Tegid, Avaggdu, was so painfully ugly that his mother resolved to compensate him with the gift of inspiration, and prepared the draught which he was to drink in the Amen cauldron. Gwion was sent to stir it, but became tempted and drank it, whereupon he was chased by Keridwen, and underwent many transformations to escape her. Finally he was swallowed in the shape of a grain of wheat by Keridwen, who had taken the shape of a hen. She gave birth to him, and cast him into the sea, where he was found by Elphin, called

Taliesin, and became a bard. The myth is connected with the Celtic idea of transmigration of souls. Keridwen was a goddess of inspiration and poetry, probably worshipped by bards. She was once obviously an earth-mother, as proved by the possession of a cauldron, the symbol of plenty, like the Roman cornucopia. (*See* Dagda.) She is described as a goddess of grain, and seems at one time to have been associated with the pig, though how such a symbol became to be connected with a deity who was afterwards regarded as the patroness of bardic art it would be difficult to say. We find the same circumstance in connection with Gwydion (*q.v.*), who appears in the same cycle of myths as Keridwen, and, indeed, the personalities therein all appear to be associated in some manner with swine. Taliesin is the son of inspiration, the ideal poet, confounded with the sixth-century bard of the same name, who was probably called after him.

Khensu. The "sailor" or "traveller across the heavens." An Egyptian moon-god, son of Amen-Ra and Mut, one of the triad of Thebes. He was sometimes confused or identified with Thoth. In the dual form of Khensu-Hor, or Khensu-Ra, he was worshipped as a solar deity. He is figured with a human head or a hawk's, surmounted by solar disk and lunar crescent, and the side-lock of youth. He was regarded as an exorciser of evil spirits in later times.

Khepera (Egypt). The form in which the sun-god arose from Nu (*q.v.*), and in which he emerged daily from Tuat at the beginning of the new day. With Khepera was associated the idea of birth and resurrection. He was self-produced from primeval matter, and the creator of all life. His emblem was the beetle, explained by the habit of the latter of rolling its eggs in a ball of dung to be hatched by the sun, giving rise to the conception of the germs of life being contained in the solar orb. As the beetle was his emblem this would seem to account for the fact that it became the symbol of resurrection in Egypt. He is seen seated in the boat of the sun.

Khnemu (Khnûm). The "modeller," ancient Egyptian cosmic deity, a personification of creative force, chief of the triad of Elephantiné. He was god of the first cataract, at which spot the Nile was of old believed to flow down from heaven. Khnemu and Ptah were Thoth's active agents in carrying out the work of creation. The universe was Khnemu's handiwork ; he formed the cosmic egg from the mud of the Nile, and shaped man on his potter's wheel. He is generally figured with a ram's head, and identified with other ram-headed Nile-gods. Later his worship was associated with that of Ra, and he is further represented with four rams' heads, as embodying the souls of Ra, Osiris, Seb, and Shu. (*See* Lanzoni.)

Kischar. *See* Cosmology (Babylonian).

Kishi Bojin. Japanese goddess, represented carrying a child and a pomegranate, with which fruit Buddha is said to have cured her cannibalistic propensity of devouring young children.

Koji-Ki. Or " Records of Ancient Matters." A Japanese classic dating from the early eighth century, containing an account of the creation and generations of the gods.

Kompira. A Buddhistic Japanese god, who has been identified with Susa-no-o, and with a deity called Kotohira, of whom little is known. His chief temple is on the island of Shikoku. He is looked upon as a patron of seafarers.

Krishna. An avatar (or partial incarnation) of Vishnu, who was re-incarnated in this form in order to destroy Kansa, a monarch against whose tyranny the earth had appealed to the gods. Kansa, being forewarned of the coming birth of his enemy, slew all the previous children of Vasudeva and Devaki, Krishna's parents, but when the latter was born, his father managed to convey him away secretly, and exchange him for the child of a cowherd Nanda, by whom and his wife, Yasoda, Krishna was brought up, the Gopas and Gopis (cowherds and shepherdesses, or dairymaids) being his youthful companions. Krishna from his earliest days possessed superhuman strength, to which he added an unusual love of prankish tricks, and the legends of his childhood, illustrative of his divine power, have always been the subject of popular delight. Among the dairymaids, his favourite was Râdhâ, and the story of their love has been the theme of poets. Krishna, among other marvellous deeds, finally slew Kansa. In one legend we hear of his carrying away the sacred tree from Indra's garden (*see* Parijata); in another it is related that Indra, jealous of the honour shown to Krishna, sent rain for seven days and nights, with intent to destroy the earth, and in order to give shelter to his companions Krishna, then little more than a child, lifted up the mountain Govarddhana, and supported it in the air with his little finger. Another of his victorious deeds was the slaying of the serpent king. His youthful career was thus passed amid pastoral scenes, and the herculean young god joined in the pastimes of his companions, and is seen among their festivities playing on the flute, for he was as beautiful and as gifted as Apollo. According to a Hindu saying " Rama is for the men, Krishna for the women " (Barnett, " Heart of India "). The gods who were pleased with his worship were generous in showering boons upon him, and the goddess Uma among her gifts is said to have endowed him with some hundreds of sons and as many thousand wives (*see* the legend of the two hairs, under Bala-Rama). Krishna belonged to the race of the Yadava, of which he was the last representative. His end was accidentally brought about by an arrow which was let fly at him by mistake. In the Mahābhārata this occurs when Krishna is in the form of a gazelle. He then ascended to his heaven Goloka. In the epic he does not appear as described above, as the young cowherd with his rural love affair ; in the earlier portions he is a powerful prince helping the Pandavas, and he and Rama in both the epics are as much human heroes as incarnations of Vishnu. It is thought that Krishna is probably a deified hero (*see* Saussaye), according to one authority (Jacobi) a legendary hero blended with a popular deity, Rama being explained in a similar manner. He is, indeed, a good example of the manner in which a hero evolves into a god, thus being directly opposed in origin to such a figure as Arthur, who exhibits the process of a hero being evolved from a god. As identified later with Vishnu, Krishna assumes a more exalted aspect, and becomes one with the supreme spirit. The tales of his youth are, it seems, later accretions to his history (*see* Wilson, " Religion of the Hindus," ii. 66).

Krishna's peculiar weapon was a fiery disk which, when flung from his hand, worked instant and wholesale destruction. Favourite representations of Krishna figure him as a child playing in various ways, or as a youth with the serpent he slew under foot, playing on his flute, and encircled by rustic dancers. (*See* " Harivamça," under Mahābhārata.)

Kubera (or Vaisravana). A post-Vedic lord of treasures and king of the Yaksas (*q.v.*). He was half-brother to Ravana (*see* Ramayana), who drove him from Lanka, which had been built by Visvarkarman (*q.v.*) and given to Kubera by his father. Kubera then took up his abode on Mount Kailasa and became regent of the north. He is described as riding on a man.

Kukulcan. The designation of Quetzalcoatl (*q.v.*) in the language of the Mayan Indians of Yucatan.

Kwannon. A Buddhist deity, by some interpreted as a god, a spiritual offspring of Amida (*q.v.*) and guardian of the Buddhist faith, but generally worshipped throughout Japan as a goddess of mercy, whose shrines are met with everywhere. She is known as the eleven-faced and thousand-handed, and the numerous hands with which she is depicted hold a variety of Buddhist emblems, and symbols of her powers and attributes. A horse's head is also at times associated with her others. Her divine ability to fulfil the desires of her worshippers has procured her the further title of Nyo-i-riw, properly the name of a gem accredited with kindred magic power (Murray). The most noted of her temples is the San-ju-San-gen-dō, founded in the twelfth century, at Kyoto. Here there are a thousand gilded images of the goddess, five feet in height, rising tier above tier, along an immense gallery. Smaller figures are on the hands, or foreheads, or nimbi of these large ones, the whole number of images numbering 33,333.

Kwan-ti. One of the state gods of China, received in 1856 the same divine honours as Confucius, because he was supposed in that year to have manifested himself during the Tai-ping rebellion and brought success to the Imperial troops. An ancient hero, he had upon several occasions appeared in the midst of the fray and, like Castor and Pollux, turned the tide of battle. A special officer with a suite visits his temple twice a year, and presents offerings and prayers to Kwan-ti on behalf of the emperor.

Kwan Yu. A mythical hero of the third century A.D., who appears in the "Romance of the Three Kingdoms." He was made the god of war of the late Manchu dynasty, with whom he was a special favourite. He is one of the "state gods" of China, and his temple is visited three times a year by a special officer of the emperor, who offers up prayers and sacrifices to his spirit on behalf of the emperor with the most elaborate ceremonial. The Chinese believe that Kwan-yu, or as he is sometimes called, Kwan-foo-tze, appears again and again in succeeding generations. But he will always be recognised by reason of his physical attributes by the more enlightened of his own generation.

Kwei. The spirits or manes of the departed in Chinese mythology. The alphabetic figure denoting it is formed from the figure of a demon's head over the legs of a man, added to another figure signifying malice. The Kwei may be regarded as akin to the Lemures of the Romans.

L

God L. This Mayan Indian deity Schellhas has designated "The Old Black God." He is depicted as an old man with sunken, senile features and toothless gums, and one half of his face, sometimes the upper, sometimes the lower, is covered by black paint. He occurs in the Dresden MS. only, and must not be confounded with God M, who is entirely black. Cyrus Thomas thinks he is the god Ekchuah, who is known by tradition as a black god, but Schellhas seems to think that this description best fits God M. Forstemann thinks L is the god Votan, so well known in Central American mythology, who is identical with the Aztec earth-god Tepeyollotl. This appears to be the more probable theory, as the word " votan " in Tzental signifies " heart," " breast," and the fact that his places of worship were always subterranean, as mentioned by Nunez de la Vega, would seem to prove. However, it is recorded of Votan by Vega that he " kept a tapir " in his subterranean temple, probably his image, which with other things was burned by the worthy bishop who writes of him in the market-place of Huehueta in 1691. If then the tapir was in any way symbolical of Votan he could not be identical with L, who has no resemblance to that animal. But there is no direct proof that the tapir was symbolical of Votan. However, it must have had some significance in his worship. This fact appears to us to place some slight doubt upon the probability of Forstemann's theory that L is the god Votan. On the other hand it must be admitted that the representation of Tepeyollotl in the Codex Borgia bears a very close resemblance to those of L in the Dresden MS. Both gods have in common the black face-markings, a similar head-ornament, and the dark hue of these deities is probably symbolical of the subterranean recesses in which they were supposed to dwell.

Lakshmi (or Sri). Wife of Vishnu, a goddess of beauty, or of good fortune, born, according to one legend, from the churning of the ocean (*q.v.*), and so called a " Daughter of the Milky Sea." She is stated however to have had several births. She is figured holding a lotus in her hand.

Laz. The wife of the Babylonian god Nergal (*q.v.*).

Leucetios. An air-god or thunder-god of the continental Celts. Very few such deities are known to Celtic mythology. His name is almost all that remains concerning him.

Llew Llaw Gyffes. Son of Arianrhod (*q.v.*), who assisted the gods Amaethon and Gwidion, his uncles, in their war against the powers of darkness. He is identical with the Irish Celtic deity Lug of the Long Hand and the continental god Lugus. The name means " He of the Steady Hand." The legend of his amazingly rapid growth from childhood to manhood goes to suggest that he was a sun-god, the appellation " Long Hand," which is the translation of his Irish name, possibly being explanatory of the long and far-reaching rays of the sun.

Llyr (or Ler). A sea-god of the British and Irish Celts, and father of Manannan. He was one of the Tuatha de Danaan in Irish myth. His myth recounts that he evinced such devotion for the children of his first wife that his second wife, Aoife, became jealous and resolved to destroy them. She took the children to Borve the Red, a neighbouring king, and transformed them into white swans. On account of her treachery she was herself turned by King Borve into a demon of the air. Lir and Borve set out to look for the children, but could not effect their disenchantment. The period of transformation, nine hundred years, passed, and the children found themselves in a changed Ireland, since Christianity had found a home in the green isle. They were now nine hundred years old, but ere their death they were baptised, and thus assured of salvation. Llyr in his British form gave his name to Leicester, or the Town of Llyr, which was a centre of his worship. The mythical King Lear, Shakespeare's wondrous creation, was confounded with him in latter times.

Lodhurr. A god of northern mythology, associated with Odhin and Hoenir in the creation of the first human pair (*see* Odhin). Another name for Loki.

Lokapalas. In Hindu mythology the eight guardians of the regions of earth.

Loki. An exclusively Norse god, belonging to a later period of myth, sometimes reckoned among the giants, sometimes among the Aesir ; of the latter he was both friend and foe ; he took part in the councils of the gods, and disturbed Aegir's feast with a murderous act and revilings ; he mingled his blood with Odhin's in a compact of brotherhood, and is found frequently in company with the latter and Hoenir, having assisted these other two gods in bestowing life on the first human pair, but at the end of all things he acts as steersman to the ship that bears the " sons of destruction " to combat with the gods. His cunning was brought into play as a help to himself and the other gods, whom he was equally ready to land in difficulties. He was pleasing in outward appearance, and could change himself into whatever shape he chose, horse, fish, flea, etc. Loki is " the great riddle of Teutonic mythology." His double nature is thought to be more completely understood by associating him with the twofold agency of fire. His name of Loki signifies the " closer," he who brings both pleasant and unpleasant things to an end (Mogk) ; he has a further name Loptr (air?) given on account of the magic shoes that carry him through air and water (Kauffmann, Mogk) ; according to Meyer, Loptr is related to the Bavarian *loftern*, i.e. *lodern*, which identifies him as a god of fire. Loki is also recognised as Logi the fire-demon, and in Utgardhaloki (*q.v.*) ; Rydberg states that the original Norse Loke-epithet *Bekki* means " the foe." According to various authorities he was originally a personification of some elemental power, or a later figure grafted on to an older fire-demon ; late enough in conception according to Bugge to be traced to Lucifer. He has been identified with Vulcan, Prometheus, the Indian god Agni, and several figures in ancient myth and epic. Whatever his original qualities, Norse mythology recognises in the developed god a spirit of opposition and evil. Further identifications of Loki are with the Mitothin of Saxo Grammaticus, who was left in Odhin's place while the latter was absent, and took the opportunity of introducing evil practices among the people ; also with Requalivahanus (" the dweller in darkness "), whose name is found in an old inscription discovered near Cologne, but in this case the identification is not, according to some scholars, sufficiently established. Loki's father was Farbauti (or Fornjotr), his mother Laufey (or Nal), and here a nature myth has been seen in the father, the lightning or storm-wind, and the mother, the leafy island or fir-tree (Nadelbaum?), and the fire engendered by them during storm. Loki had brothers of similar character to himself, Byleiptr, or Byleifstr, and Helblindi. His own evil offspring were the Fenriswolf, Midhgardh's-worm, and Hel, born of Angrbodhr, the messenger of evil, or brought forth by him after having eaten the half-burnt heart of an evil woman. His sons Nari (Narvi) and Vali (Ali) were the children of his faithful wife Sigyn, who remained with him in his captivity, for Loki, having gained access to Aegir's feast, hurled abuses at the gods, till Thor appearing he fled. For a while he escaped pursuit by changing himself into a salmon and slipping away through the water, but he was caught and chained to a rock in some abyss below the inhabited world, there to remain till the final dissolution. Over his head hung a serpent, whose venom fell on his face ; his wife caught the drops in a vessel ; when full she turned to empty it ; then a drop fell on Loki, and he shook himself and made the whole earth tremble. Among Loki's evil deeds was the slaying of Aegir's servant, Fimafengr, and of Hreidman's son Otr ; in atonement for the latter crime he had to fetch gold from the dwarf Andvari, whom he also forced to relinquish a magic ring ; the dwarf in parting with it declared that it should bring death to whomsoever became its owner. Loki's cunning on another occasion saved Freyja, who had been promised as part payment to the giant builder of the gods' stronghold, provided it was finished by a certain day. The giant depended on his fleet horse, so Loki took the form of a mare and enticed the horse away ; the bargain was lost and the giant killed by Thor. Odin's horse Sleipnir was Loki's foal. (*See* also under Idunn.) Christian influence has been traced in the account of the binding of Loki till the day of doom. "He and Balder stand in opposition to one another as Christ and Satan " (Golther). Meyer also recognises Christian conceptions in the Balder-Loki myth. That Loki is represented as one of the Aesir shows that the idea of him as a god was conceived before the belief in dualism—good and evil—was evolved in the racial consciousness. For in early times gods were not regarded as either " good " or " evil," but as possessing the virtues and vices of humanity. In many mythologies we observe beings like Loki (*see* Bluejay), and it is strange that a being who, like Prometheus, was undoubtedly connected with fire, should have been condemned by the King of Heaven to a similar fate, although no direct mythological parallel can be inferred from the circumstances.

Luck, Gods of. *See* Shichi Fukujin.

M

God M. This Mayan Indian deity is generally represented as of a completely black complexion, and sometimes as merely striped with black bars. His mouth is encircled with reddish-brown lips, the under-lip drooping heavily, and the curve of his eye ends in two separate white lines. From the circumstances in which he is found he seems to be a god of travelling merchants, and a defender and succourer of this class. Such at least is inferred from the fact that on his head he bears a roped package resembling the loads observed in the Mexican pinturas as constituting the goods of chapmen or wandering merchants; that he is found in combat with God F, who in his character of god of death by violence is the enemy of all who wander into the unknown wastes which probably separated city from city in ancient Central America; and that to-day the natives of Central America are still in the habit of conveying heavy loads in the manner described above. A deity of this character has been handed down by written tradition, and under the designation of Ekchuah is expressly described as a black god. He is further represented as pierced by the lance of God F, not as victorious over him. Regarding his blackness the opinion may be ventured that it is symbolical of the tanned or deeply bronzed skin which such of the natives of Central America as are constantly exposed to the sun through travelling or outdoor labour undoubtedly acquire, especially those who act as porters, men who seldom encumber themselves with superfluous clothing. Schellhas mentions a variant of M, with the face of an old man, the scorpion's tail, and exposed vertebræ of the death-god, bearing on its breast the head of M. M is also recognised in the Tro-cortesiano Codex as wearing the scorpion's tail. Generally M is represented as an old man with the solitary tooth in the lower jaw which the artists of the pinturas intended to symbolise old age. Might this connection allude to the perishable nature of merchandise and its proneness to decay? A stellar connection has been attributed to M by Forstemann, who thinks that a sign in the Tro-cortesianus with out-turned eye-rim alludes to a relation between him and the planet Venus. The circuit of that planet accomplished in 584 days might well be symbolised by a god of travellers, and we will recollect that Quetzalcoatl, who in his variant of Yacatecutli, the god of travelling merchants, was a great traveller, was also connected with the planet Venus, which indeed was his heart. Cholula, in Mexico, the chief seat of the worship of Quetzalcoatl, was much frequented by wandering pedlars and merchants of every description.

Maāt. Egyptian goddess of law, truth, order, and justice, the counterpart of Thoth. Daughter of Rā, lady of heaven, queen of the earth, and mistress of the underworld. The name Maāt signifies " order " or " law," and as " life by rule " was recognised as imperative by all classes in ancient Egypt she therefore enjoyed a position almost supreme. She was associated with Ptah and Khnemu in the creation of the universe, and assisted in bringing order out of chaos. She sat in dual form to hear the confession of the deceased in the judgment hall of Osiris, and she and Thoth decided on the verdict. It was she who ordered the daily course of the sun across the sky, and who rose with Rā in his boat when he first emerged from the primeval waters. Her symbol is an ostrich feather of truth rising above her head, and she is sometimes represented, like the Greek form of Truth, as having her eyes bandaged. The Greeks identified her with Themis.

Mahābhārata. The great Sanscrit epic, called the Iliad of the Indians, attributed to a mythical author " Vyasa "= " Compiler," believed to be the last who worked at the poem, which runs into 200,000 lines, having grown in length with time. The main theme is the rivalry between the Kauravas, the hundred sons of Dhritarashtra, and the Pandavas, the five sons of Pandu, the fathers being brothers, and kings in succession of Hastinapura, north of Delhi. The kingdom becomes divided between the two families, but the eldest of the Pandus, Yudhishthira, loses all his possessions at dice to one of his cousins, and he and his brothers then retire to the Kamyaka forest, where they spend twelve years filled with adventure. At the close of this period they are to be restored to the kingdom if they can remain unrecognised for a year. So they disguise and are taken into the service of Virata, King of Matsya. Now the five brothers had one wife between them, with whom the queen's brother falls in love, with the natural result that one of the husbands kills him. The Kauravas think this a good opportunity of invading the country, and severe fighting ensues, which ends with the Kauravas being annihilated, and Yudhish-thira returning to his kingdom. The Pandavas have all along had a faithful ally in Krishna (*q.v.*), who is accidentally killed, and Yudhishthira then resigns his crown. He and his brothers and wife make their way to Indra's heaven on Mount Meru; only the king and a dog who has joined them succeed in arriving there, but they are all finally reunited in the realm of bliss. Among the favourite episodes of the Mahābhārata are the tales of Savitri, who by her prayers induces Yama to restore her dead husband to life, and of Nala, who awakes one day to find her husband gone, all the incidents of her own trouble and that of the one who has left her and loves her being told with great beauty of feeling and manner.

The central theme is supplemented with many details and descriptions and extraneous matter, which help to reveal the thought and philosophy of its age, apart from its interest as abounding in legends. It is venerated as a work of religious teaching, of higher value than a mere epic poem.

The "Harivamça," a supplementary book, is the history of Krishna; in it we have an account of the fourth age of the world, the corrupt one in which we are now living, which is to be regenerated by Vishnu's next Avatar (*q.v.*).

Mama Allpa. A Peruvian harvest and earth-goddess, who was regarded as the dispenser of all human nourishment. She is depicted as having numerous breasts. She is analogous to the classical Artemis.

Mama Cocha. The Peruvian goddess of water. The Peruvian ritual described her as the mother of all mankind.

Mama Oullo Huaca. The sister-wife of Manco Ccapac, the culture-hero of Peruvian myth. As he taught the men of the country the arts of agriculture and civilisation, so she taught the women those of domestic life. (*See* Manco Ccapac.)

Manco Ccapac. The mythical founder of the race of the royal Peruvian Incas. With his sister-wife, Mama Oullo, he was the offspring of the sun and moon, and descended in the neighbour-hood of Lake Titicaca from the celestial regions. They had been instructed by the parents to traverse the country until they came to where a golden wedge they possessed should sink into the ground. It disappeared at Cuzco, the site of the ancient Inca capital, which Manco founded. He instructed the inhabi-tants in the arts of civilisation, and, having completed their

task, the divine pair re-ascended to heaven, leaving as their
earthly representatives their son and daughter. Thus it was
that all Peruvian monarchs were compelled to marry their
sisters, as it was deemed degrading to defile the heavenly blood
of the Incas with mortal contact.

Manibozho (or Michabo). " The Great Hare," a deity of the
Algonquian Indians of North America. He was a dawn or
culture-hero like Quetzalcoatl, and his connection with the hare
lies in the circumstance that the words " hare " and " dawn " are
evolved from one root. He was regarded by the Algonquians
as the inventor of their system of hieroglyphs, and indeed as a
civilising agency in general, as all arts and crafts are supposed
to emanate from him. He is also the founder of the " Meda "
or secret cult of the tribe.

Manu. Also known as Vaivasvata, son of Vivasvat. He is
regarded as a progenitor of mankind, and said to be the first
to offer sacrifice to the gods. Hindu mythology knows of six
previous Manus, the first of whom was Swayambhava. Each
Manu reigns over one of the fourteen periods into which a
Kalpa (q.v.) is divided. The present Manu is associated with
the tale of the flood (see Vishnu Avatara). To him also is
accredited the famous Hindu law-book, in which is given a
history of the creation. The " Oxford Dictionary " has an
interesting entry under " man," in which it states that Man
and Manu are usually referred to Indo-Germanic Men, Mon,
to think, which apparently connects their primary meaning
with the idea of intelligence as distinctive of the human
species. Scholars, it adds, regard this as "intrinsically unlikely," but offer no other acceptable explanation

Marduk (Merodach). The mighty lord of Babylon, the Bêl
of the Old Testament and Apocrypha. He rose into prominence under the conqueror Hammurabi (*circa* 2300 B.C.), who
brought the upper and lower states of the Euphrates valley
under one dominion and established Babylon as his capital.
Bêl of Babylon was invested with all the divine attributes of
En-lil, the old Bêl of Nippur. He was lord and light of heaven
and earth, lord of life and death, creator, in whose hands were
the decrees of fate, from whom no secrets were hid, a helper
and healer, and resuscitater of the dead. His temple was
E-Sagila, the " lofty house." Marduk had been from ancient
times a god of the morning light and of the spring sun. The

Babylonian New Year's Feast commemorated his victory over Tiamat (*see* Cosmology) and his marriage with Sarpanitum. On this occasion the other gods and the kings did homage to him, and Nebo was brought in procession to Babylon from his temple at Borsippa. The two great items of the ceremony, of which mention is found in old inscriptions, were the entry of the kings into the temple, and the clasping of the god's hand, and the foretelling of the destiny of the coming year by the great god himself.

Marduk was expressly worshipped as a god of battle by the Babylonian kings. Nabonidus dreamed that the gods Marduk and Sin appeared and told him that the Scythian power was broken (*see* Cylinder, Bab. and Ass. Room, British Museum). Some scholars identify him with Nimrod; others however identify the latter with Gilgamesh (*q.v.*).

Marduk was the son of Ea, and he partook of his father's powers; he acted as an intermediary between mankind and the latter, and like Ea was a god of the exorcist cult. He himself was father of Nebo, and husband of Sarpanitum. Marduk was identified with the planet Jupiter. The creation legend ends with a hymn of praise to this god, on whom innumerable titles of honour are lavished (*see* Cosmology).

Maruts (or Rudras). A host of deities who accompanied Indra in his warlike expeditions. They were Vedic gods of storm and wind, roaring like lions, sweeping over the atmosphere, vigorous and fertilising, of sun-bright hue gleaming like flames, their chariots yoked with ruddy horses, with spears of lightning, and hurling the thunderbolt, so that the mountains gave way before them. Their exploits were similar to those of Indra, bringing rain on earth for men, and slaying the demon of drought. Like Rudra, of whom older mythology makes them sons, Prisni being their mother, they possessed a knowledge of the healing art, and were thus kindly beneficent to men. In later myth they appear as sons of Kasyapa and Diti, and it is related that Indra, knowing the child was destined to be his destroyer, dashed the embryo to pieces with his thunderbolt, and either Indra himself or Siva converted the pieces into the Maruts, their name arising from the words addressed to the lamenting offspring bidding them not to weep.

Mâshya and Mâshyana. *See* Zoroastrianism.

Matarisvan. In Hindu mythology a divine messenger who,

Prometheus-like, brought Agni down from heaven to the Bhrigus. The name is also applied to Agni himself.

Matowelia. The principal god of the Mohave Indians, a tribe of Colorado. He was to them a species of divine cicerone, who guided them in their journeys across the boundless prairies from his home in the sky, designated by them "The White Mountain." The souls of such Indians as had received sepulture by burning fared to this divine abode, but those whose corpses were not cremated according to the tribal custom were doomed to spend their immortal existence as screech-owls.

Mehurt. Ancient Egyptian cosmic goddess, identified with other early goddesses, as Nut or Hathor, and generally figured as a cow, or with a cow's head. She was the "celestial heifer" who gave birth to the sun. Legend relates that seven children, "wise ones," were born of her who helped Thoth in his work of creation, and took the form of hawks. It was in her abode that the judgment scene depicted in the "Book of the Dead" took place.

Mendes. The sacred ram of this place was supposed to embody the souls of the four great gods, Rā, Osiris, Khepera, and Shu.

Menthu. An Egyptian god, lord of Thebes, lord of the sky. A personification of the full solar heat. Figured at times as guiding the boat of the sun and striking down Apep and Typhon. He was worshipped at Karnak, and Hermonthis, and in other Theban cities, his cult being of great antiquity. It became associated with that of the sun-god Rā. He was renowned as a god of war, and is seen with a bow and arrows in his hand, and is spoken of at times as the "Strong Bull." The bull was sacred to him, an equivalent of the Mnevis bull of Rā (*see* Bakha), and occasionally he is figured with this animal's head, but more usually with the head, or two heads, of a hawk, surmounted by a solar or lunar disk, and with two upright plumes. At one time his cult at Thebes rivalled that of Amen, and he was probably the local god of the country between Kus and Gebelên, Amen being a comparatively late interloper. His wife was Rā-t-taui.

Merlin (or Myrddin). Was a god of the British or Brythonic Celts, whose personality in later mediæval legend, like that of Arthur, degenerated into a mere wizard or necromancer. He is "the folklore representative of a great deity." He may be identical with the sun-god Nudd. Professor Rhys puts forward the suggestion that he may have been the deity specially worshipped at Stonehenge, the erection of which tradition refers to him.

Meru. In Hindu mythology a mountain supposed to be situated in the centre of the earth, the dwelling of the gods. " The Olympus of India."

Merur (Gr., Mnevis). Sacred bull of Heliopolis, in whom Rā was supposed to be incarnate.

Metztli. The moon-goddess of the Aztecs or ancient Mexicans. Her myth relates that in the absence of a luminary of day all humanity was plunged into darkness, which a human sacrifice alone could relieve. Metztli thereupon brought to the sacrifice Nanahuatl the Leprous, and cast him into a huge pyre which stood ready for the victim. She herself followed him into the furnace, and on her disappearance the sun arose. The elucidation of the myth admits of little doubt. We perceive in it the primeval idea of the spotted or starry night being slain so that the birth of the sun-god or day may be brought about. As in Egypt and many other countries the moon in Mexico was also regarded as having a distinct connection with water or moisture, probably because during the night dank and miasmatic airs and chills prevail. As the divine Tecziztecatl also, she was the goddess of generation, a quality with which water is intimately associated in the savage mind. The Mexicans painted her in two colours, to exhibit her beneficent and maleficent phases. As the beneficent dispenser of harvests and offspring she was adored, but as the ruler of the mysterious and terrifying shadow of night was sufficiently feared and placated. " We are all of us under the dominion of evil and sin because we are children of the water," says the ancient Mexican formula of baptism, and Citatli and Atli, " moon " and " water," are constantly confounded in Aztec mythology.

Mictlan. The god of the dead in ancient Mexican mythology. He is frequently represented in the native pinturas or paintings as an open-mouthed monster ever ready to devour the souls who have just left their earthly abodes. There is no reason to believe that his realm was a place of punishment, or that it had any connection whatsoever with the expiation of sin, although he was surrounded by demons called Tzitzimes, who are depicted as torturing some of its denizens. But it is likely that the conception of hell as a place of pain was a later idea borrowed from Christian belief. Mictlan, like other American hells, was

merely a place for the lowly and undistinguished. The paradise
of Tlaloc (*q.v.*) was a preserve for the rich and brave, and few
of the lower orders might enter therein. He is often alluded
to as Mictlantecutli, or lord of Mictlan (*see* reference to Central
American Hades in article " Popol Vuh.")

Midhgardh.   Middle region (Earth) of Norse mythology.

Mimir.   A Scandinavian giant, uncle of the god Odhin.
Originally an ancient water dæmon, his chief attribute was a
mysterious wisdom.   This conception is thought to be associated
with the veneration in which our forefathers held running
streams, consulting them for prediction of future events, etc.
Mimir was at one time the keeper of the magic cauldron (*see*
Odhrerir).   His well of wisdom in which all streams had their
sources lay hidden under the roots of the world tree; in it was
kept Odhin's eye, and every morning he drank from his horn of
the mead which flowed over Odhin's pledge.   In another myth we
hear how the Vanir cut off his head, thinking themselves in some
way ill-treated at the hostage that had been given them who
could answer nothing when the giant was away (*see* Hoenir).
Odhin took Mimir's head, and uttered spells over it and gave it
the power of speech.   It became the god's oracle, from which
he gathered much hidden lore, and it was consulted by him
when he knew the end was drawing near.   In the heroic saga
he is known as " Mime der Alte," and appears as a famous
smith and Siegfried's instructor.   After him was named the
magic sword Miming, which had been forged by Voland
(Wieland) and carried off by Mimir.

Min (Amsu).   An ancient Egyptian god, personifying the
generative power of nature.   God of Apu or Panopolis, he is
thought to have originated in the land of Punt (Petrie).   He
had a temple at Koptos, where archaic figures of him have been
found.   He is figured in human form, swathed, with one arm
free and raised, and a scourge above it, with two upright plumes
above his head (*see* Amon).   The Greeks identified him with
Pan.

Mithra.   A god who holds a prominent place in the later
sacred writings of the Persians, and was a deity of the Hindus and
Iranians before they separated, although it does not seem
absolutely certain that he was originally identical with the
Vedic Mitra (Lehmann).   He was a chief figure among
the Yazatas (*q.v.*).   In the Zoroastrian hierarchy his personality

gradually developed; and the Mithra Yasht speaks of Ahura Mazda having created him almost equal to himself. Mithra became the centre of a cult as a god of light, heat, and fertility, and as such the dispenser of all such good things as make for the health, wisdom, and holiness of soul and body; a powerful adversary of the wicked, above all of those who broke their faith, and to all sin and darkness he opposed to them the might of his own clear uprightness and purity of being. He was the mediator between man and god, and the old hymn describes him as thousand-eyed and thousand-eared, full of knowledge and power, neither slumbering nor sleeping. He is further described as mounted on a white horse, or in a chariot drawn by horses, armed with spear and arrows. He is thus a god of war as well as of light, and as such a favourite of the Roman soldiers to whom his worship had been introduced by foreign legionaries. Gods of light and fertility are often conceived as being also gods of war, the lightning-flash which they wield symbolising the divine spear or arrow. (*See* Ashur and Huit-zilopochtli.) He became popularly regarded as a sun-god, and was identified by the Babylonians with Shamash (*q.v.*); he is looked upon as the " Persian Apollo." Mithra was associated with the bull, and is represented as mastering, carrying, or slaying this animal; his figure is familiar in its conical cap in the act of sacrificing. The bull was a symbol of life and fecundity, and it was from the primordial ox that according to Persian cosmology (*q.v.*) sprang all living things. Reinach points out that in this act of sacrifice there is an indication of the earliest form in which Mithra was worshipped having been that of the sacred bull associated with the sun. His sacrificial act would therefore have an idea of self-immolation attached to it. The worship of this deity was carried by conquering Persians into distant dominions, and became in time an established cult in Asia Minor, and thence spread through the Roman world. The kings of Pontus gloried one after another in the name they took from this god. Christianity found the belief in Mithra one of the antagonistic faiths most difficult to overcome, partly on account of similarities in its rites and other analogies. The nature of Mithra worship is somewhat obscure, but it comprised a baptismal rite, in which bull's blood was a consecrating element, and a communion feast. Only those who had gone through all the degrees of initiation were admitted to the sacred rites or " mysteries." Mithra was one of the gods who sat at the bridge to judge the soul after death (*see* Zoroastrianism).

The sixteenth day of the seventh month was specially dedicated to this god.

Mitra. A Vedic deity, of similar attributes to Varuna, with whom he is constantly associated; he is distinguished from him as being more essentially a god of the light of day, whereas Varuna (*q.v.*) represented the night heavens.

Mixcoatl. This god, originally a deity of the Otomi aborigines of Mexico, was the Aztec god of hunting. The name signifies "Cloud Serpent," and Dr. Brinton thought that Mixcoatl represented the tropical whirlwind. He also stated in the same work, however ("Myths of the New World"), that Mixcoatl was the god of the chase, in which assumption he was more happy than in his first surmise. The hunter-god, however, is often identified with the tempest and thunder-clouds, because of the fact that the lightning is supposed to represent his arrows. He is generally depicted with animal characteristics, as a deer, for example, or even as a rabbit. Herne the hunter, for instance, has a deer's head and antlers. Mixcoatl is only the cloud-serpent in so far as he is a wielder of the lightning as a weapon of the chase. Nearly all American tribes have similar deities. He is generally represented as carrying a bundle of arrows in his hand to typify the thunderbolts. It is quite probable that Mixcoatl was originally an air and thunder god older than Tezcatlipoca and Quetzalcoatl, which is quite likely if he were an Otomi deity, and that when one or other of these gods usurped his position in the native pantheon a place had to be found for him to soften Otomi susceptibilities, and he took his rôle as god of the chase. But against this theory is the well-known fact that, unlike the Inca race of Peru, who did their best to smooth over matters with conquered peoples and admit their gods to the Inca pantheon, the Mexicans regarded subject races as so many sources of tribute, and it is unlikely that they would yield to softer impulses. Whenever the Mexicans adopted a deity from a foreign people it was usually because his characteristics reminded them of the attributes of one of their own gods, or because he filled a gap in their pantheon, or, again, mere fear of the deity of a subject or conquered people might make them adopt him as their own.

Moccus. A swine-god of the continental and British Celts, which some of the Roman authors equate with their god Mercury. Among the Celts the worship of the pig appears to have been very widespread, and may have been connected with totemism.

As some Celtic tribes are known to have abstained from eating swine's flesh, and as the Highlanders of Scotland had a prejudice against it, there would seem to be some evidence of this sort. In the myth of Diarmid the boar is a totem animal.

Monan. A deity of the Tupi of Brazil (*see* Cosmology, Tupi-Guarani).

Morrigu. A war-goddess of the Irish Celts, perhaps the consort of Nudd or Lludd. The name means " Great Queen." She delighted in strife, and hovered over the field of battle in the shape of a raven.

Mullo. A god of the continental Celts, the tutelar deity of mule-drivers, and equated with Mars by the Roman writers. He was probably of totemic origin, as inscriptions concerning him have been discovered which assist that theory.

Muspelheim. *See* Cosmology, Teutonic. Over this realm of fire presided the demon Surtr.

Mut. An Egyptian goddess, mother of the gods, mistress of the sky, wife of Amon-Ra. She was the great " world-mother," generally figured as a woman, with the vulture head-dress, the vulture being the emblem of maternity. Sometimes she is given the head of a lioness, or additional ones of a vulture or lioness. With Amon-Ra and their son Khensu she completed the divine triad of Thebes.

N

God N. Schellhas calls the Maya God N " The god of the
end of the year." The deity has the head of an old man, and
wears a peculiar head-ornament in which is included the sign
for the year of 360 days. The Mayans, like the Mexicans, had
introduced into their calendar five intercalary days which they
called Uayayab, or unlucky, and Forstemann sees in N the god
of these days. This deity or demon, Uayayab, " he by whom
the year is poisoned," they modelled in clay during the unlucky
days, and then carried it out of the village in the direction of
that cardinal point to which the new year belonged. He only
appears a few times in the manuscripts, but it is quite probable
that he has been rightly identified.

Nabu. The Nebo of the Old Testament, son of Marduk,
Bêl of Babylon, the scribe and messenger of the gods, in whose
hands were the Tablets of Fate, in whose mouth was justice,
the great god of wisdom. To him Ashurbanipal, the collector
of the library at Nineveh, tells us he owed his literary zeal.
Nabu was the upholder and guardian of the world, no decree
of heaven was passed without him, he had no equal in power,
and he lent a willing ear to suppliants. Two statues of Nabu
were found at Nimrûd (Calah), now in the British Museum. The
inscriptions accompanying them describe his attributes, of which
the above are a few, and end with the exhortation to "trust
in Nebo and in no other god" (*see* Schrader, Keilinschriften, etc.).
Nabu's ancient temple was at Borsippa (Birs Nimrûd), a suburb
of Babylon, and the traditional site of the Tower of Babel. At
the great New Year's feast his image was placed in a boat and
carried in procession to the temple of Marduk in Babylon,
where he also had a sanctuary. Marduk and Nabu were gods
respectively of the sun of the early and later year. The three
great kings Nabopolassar and his successors bear the latter's
name. Nabu was identified with the planet Mercury. His wife
was Tashmetu, interpreted as " hearing " or " audience." He
was also worshipped by the early Canaanites, and several towns
in Moab and Judah are called after him.

Nandi. The snow-white bull of the Hindu god Siva.

Nannar. *See* Sin.

Nantosvelta. A goddess of the British Celts, connected with the sun-god Sulis, who was worshipped at Bath. Her exact significance is unknown.

Narayana. *See* Brahmā.

Nefer-Tem. The third of the Egyptian deities forming the Memphian triad. A son of Ptah and Sekhet, or one other of the goddesses; he personified the heat of the rising sun and was figured as a man or a mummy, sometimes with the head of a lion. His symbol is the lotus, seen on his head or his sceptre. He was one of the forty-two assessors in the Hall of Judgment, and granted continuance of life in the world to come.

Nehalennia. A goddess apparently of fertility and navigation. She is known from monuments found on Walcheren and in Rhenish Prussia, and from the mention of her by Tacitus, who states that she was a goddess of the Suevi. She is figured with a horn of plenty or a basket of fruit, and a dog, and is found accompanied by Neptune. Her name is interpreted as the "Seafarer" (Kauffmann), and she is represented in places with her foot resting on the prow of a vessel. Her identification with other goddesses is conjectural.

Nekhebet. This goddess and Uatchêt were sister tutelary goddesses of Upper and Lower Egypt, both figured in the form of a vulture. She wears the crown of the upper or southern kingdom.

Nephthys (or Nebt-het). "Lady of the House" (of Horus), one of the great company of deities at Heliopolis, daughter of Seb and Nut, sister of Osiris, Isis, and Set, and also wife of the latter and mother of Anubis. She was the divine sister, who joined her lamentations with those of Isis over the dead Osiris. She assisted in his funerary rites, and was looked upon as a protector of the dead, and as one who had knowledge of the words of power whereby the latter were resuscitated. Dr. Budge sums up her personality as "the goddess of the death which is not eternal." She is figured as a woman, her head generally surmounted by her own ideogram, but she has at times horns and a solar disk.

Nergal. God of war and of the chase, and king of the lower regions, worshipped by the Babylonians and Assyrians. His chief temple was at Cuthah (*see* 2 Kings, xvii.) where now stands Tell Ibrahīm. Nergal as a god representing the full heat of mid-day and of the mid-year was a god of destruction, a sword being the symbol of his annihilating power. Like other sun-gods, however, he had a more beneficent side to his character as a god of fertility. The dark realms of the dead found in him a fitting king; he obtained his sovereignty by the violent means that became his character. Allatu (or Ereshkigal), the goddess of the lower world, having on one occasion sent a messenger to the gods assembled at a feast, and one of these not showing the respect to him she thought right, she demanded his death. Nergal as it happened was the delinquent, and with Ea to help him, accompanied by a host of fever-demons, he raided the kingdom of Allatu, and dragged the queen herself from her throne, preparatory to killing her. In her extremity she offered him half her kingdom as her husband, and Nergal consenting, he was enthroned as the Babylonian Pluto. Nergal was identified with the planet Mars. Another goddess associated with him as spouse was Laz. The myth signifies the descent of the sun-god into the world of darkness at night. There he could only rule for half the day — thus Allatu proffers him " half of her kingdom."

Nerthus. The "Subterranean" (Reinach), "Mother Earth." A goddess whom we are told by Tacitus was worshipped by several German tribes. At certain seasons she was borne in procession in a chariot drawn by oxen, accompanied on her route by festal rejoicings, and spreading peace and plenty over the lands as she passed along. Very sacred was all belonging to her. Only the priest might touch her chariot, and when brought back to her sanctuary at the close of her progress, goddess, chariot, and coverings were washed in a secret lake, and this hallowed ceremony over, the slaves who had assisted at it were drowned. The grove sacred to her was on the island of Seeland. Nerthus corresponds as a goddess to the god Njordhr (see this god and Freyr). In later times she was known as Herthe or Hertha.

Net, Neith. A goddess believed to be of Libyan origin, worshipped by the Egyptians, the centre of her cult being at Sais where she formed a triad with Osiris and Horus. Her worship does not appear to have developed until long after her name appears in inscriptions. Under the twenty-sixth dynasty she emerges into prominence. She was a virgin goddess, self-begotten, the mother of Ra and of the gods in general, identified by the Greeks with Athene. Herodotus describes the annual festival in her honour. There are indications of her having been a goddess associated in some way with the dead (Saussaye). She is figured as a woman holding a bow and arrows and a distaff. According to some she may have been a goddess of war. She became identified with Isis and other goddesses, especially the sky-goddess, when she is represented as a cow.

Niflheim. (*See* Cosmology.) In Norse mythology a world of mist and cold and darkness, an underworld, distinguished from Hel (*q.v.*). In the midst of Niflheim was Hvergelmir, the fountain from and to which all waters found their way. From it flowed the rivers Elivagar (*see* Ymir). When Hel was born, the offspring of Loki, the gods cast her down into Niflheim and gave her power over nine worlds, among which she distributed the dead. Apparently the dead all traversed the same road for a while, whatever their final destination — Asgardh, Hel, or Niflheim—till they reached Urdhr's fountain, where the gods assembled daily to deliver justice. They passed through dark valleys till they reached the border river Gjoll, spanned by a golden bridge, a silent company travelling on foot or on horseback, warriors with their arms and women with ornaments. Their ways parted at Urdhr's fountain, where they received their doom, still in silence, unless they knew certain runes to help in their defence (*see* Rydberg, 333 ff.). The wicked were sent on their dismal journey to the Na-gates, set in the high dark walls of the gloomy abode awaiting them. Huge dogs were here on guard, and winged demons stood in readiness to carry them off to their several places of punishment. Niflheim was the abode of the dragon Nidhogg, that sucked the blood of corpses, and the fierce Fenris-wolf. There too was the dreadful river, Slid, through which the worst criminals had to wade. The hall of Nastrand, one of the divisions of this lower world, is described in Voluspa as entwined with serpents' backs, while venom drops from its roof.

Ninâ. Patron goddess of Ninâ (Nineveh). The ideogram of the goddess and of the famous city of Assyria signified " house of the fish." She was the daughter of Ea, the god of the deep, and according to Jastrow differed from Ishtar in this connection of hers with the lower realm of waters. Ninâ was, however, subsequently merged in Ishtar, whose " beloved city " was Nineveh. It is a question whether the city where the Babylonian goddess reigned was the Ninâ of Assyria or a town of that name in Babylonia.

Nin-gal. Wife to the moon-god Sin (*q.v.*).

Ningirsu. Lord of Girsu, a district of the town of Lagash (or Shirpurla), now known as Telloh, where a large library of tablets was found dating back to its ruler Gudea (*cir.* 2500 B.C.); the latter built temples to this god and the goddess Bau. Ningirsu was a double or counterpart of Ninib, a sun-god, a god of agriculture, and a god of war.

Ninib (or Adar). Another sun-god, of Babylonian origin (*see* Nergal), and, perhaps, a god of western origin, who had migrated to Babylonia" (Paton). He was the firstborn of En-lil, and had his temple also at Nippar. Like most sun-gods, Ninib was a grim and mighty warrior, heralded by storm, and especially worshipped by the Assyrian kings as the lord of battle and of chase, and equally a beneficent deity of vegetation and fertility, and in partnership with his wife, Gula, associated also with the gift of healing. Another consort was Bau. One of his temples was at Calah (*see* Genesis x. 11), the site of the present mound of Nimrûd, residence at one time of the kings of Assyria. The winged bulls at the entrance to the doors of the royal palaces are thought to be symbolic forms of Ninib.

This god has been identified with the planet Saturn (*see* Flood).

Ninigi-no-Mikoto. Grandson of Ama-Terasu, the Japanese sun-goddess, and ancestor of the Imperial family of Japan. He descended from heaven and Okuni-Nushi (*q.v.*) resigned in his favour. His grandmother gifted him before his departure with the three symbols of imperial power, the jewel, mirror, and sword. He landed on the summit of the volcano, Takachitro.

Nin-Khar-sag. *See* Nin-lil.

Nin-lil. The goddess of Nippar, wife of the Babylonian god En-lil, also known as Nin-Khar-sag, "Lady of the great Mountain," as the consort of the great god.

Njordhr. One of the chief representatives of the Vanir (*q.v.*). A close relationship, not entirely clear, exists between this god, Freyr, his son, and Nerthus. He was a god lavish of riches, but whether originally a god of fertility or associated with the sea is uncertain. In Sweden and Iceland we find him a protector of seafaring men, in his home Noatun (=ship place, Kauffmann), with rule over sea, winds, and fire. His wife Skadi was the daughter of the giant Thjazi, whom he married as an atonement to her for her father's death (*see* Idhunn); when choosing her husband from among the gods Skadi was only allowed to see their feet; she chose the whitest, thinking they were Balder's. She and Njordhr were not a well-matched pair; he disliked the snow mountains and their wolves, while she delighted in racing over them in her snow-shoes and hunting, and objected to a warmer climate and the cry of sea-birds. So they arranged to spend nine nights in her abode and three in his, that is the winter in one and summer in the other. Meyer regards Njordhr as an idealised elf of the wind, with many characteristics of the wind god but in a milder form.

Noncomala. The creative deity of the Indians of Costa Rica. In the beginning he shaped the earth and created the waters, but darkness reigned over all. By Rutbe, a water-spirit, he had twins, the sun and moon. Later, men were created, but their conduct angering Noncomala, he flooded the earth, thus destroying all human beings. Nubu, a beneficent deity, however, succeeded in saving the seed of a man, which he sowed in the earth after the flood had abated. From that which ripened sprang man, and from the more abortive shoots came the apes.

Norns. In Norse mythology the three Fates, the dispensers of destiny, Urdhr, Verdandi, and Skuld (present, past, and future), who were descended from the giants. They sit by Urdhr's spring, and are also known by the general name of Urdhr.

Nu, Nun (Egypt). Father of the eight ancient cosmic gods of Egypt at Hermopolis. A personification of the inert primeval mass of waters in which were contained the germs of all existence. Out of Nu, on the first day of creation, rose the sun-god in the form of Khepera (q.v.). Nu had been from the beginning, and is described as self-created, both male and female, able of himself to conceive and beget.

He is figured as a man, with a solar disk and plumes on his head. The goddess Nut was regarded as his female principle.

Nuada. See Nudd.

Nudd (or Ludd). A deity of the British Celts, confounded in later times with a legendary British king of the same name. It is supposed that his temple stood on Ludgate Hill in London, and that he was worshipped chiefly at Lydney in Gloucestershire, where the remains of another temple to him have been found with many inscriptions which mention him by name. He appears on these as a sun-god, his head surrounded by bright rays. His Irish equivalent is Nuada Argetlam (Nudd of the Silver Hand).

Nusku. Babylonian fire-god, with attributes similar to those of Girru (*q.v.*). The " offspring of Anu," "first-born of En-lil," " created one of Ea " (*see* tablet, Nineveh Gall., British Museum). Nusku was also associated with the moon-god Sin, and appears sometimes as the latter's son. He was identified with Nabu.

Nut. An Egyptian goddess, one of the great company of Heliopolis, wife of the earth-god Seb (Keb), daughter of Shu and Tefnut. She personified the vault of heaven and may be seen as such with raised body studded with stars, and pendant legs and arms, arched over the recumbent figure of Seb. It was Shu (*q.v.*) who separated these two, and forced Nut into this posture, and was said therefore to be commanded by Ra to remain for ever as her support. Another idea pictured her as sinking down nightly to her husband and thus bringing the darkness. Nut was the primeval mother of the gods and mistress of the sky, figured at times as the celestial cow; her five children were Osiris, Horus, Set, Isis, and Nephthys. She became identified with the other chief native goddesses. Apparently she is not identical with the Nut who was one of the ladies of the sycamore and provided refreshment for the soul before it started on its dismal journey after death. The latter may be seen amid the foliage holding a plate of bread and pouring water on the hands of the deceased.

O

Goddess O. Goddess O, a Mayan deity, appears only in the Madrid MS., and is represented as an old woman by the usual method of providing her with a single tooth in the lower jaw. She is not to be confounded with the pictures of goddesses wearing the serpent head-dress. Few pictures of her exist, and but little can be said of her, but it appears likely that from her avocations of spinning, etc., she is the deity of feminine old age. She may be a sort of earth-mother who had become domesticated.

Odhrerir. In Norse mythology the name of the cauldron containing the magic potion, the mead of poets, prepared by the dwarfs, Fjalar and Galar, from honey mingled with the blood of Kvasir, the wisest of men, who had been created from the spittle of the Aesir and Vanir, the treaty of peace between them having been sealed by each side expectorating into a vessel. The liquor conferred wisdom, knowledge of runes and magic charms, and the poetic faculty on those who drank of it. Odhin, aware of its potency, having himself drunk of it, determined to secure it for his own. The cauldron belonged to the giant Suttungr, whose daughter Gunnlodh was set to guard it. Odhin, who could take what form he chose, transformed himself into a snake and bored his way through the rock to where Gunnlodh sat on her golden stool. She gave him to drink and he lay in her arms for three days, and then having drained the cauldron dry he flew away in the form of an eagle, and on his arrival in Asgardh spued the liquor into a vessel. He left Gunnlodh in tears, but he showed no godlike gratitude nor godlike truthfulness when questioned concerning what had occurred. We find a similar occurrence in Celtic myth (*see* Keridwen).

Odhin (Odhinn), Norse form of Anglo-Saxon, Woden; H. G., Wuotan (from Sanscrit root signifying " to blow," or perhaps " motion," to infer a supreme spirit penetrating and circulating everywhere). Latin Vates is etymologically closely akin according to Kauffmann, but Saussaye considers this connection untenable. The old wind-god, associated in later legend with the wild huntsman who sweeps through the air with

his phantom hosts, familiar to all German tribes. ". . . no doubt
at an earlier stage the god of spirits and the guide of the dead
after the manner of the Greek Hermes Psychopomp. He is at
once an atmospheric, nocturnal, and infernal god " (Reinach).
The fertilising showers that follow in the god's train led to
his being also looked upon as a god of agriculture, and to him
was dedicated the last sheaf of the harvest field. In his less
mild aspect he was a god of storm and war, the leader of hosts,
giver of victory, in whose name the old tribes took possession
of our country, from whom both the royal houses of the rival
kingdoms of Deira and Bernicia claimed descent, the great
chief of Valhalla. The slain on the field of battle were his,
and prisoners of war were sacrificed to him. In heathen times
all those who died a violent death were supposed to go to him,
and he was especially the god of those who were hanged, the
gallows being known as his steed; it was an old saying in
Germany when a violent wind blew that some one had hanged
himself (Mogk). Those likely to die a straw death are said
to have purposely put a more violent end to themselves in
order to go to Odhin. This supreme god of the north, creator,
all-father, god of the dead, was rich in runic lore and versed
in magic and song, a father of spells and source of all poetic
faculty. His mysterious wisdom came to him when as young
he hung for nine days on the gallows tree, pierced through
with a spear which he had dedicated to himself, until " he
caught up runes " and fell. The meaning of the lines which
relate this curious myth can only be conjecturally interpreted.
Mimir gave him to drink from the cauldron Ödhrerir (q.v.)
which increased his wisdom, and of this magic mead he finally
became entire possessor. The All-father, according to the
Eddic tale, went to Mimir one day and begged a draught
from the well of wisdom, of which the latter was owner, which
he obtained, but only on condition of having one of his
eyes as a pledge for it, hence the god is often represented as
one-eyed. " Here he changes his character and represents the
sun, which becomes one round eye only when reflected in any
well " (Poor). From his throne (Hlidhskjalf) he kept a daily
outlook over the world, and every night his two ravens, Huginn
and Muninn (Thought and Memory) perched on his shoulder
and told him all the news they had gathered from below during
the day's flight over the fields of earth. Two wolves were also
his companions. Popular imagination pictured Odhin as a
wise and kindly god; old, with long white beard, a broad-

brimmed hat drawn low over his face, and a large dark cloak. As god of the wind he rode on a white, eight-hoofed horse (Sleipnir); his weapon, a spear (Gungnir), was forged by the dwarfs, and the first war of the world began by his hurling it into the ranks of the Vanir. As the warrior he was clad in golden helmet and breastplate. Odhin could assume what form he chose from snake to eagle; he was fond of coming down to earth and wandering about as an ordinary traveller asking for shelter, or seeking knowledge in disguise (for the wind must wander), as does the Mexican wind-god Tezcatlipoca; so he sits as a stranger and minstrel in the hall of the Norwegian king, Olaf Tryggvason; appears as a beggar to King Geirrödhr, who treats him badly and kills himself when he finds out who the beggar really is; as an old, one-eyed man to young Hadding, whom he carries with him on his horse over the sea; as a wanderer to the giant Vafthrudhnir, with whom he exchanges questions as a test of wisdom, the giant losing his head, the agreed forfeit of the one who cannot answer. Odhin was one of the three sons of Borr, the son of Buri, said to have been licked out of the salt ice-block by the cow Audhumla. The giants Bolthorn and Mimir were his maternal grandfather and uncle, his wife was Frigg (*q.v.*), and his son Balder. With the help of his two brothers Vili and Vé he lifted the earth out of the waters, and he and two other gods, Hoenir and Lodhurr (probably other names for his two brothers, Kauffmann), finding a couple of inanimate figures which the dwarfs had fashioned out of trees, gave them respectively breath (or spirit), understanding, and good colour (or " the appearance (image) of gods," Rydberg); thus were created the first pair of human beings, Askr and Embla.[1] Odhin was, further, the inventor of the mystic runic alphabet. He is the god of wisdom because the sun can peer into every corner and cranny.

The " Dies Mercurii " of the Latins became among the Norse Teutons and the tribes of lower Germany Odinsdagr, Wôdenes-doeg, etc., our Wednesday. Mogk considers Wodan, like Thor, the development of one aspect of the sky-god Tiwaz, associated with additional attributes. (*See* Mimir, Odhrerir, Valhalla, Hoenir, and Lodhurr.)

NOTE.—Both human sacrifice and self-immolation were associated with the cult of Odhin. Prisoners of war were sacrificed to him, either by hanging or stabbing (*see* Chadwick, " Cult of

---

[1] The origin of man from plants is a myth of ancient Aryan origin (*see* Rydberg, 84-85).

Othin "); sometimes the " blood eagle " was carved on their backs. The inhuman practice among the Vikings of tossing up young children and catching them as they fell on the spear point was possibly a kind of human sacrifice. Prominent among the tales connected with these offerings to Odhin is the saga of King Vikarr. He and his comrades were detained by contrary winds, and consulting the oracle were told that Odhin demanded one of their number as a sacrifice, to be chosen by lot and then hanged. The lot falls on the king himself. Starkadr (q.v.) is the executioner; Odhin had asked him to make a return for the benefits he had bestowed on him, to which Starkadr gladly consented, and the god gave him a javelin which had the appearance of a cane-reed only. Starkadr climbs a rock, pulls down the branch of a tree, and fastens Vikarr to it with the entrails of a newly-killed calf, pretending it is but a mock sacrifice. Then he thrusts him with the cane which turns into a javelin, and pierces the king, exclaiming as he does so, " Now I dedicate thee to Odhin; " the entrails turn into strong withes, the branch flies back, swinging the hanging king into the topmost boughs, and he dies.

King Aun, or On, of Upsala sacrificed nine of his sons in turn to Odhin in order to prolong his own life ; the death of a son gave him ten extra years, and before the end he was bedridden, and had to be fed like a weaned child ; his people would not allow him to sacrifice a tenth son, so he died. Kings in ancient times were supposed to be responsible for weather and crops, and in two instances they were offered to Odhin in order to put an end to a famine, one victim being King Domalde of Sweden, the other King Olaf ; in the latter case they surrounded the king's house and burnt him in it. As regards self-immolation the idea was to consecrate oneself to Odhin, " to mark oneself with the spear point," so as to be admitted among the Einherjar, or in some cases to leap from a height and so go straight to Odhin. The custom of marking with the spear point was traditionally derived from the god himself, who in the Ynglinga Saga and elsewhere appears as a king ruling over Sweden. As he drew near his end he had himself marked with the point of a javelin, and all who died by arms were by this act dedicated to him.

Ogmios. A continental Celtic deity of agriculture. He is equated by the Roman authors with Mercury, and is represented, like him, with club and lion-skin. Strangely enough he also possessed the qualities of a god of eloquence, and is depicted as drawing men after him, their ears being attached to his tongue by golden threads. He is the same as the Irish Ogma, the god of poetry and eloquence.

O'Harai. A Shinto ceremony of general purification which took place twice a year, when all the people brought expiatory offerings, and the emperor himself, or his representative, gave the absolution. A work of the tenth century has preserved the ritual or formula (Norito) used on this occasion.

At the present day pilgrimages are made to the great temple in Ise, on the occasion of the half-yearly purification festival, in order to obtain sacred charms, which are brought home and placed on the " god-shelf " for the protection of the household.

Ohonamochi (Onamuchi or Okuni-Nushi, etc.). The earth-god of Japan, sometimes identified with Daikoku (*q.v.*). His great shrine was at Kitzuki, in Idzumo, and was the second in importance in Japan. He was son of Susa-no-o (*q.v.*) and resigned his throne in favour of the ancestor of the present emperor, who is derived from Ama-Terasu. Thousands of pilgrims flock yearly to this shrine, which has many smaller temples round about. According to legendary belief these are visited by the whole host of gods during one particular month of the year, when heaven is therefore uninhabited. There is a long legend connected with this god which tells of his descent into Yomi where he marries Susa-no-o's daughter, and is put to tasks by this god which his wife helps him to accomplish; finally he escapes with her. A great festival is held in Tokyo in honour of this god, who is looked upon as the guardian deity of the city.

Omacatl. A name which signifies " Two Reeds," was the Mexican god of joy, festivity, and good cheer. He was worshipped only by those who came under his direct influence, that is to say, the rich and those whose means permitted them to render homage to him in splendid banquets and feasts. Persons of convivial habits gave periodical festivals in his honour, embellishing their mansions for the occasion with heaps of flowers, and engaging the services of professional singers and dancers. The day of rejoicing having been fixed, the image of the god was placed in the domicile where the feast was to take place. Sahagun states that it was believed by the Mexicans that if his celebrants were in any way wanting in respect to the deity, or failed in any way to render him his due, that Omacatl would appear at the banquet, and in stern tones would reproach the offender in the following terms: "Wicked man, for what reason hast thou omitted to honour me with respect? I will hence-forth abandon thee, and thou wilt pay dearly for the injury thou hast put upon me." Illness would later be the lot of each member of the convivial party—an indisposition the symptoms of which were dizziness and falling sickness. The idea of com-munion which appears to have instigated nearly all of the religious feasts of the Mexicans was apparently present in these banquets. Before the banquet to Omacatl the notables who took part in it fashioned a great bone from maize paste, and pretended that it was one of the bones of the deity whose jovial rites they were about to celebrate. This they ate, to the accom-paniment of large draughts of pulque. Provisions were stuffed into the belly of the idol of Omacatl, possibly hollowed out for the purpose. The idol was represented as a squatting figure, painted black and white. A paper crown enriched with emeralds surmounted its head, and paper of divers brilliant hues was hung round the figure. A cloak fringed with flowers and a sceptre completed the costume of this Mexican Bacchus.

Oni. In Japanese mythology a general name for demons, goblins, etc., and all other spirits of evil and darkness.

Onniont. In Huron Indian myth a gigantic snake having on its head a great horn which pierced mountains and rocks which intercepted its path. This horn was regarded by the Hurons as a symbol of great good luck, and to obtain a portion of it was the desire of at least every male member of the tribe. The medicine-men were wont to persuade the warriors before going on the war-path that they were in possession of it, and pretended to give them pieces of it pounded down in water as "war-physic."

Oonawleh Unggi. "The Oldest Wind," a wind-god worshipped by the Cherokee Indians. He is identical in character with most other American wind-deities. (*See* Tezcatlipoca.)

Opochtli. A name which signifies "The Left-handed," was the Mexican god of fishing and bird-snaring, and during the somewhat prolonged period when the Aztecs dwelt in the marsh-lands surrounding Mexico-Tenochtitlan, he must have been a deity of some importance to this people who depended for their livelihood and the very tribute they paid to their overlords upon the industries of which he was the patron. To him was attributed the invention of the fishing-rod and harpoon, or minacahalli, a description of trident, as well as the nets in which birds were snared and those with which fish were caught. The fishers and birdcatchers of the surrounding country offered up an occasional feast to Opochtli, the constituents of which were eatables and a beverage called octli. Maize, flowers, tobacco, and copal gum, as well as an aromatic herb called yiauhtli, a species of absinthe, were also offered up. A procession was formed in which marched elderly persons who had set themselves apart for the worship of the god. Opochtli was represented as a naked man painted black, his head surmounted by the plumes of the wild birds of the country. He was also crowned by a paper coronet in the shape of a rose. He was encircled with green paper which fell to the knee, and was shod with white sandals. In his left hand he held a shield painted red having in the centre a white flower with four petals placed crosswise, and in the right hand he held a sceptre in the form of a cup.

Osiris. The Egyptian god of the dead, son of the sky-goddess Nut and the earth-god Seb; brother and husband of Isis. His original significance has been variously interpreted; by some as a solar deity or developed as such from a god of the night sky, by others as an ancient god of the Nile waters. But he is undoubtedly the sun who is overcome by the night, and rises again on the following morning. He became gradually transformed, and was associated in extremely early times with the idea of immortality. As the deity worshipped in this connection he was both man and god, a creator possessed of all the powers of the highest divinity, addressed as " god one," and above all the god who had overcome death. The hope of life after death was rooted in the dependence on this god who had not seen corruption. Every one who died hoped to become an Osiris, that is, he trusted that the same divine and wondrous miracle of the god's death and resuscitation would be repeated for him. The cult of Osiris was national, but the classic centre of his worship was at Abydos. Busiris was also an ancient shrine of the god, where he was symbolised by a hieroglyphic sign, which is thought to have represented a leafless tree, but was interpreted after the Osirian myth had been established as the god's back bone. Osiris was believed to be embodied in the sacred ram of Mendes (*q.v.*). He became the chief god of the dead, absorbing or becoming associated with other rulers of the underworld. The myth connected with Osiris and Isis is fully detailed by Plutarch; Ra, the sun-god, in anger with his faithless spouse Nut, declared that her child should not be born in any year or any month. Thoth on behalf of the goddess played with the moon for a seventy-second part of every day, and eventually he made up five extra days beyond the usual length of the year, and on one of these Osiris was born. Osiris was a kind, wise king of Egypt, and he travelled about his realm to spread the advantages of civilisation. His brother Set was evilly-minded, and plotted mischief against him. He secretly took his brother's measurements and then had a handsome coffer made to the same. On a night of feast he offered the coffer to the one it would fit, and Osiris took his turn at lying down in it. Set and his accomplices instantly rushed forward and fastened the lid over him, and afterwards threw the coffer into the Nile. Then began the sorrows of Isis, and she wandered far and wide seeking the body of her husband. She sought shelter in the swamps of the Delta and there gave birth to her son Horus. The coffer floated to Byblus, and Isis heard that a beautiful tree had grown up on the spot enclosing it within its trunk. The king had so admired it that it had been cut down to serve as a pillar in his palace. Thither Isis repaired and obtained admittance to the palace, and finally making herself known was allowed possession of the pillar. Opening the trunk she took out the coffer and placed it in a boat. But her sorrows were not over, for leaving it a while in order to visit her son, Set and his companions, who were out one moonlight night, came across it, and recognising the body of Osiris, cut it up into fourteen pieces. Isis went about the marshes in a boat of papyrus gathering up the fragments, and burying each as she found it, which accounts for the many places claiming to be the burial spot of the god. The chief account relates, however, that on finding the body Isis and her sister Nephthys sat down and uttered a lament, which for ever after was the received funeral dirge of the Egyptians, and that then with the help of Anubis, Thoth, and Horus—all of whom appear in later scenes in connection with the dead—the body was put together and swathed and the due funerary rites performed. Then came to pass the great miracle of the resuscitation—by the fanning of her wings, by the utterance of magic words, Isis brought the dead king to life again. He rose from the dead and became the king of the underworld. The reconstitution of the body was supposed to have taken place at Tettu. A yearly festival commemorated the death and resurrection of the god. Horus later avenged his father by the slaughter of Set. Osiris, when figured in connection with funeral rites, appears as a mummy wearing a white crown; otherwise he is figured as a man. The Greeks identified his parents with Kronos and Rhea, and the god himself with Pluto and Dionysus (*see* Herodotus, ii. 144). The myth of Osiris is allied to that of Adonis.

P

God P. Schellhas alludes to P, a Mayan deity, as " The Frog God," because in the Codex Tro-cortesianus he is represented as having the fins of a frog, and the blue background which represents water is present. He is unquestionably an agricultural deity, as he is found sowing seed and making furrows, and in this connection we can have no difficulty in placing him when we recollect the very prominent part the frog-like water deities of Mexico play in the agriculture of the country. He also wears the 360 day sign in his head-ornament, probably with a seasonal reference. Seler asserts that this god is none other than Kukulcan, but for this idea there is absolutely no ground.

Pacari Tampu (House of the Dawn). Was a mythical cave, whence issued the four brothers and sisters who initiated the four various Peruvian systems of worship. The eldest ascended a mountain, and cast stones to the four points of the compass to indicate that all the land was his. But the youngest of the four, who was of a cunning disposition, succeeded in enticing the eldest into a cave, which he sealed up with a great stone, imprisoning him there for ever. He persuaded the second to climb a lofty mountain, from which he cast him, changing him into a stone in his descent. The third brother not unnaturally fled on beholding the fate of the others. The first brother would appear to represent the oldest religion in Peru, that of Pachacamac, the second that of a fetishtic stone-worship, the third that of Viracocha, and the last sun-worship pure and simple. The " official " legend concerning the brothers, however, states that the sun had three sons, Viracocha, Pachacamac, and Manco Ccapac. To the last the dominion of mankind was given, whilst the others were concerned with the workings of the cosmos. This politic arrangement placed all the temporal power of the country in the hands of the descendants of Manco, the Incas.

Pachacamac (or " Earth-generator "). Was the name of the Peruvian god of earthquakes in Incan times. The chief centres of his worship were in the valleys of Lurin and Rimac, near the city of Lima, and in the latter valley a great temple of which he was the tutelar stood in the time of Pizarro, and is now reduced to ruins. He had a great reputation throughout old Peru as a great civiliser, and was a rival to Viracocha, whom he defeated, recreating the world to his own liking. Like his rival he was a god of fertility, but was evidently the concept of a separate caste of priests. As the god of earth-disturbances, however, he was naturally hostile to the god of water. At his mutterings in the centre of the earth the Peruvians prostrated themselves in dread. In some respects Pachacamac had an oracular significance, the murmuring or rumbling of the earthquake being regarded as the voice of the deity.

Panis. *See* under Indra. Pani signifies "miser," and is used to denote the man who makes no gifts to the priests (Bergaigne).

Parasu-Rama (or Rama of the Axe). *See* under Vishnu Avataras.

Parijata. In Hindu mythology a sacred tree produced at the churning of the ocean. It was planted in Indra's garden. Krishna, having been entertained at Swarga, was instigated by his wife to carry off the tree, which he did after a serious fight with Indra whom he overcame. It was not returned to its rightful owner till after Krishna's death.

Parjanya. A lesser Vedic god of rain, a personification of the rain-cloud. Ideas associated with this deity connect him with Indra.

Parvati. A name of Siva's wife, indicating her connection with the mountain (*see* Uma, Durga, and Kali).

Patala. The lowest division of the underworld or the infernal regions generally in Hindu mythology, inhabited by Daityas, Danavas, serpent-gods, etc. ; it is described as a place of enticing delights in the shape of women, music, feasts, etc.

Phan-Ku. In the later Taoist mythology of China the first man, and the head of the triad which governs the Taoist pantheon. He is usually depicted as a dwarf Heracles, and is supposed to personify the creation of the universe from Chaos. He is popularly regarded as the Chinese Adam. By some authorities he is described as analogous to Chaos. In Taoist drawings he is pictured as a shaggy bear-like being, armed with a huge hammer, with which he is breaking the primeval rocks.

Pillan. The supreme being of the Araucanian Indians of Chili. The name is derived from the word pilli, the soul, and signifies "Supreme Essence." He is unquestionably a thunder-god, similar to the Tlaloc of the Mexicans or the Con of the Peruvians. Supernatural beings of this type are usually described by the Indians as being red in colour (the lightning flash), quick-moving, and limbless, difficult of approach because of their irascibility, and generally placated by potations of spirit poured into the pools on the mountains where they are supposed to reside. They are usually roused to activity for the purpose of making rain in a droughty season by the priests or medicine-men of a tribe. The entire economy of an Arau-canian tribe was modelled upon the celestial plan of Pillan. That is to say, the deity was supposed to have his chiefs and sub-chiefs, and to live in every respect like an Araucanian potentate.

Pitris. In Hindu mythology fathers or progenitors; also manes.

Popol Vuh (The Collection of Leaves). A sacred book of the Kiche Indians of Guatemala, rediscovered in 1854 by an Austrian scholar, Dr. Scherzer. It is written in the Kiche Indian dialect of Mayan, and in four books gives an account of the traditional history and mythology of that people. The first book deals with the creation of the Indian races prior to the flood, and the punishment of the earth-giant Vukub-Cakix, and his sons Zipacna and Cabrakan, earthquake monsters. The second and third books are concerned with the deeds of the hero-gods Hun-hun-ahpu and Vukub-hun-ahpu, who are challenged to a game of ball with the lords of Xibalba or the underworld, are defeated by guile, and imprisoned in the dreary Kiche Hades. They are rescued, however, by the sons of the former, Hun-ahpu and Xbalanque, who descend to Xibalba, and after beating the lords of Hades at ball, free their father and uncle, and are transformed into the sun and moon. The portion of the book thus outlined resolves itself into a fable of the "harrying of hell," which was often invented by pagan races for the purpose of heartening themselves against the terrors of death. (*See* Lewis Spence, "The Popol Vuh," Nutt, 1908.)

Pradhana (Prakriti). In Hindu philosophy primeval, un-evolved matter, "a non-intelligent principle, the causal sub-stance of the material universe." (*See* Winternitz, "Index, Sacred Books of the East.")

Prajāpati. A supreme Vedic god, " lord of creatures," creator of heaven and earth, father of gods and men. According to one legend of the creation, Prajāpati was formed by the gods ; according to another a golden egg came into existence in the primeval waters, whence issued this god. The term was originally employed as a name of Savitri and Soma, as well as of Brahmā and Hiranyāgarbha, but later came to imply a separate deity. The mysterious Ka (Who?) of one of the Rig-Vedic hymns is declared in the same to be Prajāpati. As the first man identical with Purusha, he spoke the three words which brought the universe into existence. In the plural, the Prajāpatis are the mind-born sons of Brahmā. Prajāpati is often identified with the universe, and may have implied " matter " or " substance."

Prisni. Mother of the Maruts (*q.v.*) ; name used also for cow, cloud.

Prithivi. A Hindu manifestation of the earth. Generally associated with Dyaus (*q.v.*); addressed as " the mother." Later myth explains her name as derived from Prithu, a king, who when famine raged pursued her, and only granted her life on condition of her again yielding her fruits, and so became in a way her father.

Ptah. An Egyptian god, chief of the great triad at Memphis. The self-created " Father of Beginnings," architect of the universe, the sculptor or potter who formed the egg of the sun and moon. He is said, in conjunction with Khnemu, to have carried out the active work of creation at the command of Thoth (*q.v.*). This god is usually figured as a mummy. He was identified by the Greeks with Hephaistos (the Latin Vulcan). He was also in a measure a god of justice, whose rule he is said to have established on earth. Doubtless his reputation as an architect, or constructor, would bring him this added honour, stability or balance being imagined as the basis of justice.

Ptah-Seker-Osiris. The form under which Ptah symbolised the mummy-shape of Osiris. Images of this composite deity are common, and were frequently hollowed out to contain papyri on which were written certain chapters of the " Book of the Dead."

Ptah-Tenen. The latter was an ancient cosmic god, described as " old from all eternity " with whom Ptah was early identified.

He is figured as a potter shaping the egg of the world on his wheel.

Purusha. In the Rig-Veda a primeval giant whom the gods slew for sacrifice, and from his limbs created the world. In Hindu philosophy, spirit, or the " universal soul," as distinguished from Pradhana (*q.v.*). A celebrated hymn of the Rig-Veda dedicated to this abstract being states, " Purusha himself is this whole (universe) whatever has been, and whatever shall be " (Muir, v. 368). According to Mann, Purusha is Brahmā, and he further states that Brahmā divided his body into two halves, of which one became a male (Purusha), the other a female (Viraj). Purusha and Viraj are also said to spring from one another. (*See* Skambha and cf. Ymir.) By some he is regarded as a variant of Vishnu.

Puranas. Later Sanscrit works, dealing chiefly with the origin of the world, written in epic verse. They contain popular versions of ancient myths, legends of gods and heroes, as well as the cosmogonic tradition. Vishnu is the most prominent god throughout them, and there is an account of his avataras.

Pushan. In Hindu mythology the sun, and a brother of Indra. He is invoked as a protector of travellers and the newly married, and against evils that walk in darkness and oppressors. He took part in the affray at Daksha's sacrifice, where he lost his teeth, and he is figured toothless.

Pwyll. Lord of Annwfn, the otherworld, or realm of the dead, in British Celtic myth. His wife is Rhiannon, or great queen (*q.v.*). He carries on an unceasing warfare with the sons of Don, and is an ally of the children of Llyr, the sea-god, as a god of death naturally abhorring light and favouring darkness.

Q

Quahootze. One of the chief gods of the Indians of the Nootka Sound country in North America. It is conjectured that he is a war-god from the nature of the addresses offered up to him by the native shamans.

Quetzalcoatl. An important deity of the Nahua or Aztec people of ancient Mexico. The name signifies " Feathered Serpent." He was probably a god of a still older race, the Toltecs, whose civilisation the Aztecs profited by. By the sorceries of the Aztec god Tezcatlipoca (*q.v.*) he was driven from the land of Mexico, and returned to the fabled country of Tlapallan, whence he had come. But he promised to return, and the advent of the Spaniards was held by Montezuma and the Aztecs of that period as signalising his second coming. Other accounts state that he cast himself upon a funeral pyre and was consumed, and that his heart ascended into the sky and became the morning star. Some authorities regard him as a sun-god, and point to the circumstance of his returning to the east, his native home. Others regard him as a god of the air. He is, they say, connected with the cardinal points, and wears the insignia of the cross which symbolises them. Still others see in him both a wind and sun-god. He was like all the dawn-heroes, clothed in long, white robes, they say, and wore a full and flowing beard. A last theory derives Quetzalcoatl from a culture-hero who really existed, and some of the early Spanish missionaries professed to see in him the apostle St. Thomas, who had journeyed to America to effect its conversion. With all due regard to those various theories it is much more probable that Quetzalcoatl was a " Man of the Sun," who has left his divine sphere for a season for the purpose of instructing mankind in those arts and customs which go to make up civilisation. Quetzalcoatl was represented as a traveller with staff in hand, and this is sufficient to denote his solar significance, as is the assertion that the fruits of the earth grew more luxuriously under his rule than before or after. He is almost always shown with the solar disk or semi-disk, but he is pictured as emerging from the luminary in many of them, and it is evidently regarded as his dwelling place, not he as a personification of it. He is the sun-dweller, the being of a higher sphere, who has come to earth to instruct and civilise mankind. He it was who was regarded in Guatemala as Gucumatz, and in Yucatan as Kukulcan, both of which names are literal translations of his title of Feathered Serpent.

R

Ra. The great sun-god of the Egyptians, supreme among
the gods, whose existence dated from all time. He is pictured
as travelling in his boat across the celestial waters by day, and
along the Tuat (*q.v.*) by night, and with these day and night
journeys were associated ideas of life, death, and resurrection.
Through the night he fought with evil powers whom he left
behind him vanquished when he appeared afresh at dawn,
issuing from the dark valley. Ra was worshipped under
different forms, symbolic of the stages of his course (*see* Khepera
and Tem). He himself represented the full glory and heat of
the sun. Other gods became in time secondary forms of Ra,
to whom every attribute of divinity was ascribed. The chief
centre of the sun-god's worship was at Heliopolis (Egyptian,
Annu or An; Hebrew, On), and here his cult absorbed that of
other deities, among them that of Tem, the local god of Heliopolis, and the double god Rā-Tem was worshipped as the one
primeval god. In the same way his cult was mingled with that
of Amen (Amen-Ra) and others. Ra is figured as a hawk, or as
a man with a hawk's head, surmounted by the solar disk and
uræus, typical of the bird which strains in its flight towards
the sun.

Rā-t, represents the feminine principle of Ra. She was
evolved more from an idea of the priesthood than from any
spontaneous conception of godhead.

Ra is associated with the myth of the destruction of mankind.
Here as in another tale (*see* under Isis) Ra is represented as
sharing man's infirmities, for it is when he is growing old
that he feels that mankind is beginning to treat him with less
respect. By advice of the gods he sends out Hathor-Sekhet,
and she accomplishes the task of destruction imposed on her so
thoroughly that she is soon wading in the blood of humanity,
and no creature would have escaped had not Ra relented at
the last moment. Then he has quantities of beer brewed with
which the earth is flooded, and the goddess drinking the intoxi-
cating liquor forgets to carry on her work. Ra, however, the
tale continues, still wished to resign his sovereignty over the

world, and so withdrew to upper regions and there chose a spot
for his abode, the fields of peace, where the blessed resort
after death.

Ra possesses all the attributes of the typical sun-god. His
boat, his nightly combat with the powers of darkness, and his
ultimate victory are parallels with the attributes of many other
sun deities. His growing old is a frequent phenomenon amongst
cognate deities. Primitive people believe that unless the sun
is regaled with the blood of mankind that he ages rapidly.
Hence the myth of the sending of Hathor-Sekhet to earth, and
the holocaust of humanity. Such sacrifices on a large scale
were frequent in ancient Mexico, and on one occasion some
70,000 people were immolated on the altars of the war-god
Huitzilopochtli, the procession of victims stretching for over
two miles! Primitive man imagines that unless the sun is
sacrificed to he will refuse to mature the crops, and it is likely
that the myth of Ra and Hathor-Sekhet commemorates some
real act of extensive immolation.

Ragnarök. In Norse mythology the Twilight, or Doom of the
Gods. There had been a foreshadowing among the gods of the
irresistible fate awaiting them, and at last the day came when the
powers of chaos were let loose and destruction fell on them and
the world. The last decisive battle was preceded by a desolating
period of continuous winter, of snow from every quarter, of frost
and piercing wind, three long years, followed by another three
when no summer intervened to lessen the dreariness of the sun-
less earth. A demoralisation set in among mankind, which
destroyed the natural feeling of child to parent, of brother to
brother ; war was abroad throughout the world. But the end
was not yet. Sun and moon are each swallowed by two wolves,
Sköll and Hati, offspring of a hag who dwelt in the Iron wood,
to the east of Midhgardh ; the foundations of the earth and the
world-tree tremble, the stars fall, the mountains come crashing
down ; the Midhgardh-serpent rises from the raging sea and
spreads over the earth ; no bond or chain can longer hold, and
the Fenris-wolf breaks loose ; Naglfar, the ship made of dead
men's nails, is launched with the hosts of the frost-giants, and
the troops of Hel, lead by Loki ; from the south rides Surtr,
his fire-sword flashing, followed by the sons of Muspel ; the
open jaws of the Fenris-wolf stretch from heaven to earth ;
the Midhgardh-serpent blows venom over air and sea. Odin con-
sults Mimir's head. The Aesir and Einherjar arm for battle,

for the gold-combed cock has crowed, and the hell-dog Garm is barking. The gods meet their adversaries on the battle-field of Vigridhr (or Oskopnir) ; Odin and the Fenris-wolf encounter one another, the god is destroyed, but Vidharr revenges his father's death by tearing the monster's jaws asunder ; Tyr and Garm kill one another, as do also Loki and Heimdall ; Thor slays the Midhgardh-serpent, but falls dead from the flood of venom it outpours ; Freyr fights with the fire-demon Surtr, and being without a sword, falls. Surtr flings his fire over the world, the flames rise to heaven, and the earth sinks into the sea. Only the primeval realms of Muspel and Niflheim remain. When the great convulsion subsides a fresh and purified earth rises again, to be peopled by a new race of men, offspring of Lif (Life) and Lifthrasir (Desire of Life), who had been safely hidden in Hoddmimir's grove (World ash) and nourished with morning dew. A sun, the daughter of the old one, shines again ; Vidharr and Vali have survived the catastrophe, and again on the Idafield the gods meet, for thither come also Modi and Magni, sons of Thor, inheritors of their father's hammer, and Baldr and Hodhr, set free from Hel. They find again the golden tablets they had possessed, and all once more is plenty and peace. In Voluspa it further states that a supreme god, above all the Aesir, will reveal himself and rule for all eternity, and the blessed shall dwell in Gimlé, a hall fairer than the sun, the highest abode of light, and the dragon of darkness will be for ever sunk in the abyss. In the myth of Ragnarök we find all the elements of a story of cosmic change. To the mind of early man the idea of eternity was unthinkable, and he almost invariably broke up his mythical chronology into æons which usually ended with the complete annihilation of the current condition of things, and the creation of a completely new heaven and earth. The heavenly bodies share the destruction of earth. But we have in the myth of Ragnarök probably the most complete conception of cosmic destruction to be met with in the annals of mythology. Whether it has been in any way sophisticated by later Christian influences it would be extremely difficult to say. But such influences are by no means markedly discernible. But it is seldom that another pantheon of gods takes the place of that already existing. Hindu mythology allows for the displacement of certain deities by others more firm and worthy at certain stated intervals. The Mexicans believed that eternity was divided up into four such cycles, each governed by a separate sun, and ending in a general catastrophe caused by flood, fire, or famine, and the Kiches of Guatemala conceived the idea of a new condition of things, where the first men shaped from wood were replaced by giants who in their turn were overthrown.   But nowhere do we meet with such a complete and exact conception of cosmic change as that under review, which indeed overshadows the whole of Scandinavian mythology, and probably did much to colour the later northern conceptions regarding the end of all things temporal.   (*See* W. Farday on Axel Olrik's " Om Ragnarok," " Folklore," No. 15.)

Rakshasas, Rakshas.   In Hindu myth, evil spirits or demons which assumed various forms.   The gods in turn waged war against them.

Rāma Chandra.   Seventh avatara of Vishnu (*q.v.*).

Rāmāyana.   The epic of South India, rewritten by the poet Valmiki, who flourished about the close of the Buddhist period, or the beginning of the Brahmanist revival.   He probably reconstructed it from an older Vedic rhymed tradition.   The leading theme is the rescue of Rama's wife, Sita, from Rāvana, the demon king of Ceylon.   Rama, through the machinations of his step-mother, is banished from Ayodhya (Oude), where his father, Dasaratha, reigns as king.   During his exile, Rāvana, brother of a female demon whose anger Rama has provoked, at her instigation carries off Sita.   The monkey king and his general Hanuman help in the pursuit for her recapture.   They assault Lanka (believed to be Ceylon) and make a causeway over to it from the mainland by throwing rocks into the sea, the passage being still known as Adam's or Rama's bridge. Finally the demon antagonist is killed and Rama returns home and is installed as rightful king.   The later incidents of the banishment of Sita, of her meeting with Valmiki, of the birth of her two sons, who are brought up by the poet, and the final reunion with her husband, are not thought to be part of the original work, the genuine Rāmāyana, which, according to internal evidence, is believed to date from pre-Buddhistic times (Macdonell).   The old tradition relates that the poem was originally handed down orally by Rama's two sons, who had learnt it from Valmiki.   It is extant in three versions.   The poem is thought to outline the struggle between the incoming Aryans and the aborigines of India.   But it had, as treated by Valmiki, a lofty religious purpose.   " He wished to afford consolation to the soul," says Wheeler, " when the world seemed to be going wrong and the divine government doubtful." Rama must be regarded as an incarnation of Vishnu, and Sita of Lakshmi. Rama is sent into the world to force the Brahman from the persecution of the Buddhists (Poor). The Rāmāyana " teaches the hopelessness of victory without purity of soul and abnegation of self " (Monier Williams). As stated above, the original poem is probably pre-Buddhistic, but for religious and topical purposes Valmiki framed it into the epic of Brahmanism at bay against the inroads of Buddhism. Behind all, however, the solar myth is discernible. Rama is the sun, " His birth is supernatural, he wins his bride by bending a bow, he suffers for the good of others; he fights with the powers of evil and darkness; he wins by a magical weapon, which he alone can use." His bride is Sita, " furrow," therefore the earth wed to the sun.

Ramman. *See* Adad.

Ran. *See* Aegir.

Rashnu. Worshipped by the Persians as a god of justice; he and Mithra are the two judges who decide the fate of the soul after death (*see* Zoroastrianism).

Reret. Egyptian hippopotamus-goddess, a form of Ta-urt.

Rhiannon (" Great Queen "). Wife of Pwyll, Prince of Annwfn, the monarch of the British Celtic Hades.

Ribhus. The three great artificers of the Hindu gods. They were sons of Sudhanvan, and acquired their skill, according to one account, from Tvashtri (*q.v.*). The excellence of their handiwork is said to have procured them the gift of immortality. They fashioned the Asvin's chariot and Indra's horses (chariots and horses, Bergaigne writes, were primitively the prayers with which the Ribhus led the gods to sacrifice). The Ribhus are said to have been ancient sacrificers. The most wonderful of their works was the conversion of a sacrificial cup made by Tvashtri into four. They are said to have won the privilege of drinking Soma, and were enabled to bring youth back to their parents. The Ribhus are celebrated in several of the Rig-Vedic hymns. The word Elf is sometimes compared with the Sanscrit Rbhu, " the three genii of the seasons in Hindu mythology " (" Oxford Dictionary ").

Rishis. Seers, sages. The seven chief Rishis were the mindborn sons of Brahmā (*see* Prajāpati), and Hindu astronomy associates them with the stars of the Great Bear. To them were revealed the hymns and other parts of the Vedas.

Rudra. The "Howler" or "the Ruddy One" (*see* Macdonell), "boar of the sky," a Vedic god of storm, "the wild huntsman of Hindu mythology" (Saussaye). Rudra did not originally hold such a high position as was accorded him in the post-Vedic age, when he shared the honours bestowed on Vishnu. He is described by many contradictory epithets, strong and glorious, fierce and bountiful, a destroyer and plunderer, a divine physician and a deliverer. He is pictured as red-coloured and blue-necked, wearing a garment of skin. Later myth made him the offspring of Brahmā, or Prajapati, and the many titles he bears is explained by the legend that at his birth he wept eight times, each time asking for a name. He is said to have sprung from a drop of blood belonging to Brahmā, who, when wiping perspiration from his brow with a piece of wood, scratched the skin and drew blood, which fell into the fire and became Rudra. The fact that he is red proves almost beyond doubt that he is a lightning or thunder god, which class of deity is usually described in many mythologies as being ruddy in colour, quick-moving, and irascible. A further myth in relation with him states that he divided himself into two, male and female, from each of which sprang eleven beings, some dark, some fair, with characters to correspond. He was early identified with Siva and later became merged in Siva. A bow and arrows are his chief accompaniments. He (or Siva) was the god who rushed in on Daksha's feast (*see* Daksha). Rudra was father of the Maruts (*q.v.*) or Rudras.

S

Sâkyamuni. Chinese name of Gautama Buddha.

Sambara. One of the demons of Hindu mythology slain by Indra.

Saoshyant. In Persian belief the saviour born towards the close of the third millenium to save the nations upon whom distress has fallen. (*See* Zoroastrianism.)

Saranyu. In Hindu myth wife of Vivasvat (Sun) and daughter of Tvashtri. She bore twins, Yama (*q.v.*) and Yami, and then left her husband, leaving behind a double of herself, and fleeing in the form of a mare; as such she became the mother of the Asvins (*q.v.*). The later tale of Surya and Sanjna is similar; here it is explained that the wife left as she was not able to bear her husband's effulgence; the sun in order to enable her to return parted with some of his brightness, and from the detached fragments were fashioned Vishnu's disk, Siva's trident, and the weapons of Kartikeya and Kuvera. She is probably the dawn, who bears to the sun-god the twins day and night.

Sarasvati. The wife of Brahmā and the Hindu goddess of wisdom and science. She is regarded as the inventor of the Denanâgri letters, and thus as " the Mother of the Vedas." Pictured as a young woman of fair countenance with four arms, she is never represented as without her husband. She holds a book of palm-leaves, symbolical of her powers of erudition. She was supposed to have sprung from the essence of Brahmá himself. She was originally a river-deity, as her name " the waters " implies. Indeed the river called after her in the Brahmāvartta region was to the Vedic Hindus what the Ganges became later to their descendants. She is identified with Vâch, the goddess of speech. It is not easy to say in what manner she evolved from a river-goddess into a goddess of wisdom. In Celtic myth we find knowledge and inspiration associated with running water, or in the myth of the goddess Sinend, daughter of Lodon, son of Lir, who sought and found Counla's Well beneath the sea. A myth connected with her states that on one occasion she was late for certain rites, and her husband, Brahmā, irritated in consequence, took a milkmaid, Gāyatri, to wife, and installed her in Sarasvati's place. The goddess beholding this in her wrath placed a curse upon Brahmā, that he should be worshipped on one day only in the year. Vishnu she doomed to be born as a mortal, and Agni to be a devourer of unclean things. She also placed the curse of barrenness upon the goddesses. But Gāyatri modified the curses considerably.

Sarpanitum. Wife of Marduk, the Succoth-Benoth of 2 Kings xvii. 30. (*See* Rawlinson's " Herodotus," 1875, vol. i., app. 653, and Hastings' " Dictionary of the Bible.")

Saruto-hiko. According to Japanese mythology the leader of the host that accompanied Ninigi-no-Mikoto (*q.v.*) when he descended to earth.

Satarupa. Brahmā in the beginning divided himself, and became twofold, one half a male (Swayambhuva) who was himself, and the other the first woman, Satarupa. (*See* also Viraj and Purusha).

Sati (Satet). An Egyptian goddess, who with the goddess Anqet and the god Khnemu formed the triad at Elephantine. She was associated with the Nile waters, her chief centre of worship being on the island of Sāhal, near the first cataract. She is figured with the crown of Upper Egypt, and two horns. Sati was, like other goddesses, spoken of as a form of Isis, and is mentioned in some papyri as the daughter of Ra.

Sati. Another name for Siva's wife, Uma ; she was daughter of Daksha, and when her husband was treated by the latter with indignity, she consumed herself on the sacrificial fire, according to one account, or was consumed by her own glory. The name means " true or virtuous woman," and was formerly applied to those widows who were voluntarily burned on the funeral piles of their husbands. (*See* Ambika, Parvati, Uma.)

Savitri (Savitar). Generator, quickener. A Vedic deity. Identified with other gods, among others with Surya (Sun) and with Tvashtri. According to Saussaye " he does not represent the concrete figure of the sun, but its movement, rising and setting . . . the principle of activity." In the Mahābhārata over one hundred names are enumerated for the sun-god.

Schala. Wife of the Babylonian god Adad.

Seb (Geb, Keb). Egyptian god of the earth, one of the great company of gods at Heliopolis; son of Shu and Tefnut, father of Set, Nephthys, Osiris, and Isis; identified by the Greeks with Kronos. He and Nut had been joined in the primeval abyss, and had been separated by Shu (*q.v.*). Dominion was given him over all things of the earth, which was known as the " horse of Seb." Among his titles were " Hereditary Chief of the Gods " and " the Great Cackler," as he was attributed with the production of the great cosmic egg. He is present at the weighing of the heart in the judgment hall of Osiris. He is usually figured as a man, with crown and disk on his head, whereon is his symbol the goose, and may be seen as described under Shu.

Sebek (Gr., Suchos). The crocodile-god of the Egyptians, worshipped at Ombos and in other towns of the Fayum. His cult at one time was an important one, and in combination with Ra he became a solar divinity, Sebek-Ra. There was, however, another aspect of the god, for he was identified with Set (*q.v.*), a fellow-deity at Ombos, and elsewhere in Egypt crocodiles were considered emblematic of evil powers. Wiedemann thinks that we have here two different gods rather than two aspects of the one.

Sebek is figured as a man with a crocodile head, or as a crocodile. There is no difficulty in seeing in this deity a crocodile totem which has achieved godhead.

The crocodiles sacred to him in the lake of his temple were fed by priests and hung with jewels.

Seker. The " closer of the day," an Egyptian god of the dead, worshipped at Memphis. His kingdom is described in the Book of the Dead as a land of hopeless darkness, where the dwellers remain sunk in deathful sleep. The soul had to make its way thither past evil spirits and noxious reptiles. For a short interval the melancholy inhabitants had a return of light as Ra passed through Seker's realm in the course of his night journey.

Seker became associated with Ptah and Osiris, forming with them a triune deity (*see* Ptah). He is figured with a hawk's head; sometimes as a mummy holding symbols of power, or a mummified hawk. In the latter form the god is seen borne along in his sacred bark.

Sekhet. " Lady of the West." Egyptian goddess, wife or sister of Ptah, the second deity of the Memphian triad, and mother of Nefer - tum and Im - hetep. She personified the destructive heat of fire and sun, and was Ra's minister for the punishment of the wicked. She assisted Hathor when the latter was sent by Ra to annihilate mankind, and was indeed a form of this goddess (*see* under Ra). Sekhet is figured with the head of a lioness, surmounted by the solar disk and uræus; also as the eye of Ra (*q.v.*), having an eye for a head with a hawk behind her (*see* Lanzoni).

Sekhet-hetep. Field of Peace (or Hetepet=offerings), part of the kingdom of Osiris, known as a whole by the name of Sekhet-Aaru (or Aalu), Field of Reeds (or plants). This elysium was pictured as a fruitful and well-watered land, with a heavenly Nile flowing through it, its fertility corresponding to that of the Delta, in which region the realm of Osiris was originally placed. It was rich in all material blessings, and the dead, clad in white robes, lived in companionship with the gods, occupied with the same pursuits that filled their time on earth, hunting, playing chess, sowing and ploughing, etc. Their bread never grew stale or their wine musty. To ensure them perfect ease, figures of clay or wood (Ushabti figures) were sometimes placed in the tomb, in order that the doubles (Kau) of these might act as slaves to the deceased. Ideas as to the position of this paradise differed from time to time. It was moved from the marshes of the Delta, and found a place in course of time near the Great Bear. The conception of a celestial abode above the sky, which served as its floor, obliged the deceased to mount by aid of a ladder, and even Osiris is said to have employed this means of climbing to heaven. According to another system of belief the soul on quitting the body travelled to the west, and entered the Tuat (*q.v.*) at a gap in the mountains near Abydos (*see* further under Ba). The best account of it is contained in the legend of " The Destruction of Mankind," the papyrus of which was found in the tomb of Seti I. (*circa* 1366 B.C.). Aaru, it states, was surrounded by a wall of iron broken by several doors, the ways to which were mysterious.

Sengen. Goddess of the famous mountain of Fuji in Japan, the highest in the country, and at times an active volcano. The most recent eruption was in 1707. Pilgrimages are made to the summit of this sacred height.

Serapis. *See* Hap.

Sesha. A serpent-deity of Hindu mythology incarnate in Bala-Rama (*q.v.*). He was chief of the Nagas, or snake-gods.

Sesha was used for the churning of the ocean (*q.v.*), and the earth, in later mythology, is sometimes figured as resting on Sesha's head. Vishnu is seen reposing on the serpent's coils during Brahmā's night, the belief being that creation at the close of each day is destroyed by the fire that issues from its mouth. "Generally only a designation of the demon Vritra" (*q.v.*) (Macdonell). The serpent is spoken of as encompassing the waters (*see* Indra). He is figured with a thousand heads.

Set (Sit, Sati). An Egyptian god, one of the great Ennead at Heliopolis, son of Seb and Nut, brother of Osiris, Isis, and Nephthys, also husband of Nephthys and father of Anubis. Identified by the Greeks with Typhon, and by the Syrians with Baal. A "god of the prehistoric inhabitants before the coming in of Horus" (Petrie). Maspero thinks that he was originally a dæmon of the sandy desert. His conflict with Horus (*q.v.*) is believed to be reminiscent of a tribal warfare: according to one account Thoth intervened and Egypt was divided, the upper kingdom being given to Set and the lower to Horus; this coincides with history, the country in ancient days was governed by two separate rulers, the divisions being known as the two halves of Horus and Set. Set was at one time worshipped at Tanis as a sun-god, "the beloved of Ra." The Hyksos identified him with their chief god, and Saussaye thinks that this accounted in some measure for the character of darkness that was later assigned to him; there was no redeeming side to it as he appears in connection with the Osiris myth. In his serpent form, Apep, he was nightly annihilated by Ra. As an evil power, inimical to the sun-gods, his emblem is a peculiar animal not exactly identified (the jerboa and okapi have been suggested), and the god is figured as a man with the head of this creature. In later times he was regarded with abhorrence, and his name erased from the monuments. This was, of course, when the growth of the idea of dualism made it possible for him to be regarded as an active agency of evil rather than a mere personification of darkness.

Shamash. The sun-god worshipped by the Babylonians and Assyrians; the son of Sin and brother of Ishtar. Identified by some scholars with the Sepharvaim of the Old Testament. He had the usual attributes of a sun-god, beneficent, healing, and life-giving, and inimical to all darkness and wickedness. He was above all looked upon as the great judge of the universe. His chief temples were at Larsa in the south and at Sippar in the north of Babylonia. In the "Sun-god Tablet" in the British Museum (Bab. and Ass. Room) the King Hammurabi is seen receiving the laws, which were drawn up by him, from the hands of Shamash. He was also worshipped in Canaan, sometimes under the name of Heres.

Shen-Nung. A Chinese patriarchal emperor 2838-2698 B.C., who taught his people agriculture, and was later deified as the tutelary deity of that art. A typical prayer to him runs: "My fields are well tilled, and this causes much joy to my husbandmen. Let us invoke the Father of Husbandry with the music of lutes and the beating of drums. We will pray for rain so that our millet fields may increase, and in order that my labourers and their wives may be blessed."

Shichi Fukujin. Seven Japanese gods of luck. They include one goddess, Benten, generally seated on a dragon; Daikoku, god of wealth and good fortune, figured seated on rice bags; his figure is said to be often seen among the household gods; Ebisu, figured with a fishing-rod and fish; Fukurokuji, god of wisdom and longevity, or popularity (Papinot), figured with bald, high head; Bishamon, god of war, figured in armour, holding a spear and a pagoda; Hotei, god of ease and joviality, a corpulent figure; Jorōjin, figured with accompaniments of stag and crane, "as a sign of longevity" (Papinot).

Shih King. An ancient Chinese classic, the title of which signifies "Book of Poetry." It contains 305 pieces, dating from the sixteenth century B.C. to the sixth. They are very valuable from a mythologic point of view, and contain, beside much rhetorical matter, a remarkable document called the "Establishment of Government," in which the founder of the Chow dynasty gives a précis of the history of the kingdom down to his own time.

Shinto (Way of the Gods). A Chinese word, of which the Japanese equivalent is Kami-no-Michi. Shintoism is the name given to the indigenous polytheistic nature and ancestor worship of Japan. It was the sole religion of the country until the introduction of Buddhism in the sixth century, which gave rise to religious factions; Buddhism however continued to spread, and finally all further rivalry was averted by the Buddhist priests taking over the Shinto gods as avatars or manifestations (Gongen) of their own deities. Under this foreign influence pure Shintoism developed into Ryōbu-Shinto. During last

Non-Classical Mythology 157

century the two religions were officially separated, and Shintoism proclaimed the sole religion of the state. Shintoism is an undogmatic religion, and possesses no special code of morals, such, according to Shintoist idea, being superfluous for creatures of understanding and reason. Its divinities are countless, the earliest tradition numbering them at eighty to eight hundred myriads. They include chief gods of the sun, moon, and earth, gods of the elements, gods of the house and locality, of all things connected with household life, and of abstract qualities. Nothing escapes having a god attached to it from the thunderstorm to the pots and kettles on the hearth. Deified kings and lesser mortals help to swell the host, and the pantheon still has room for certain animals among its Kami, the general name for the gods, or for anything possessing supernatural power or arousing fear or wonder (*see* Aston, pp. 7-10).

The more primitive deities were nature-gods, the foundation of the religion being animistic ; a circumstantial account of their creation is given in an ancient work (*see* Koji-Ki). From the chief of these is descended the imperial dynasty, the emperor himself being high priest as well as temporal ruler, and certain castes of priests, the priesthood being hereditary, also claim divine ancestry or some particular connection with a god. Ancestor-worship appears to have grown more pronounced as time went on, and is now a prominent feature of Shintoism. Shinto temples are plain and unadorned, and without idols, ornamentation and representations of gods being Buddhist innovations. Mr. Aston ascribes the lack of images purely to the state of low artistic development among the Japanese before China had exerted its influence. Within the sanctuary of the Shinto temples, is preserved the Shintai, or " God-body," the symbol or representative of the deity, or rather of the Mitama, the " August Soul " or spirit of the deity, serving as intermediary between the latter and his worshippers. In old tales the god's Mitama appears as his guide and assistant; sometimes it has a double form of antagonistic qualities. The Shintai varies in kind and may be a stone or pillow, etc. The special Shintai of the Sun-goddess is a mirror, preserved in her temple at Ise. The Shintai is never exposed to public view, but is kept wrapped up in some rich material and enclosed in a casket of precious wood. Shintoism is a household religion, and every Japanese family has its small shrines, or tablets inscribed with the names of certain deities, kept on a shelf in one room of the house, to which votive offerings are daily made. It is a cult rich in festivals—at blossoming time and harvest, at the ingathering of the rice and the New Year, and in honour of local deities, who on these occasions are carried in procession; formerly several were dedicated to elemental gods in order to secure prosperity and to ward off evil. The greater festivals are accompanied by music and dancing; one dance or mime in particular being performed which is said to be the one that drew the sun-goddess from her cave (*see* Ama-Terasu). A general purification ceremony takes place twice a year (*see* O'Harai). Besides the temple festivals, others are celebrated in the sacred hall of the imperial palace, where stands an altar to the sun-goddess, in which the emperor himself takes part. Beginning with New Year's Day, when he prays especially for the peace and prosperity of the realm, they continue at intervals throughout the year, generally in honour of an imperial ancestor, or of the host of ancestors in general. These celebrations are observed as national holidays. Offerings, generally of articles of food and drink, which are prepared and received with great care that no defilement may be caused by the breath, are the chief feature of Shinto ritual. Those well acquainted with the Japanese lay stress on their cleanliness, which is an essential principle of Shintoism. Defilement caused by contact with blood, however slight—Florenz speaks of a drop or two caused by a slight injury—or with death, necessitates ablution before a temple can be entered, and exclusion from it may last for weeks. Formerly houses were set apart for child-birth and for the dead. Shintoism has no very definite idea of a future state, or any distinct doctrine as regards sin and punishment, or heaven and hell. The Shinto form of disposing of the dead is by burial, cremation having been introduced with Buddhism. The ancient practice of sacrificing wives and others at the grave may, according to Mr. Aston, have had another reason than gratifying the dead in the next world. Food and ornaments were, however, buried with the dead, and shoes have been found, which suggests the idea of helping the departed on his journey into the vague beyond. Nothing certain can be gathered from old writings as to ideas concerning immortality; and " even to this day," writes Hearn, "Shinto belief represents the pre-Homeric stage of imagination as regards the supernatural." Certain days are set apart for honouring the dead, following each other with less frequency as time elapses, and every Japanese desires a son for the observing of these pious rites, and the maintaining of the family cult. Shintoism is a relic of spirit worship and appears to be an atrophied form of that phase of the evolution of religion in which the animistic spirit had as yet scarcely evolved into the god. As such it possesses affinities with Chinese aboriginal religions, and several African and South American forms. But never has such a comparatively simple type of religion been preserved so long or surrounded itself with such a semblance of the forms of the higher religions.

Shu. One of the " great company " of Egyptian gods at Heliopolis ; son of Rā or Tem. He personified the atmosphere, or the space dividing earth and sky ; his " pillars " supported the heavens. He interposed between Seb and Nut (*q.v.*), and is figured upholding the latter's arched body. One version of the tale relates that he had to make use of a ladder to lift Nut's body, and he is mentioned as one of those who helped the deceased to mount the ladder to heaven. He was a twin god with Tefnut, both being symbolised by a lion. Shu is figured as a man with an upright feather on his head. He is frequently represented as placing the sun in its correct position between heaven and earth.

Shu-King. A compilation of ancient Chinese documents and books. The title signifies " The Book of History." The first two portions cover an historical period of 150 years, and recount the events in the reigns of the rulers Yao (2357 B.C.) and Shun (2207 B.C.). They were edited by Confucius (*q.v.*). In it there are numberless references to the ancient faith, and many expressions are employed which seem to be a re-echo of the primal revelation.

Sien-Tsan. Chinese goddess of silk-culture. She was the wife of the Emperor Hwang of the Chou dynasty (2838-2698 B.C.) and arose as a deity along with other similar conceptions, notably Shen Nung, the tutelary deity of agriculture. In some measure she is an elemental deity, but it is not difficult to suppose that she was a veritable personage whose patronage of the culture of silk in early China caused her to become confounded with a divinity more or less identified with one or other of the forces of nature.

Sin (or En-zu). " Lord of Wisdom." The Babylonian moon-god, chief of the second divine triad composed of Sin, Shamash, and Adad, or Shamash and Ishtar. The Babylonian calendar was regulated by the moon, hence the prominent place held by this god in the national pantheon. He was the firstborn of

En-lil, the Bêl of Nippur, the father of Shamash, the sun, and of Ishtar. Sin was surrounded by the high mystery that accompanies the majesty of a supreme deity. A prayer in the library of Ashurbanipal speaks of him as a " divinity . . . full of love, like the far-off heaven and the broad ocean . . . whose deep inner being no god understands." (Roger, "Rel. Bab. and Ass.") A chief and probably most ancient seat of worship of the moon-god, known here as Nannar, was at Ur ; another at Harran. Sin held a less exalted position in the Assyrian pantheon, where Ashur overshadowed the other gods. A temple was erected to him in Khorsabad. Sin's wife was Nin-gal.

Siva (Civa). A development of the Vedic god Rudra (*q.v.*) ; the third of the great Hindu triad, the destroyer, or regenerator. In the epic he and Vishnu are rivals, or sharers of the honours paid to the " all-god." Maha-deva, the " Great God," is one among his thousand names.

His name Siva signifies " kindly, gracious, propitious," but though a god of reproduction, and a deliverer and restorer, he had terrible aspects to his character, even as Rudra had his twofold nature. He is a god of arts and learning, of dancing and revelry, and the god of asceticism (Maha-Yogi). His dwelling is on Mount Kailâsu, in the Himalaya, hence his title of " Lord of the Mountain." His sacred animal is the bull Nandi. He is represented girdled with serpents, hung with a necklace of skulls, sometimes with several faces, clad in an elephant's skin, holding a discus, trident, club, sword, or bow, etc. He can laugh and sing, and join in revelry and dancing, but at other times haunts cemeteries and other gruesome places, and goes naked smeared with ashes. He has three eyes (*see* Kama), is " blue-throated," or ruddy, or livid white, his hair plaited like Rudra's. It was he who cut off the fifth head of Brahmā (*q.v.*), which he was not able to get rid of till having fled to Benares he there obtained absolution. His wife is known under different names (*see* Uma, Parvati, Durga, Kali) ; his two sons are Ganesa and Kartikeya. Combined with Vishnu the dual deity is known as Hari-hara ; as the creative principle he is both male and female. Siva is worshipped very generally under the form of the Linga. Bloody rites have been associated with the cult both of him and his wife (*see* under Daksha and Ganga).

Skambha. In Vedic mythology the appellation of the supreme being, and apparently identified with Purusha (*q.v.*). Muir describes him as " a vast embodied being co-extensive with the universe."

Skanda. *See* Kartikeya.

Skrymir. A Norse giant. The old myth runs that Thor, travelling to the land of giants with his usual companions, sought shelter from an earthquake in a house, on leaving which the following morning he found a gigantic man asleep and snoring. When the latter awoke he asked what Thor had done with his glove, whereupon the god saw that the glove had been their house of shelter, and that he had passed the night in its thumb. The giant travelled on with them, carrying food for the party, and that evening when they were resting under a tree he fell asleep. Thor wanting food, found the straps of the giant's wallet too hard to undo, and in a temper struck Skrymir on the forehead with his hammer. The giant awoke and asked if an oak-leaf had fallen on him. Thor struck him again twice, but with as little effect as the first time. On the morrow they parted company. Thor went on to another giant, Utgardhaloki, to whom Loki showed his skill in eating, Thjálfi in running, but both were outdone. Then came Thor's turn to show his drinking powers. The latter, however, after three draughts from the long drinking-horn, found the liquor only a little lower. Then a cat ran in, and Thor trying to lift her could only raise one of her feet from the ground ; a worse humiliation still was his overthrow in a wrestling match with an old woman, his nurse. Later on the giant confesses to Thor that the end of the drinking-horn lay out in the sea, that the cat was the Midhgardh's serpent, and the old woman, age.

Soma. An ancient Vedic god, the deified fermented juice of the plant of this name ; " the Indian Bacchus." The hymns in the ninth book of the Rig-Veda are entirely devoted to its honour ; they were intended to be sung during the preparation of the sacred drink, which was accompanied by a religious ceremony. Soma the god was accredited with every attribute of a supreme deity, and he was closely allied with Agni. Various legends are associated with the bringing of the Soma to earth, in which a bird of some kind is introduced, reminiscent of the nectar-bringing eagle of Zeus. Varuna was supposed to have placed it in some distant region on a mountain, or in some high heaven. According to one account an eagle or falcon brought it thence for Indra. The daughter of the sun, through whose filter it was passed for purification, is related elsewhere to have brought it from some spot where the rain-god had nourished it; and another tale speaks of it as placed under the care of the Gandharvas (*q.v.*); Gayatri (*q.v.*) in the form of a bird flew to bring it away but was prevented; finally this myth winds up with the Gandharvas allowing Vach (*q.v.*) to carry it away. Soma was said to cure all ills, and to confer vitality, inspiration, and immortality; for men to drink it was to " feel the god within their veins." Indra drank freely of it in preparation for his martial exploits. The blessed drank it in Yama's realm and became immortal. It was offered in daily libation to the gods, and played an important part in the sacrifices. In later mythology the name Soma was given to the moon; the identity of the two results from the deity's being created a moon-god at a period when intoxicants were in disuse. An astrological significance may attach to the connection, as plants are often identified with heavenly bodies not only in primitive communities but in a much more advanced condition of society than obtained in ancient India.

Sraosha. The Yazata or Angel of Obedience in the celestial hierarchy of Persian theology. He becomes prominent in the Younger Avesta, where he has assumed a priestly character, and is associated with sacrifice, and in this respect reminiscent of Agni (*q.v.*) (Lehmann). He is a more interesting figure as the angel who bears the soul aloft after death (*see* Zoroastrianism), and as the valiant supporter of Ahura Mazda in the last days of final combat, when he fights with opposing demons. He was supposed to keep guard over the world during the night-watches.

Starkadhr. A giant's son, and favourite of Odhin. In the legend concerning him Thor appears as the adversary of Odhin, for in some way he caused all the latter's good gifts to Starkadhr to be balanced by some evil. Odhin granted him a life of three generations; Thor decreed that in each he should commit a dishonourable act; Odhin decreed him victory and treasure, Thor grievous wounds and discontent; and worse still, Odhin granted him the gift of poetry, while Thor caused him to forget the poems he made.

Starkadhr was a famed legendary warrior, the last of the old stern, heroic kind. His body, it is said, continued to fight after his head was cut off. (For Starkadhr's connection with Vikarr's sacrifice, *see* under the latter's name.)

Sua. A culture-god of the Muysca Indians of Central America, sometimes alluded to as Nemquetaha or Bochica. The name signifies " day," and shows his solar significance. He is analogous to Quetzalcoatl and other Central American sun-gods.

Sugawara Michizane. *See* Tenjin.

Suitengū. A Japanese god of the sea. Popular belief however maintains that he is the young Emperor Antoku, drowned in 1185. Dr. Florenz connects him with the Indian Varuna. His temple is at Tokyo. There are three other gods of the sea, worshipped at Sumiyoshi.

Sulis. A sun-god of the British Celts, whose place of worship appears to have been at Bath.

Supay. The god of death of the Incan Peruvians. All souls who did not fare to the home of the sun were destined to dwell in his shadowy subterranean abode. He is analogous to the Mexican Mictlan (*q.v.*). Like Pluto and other deities of the underworld, the Peruvians believed he had power over the crops.

Surya. The sun. One of the three chief Vedic gods (*see* Agni and Indra), son of Dyaus, or of Aditi, or child of Ushas, the dawn, who is also spoken of as his wife. He is described as a far and all-seeing god and as " the eye of Mitra and Varuna." Seven ruddy or " lucid " mares draw the chariot of this god with flaming hair. For a later legend of his wife, *see* under Saranyu. He is perhaps the sun in his aspect of rising and setting.

Susa-no-o. A Japanese god born from the nose of Izanagi (*q.v.*). He was originally appointed to be ruler of the sea, but he expressed his wish to join his mother in the nether-world, which he finally did. He is therefore looked upon by some as a god of the underworld (Florenz); by others as god of the moon, or of the rain-storm. He was of a violent disposition, and before passing down to the nether regions he went to visit his sister Ama-Terasu (*q.v.*). At first he proposed that they should beget offspring by chewing parts of the jewels and swords they wore (his sister knowing his character had armed herself) and spitting them out; the result was eight children, from one of which the Mikado is descended. Susa-no-o's deeds after this became so alarming and destructive, and he behaved so offensively to Ama-Terasu, that she retired into a cave. Susa-no-o was banished and retired to Idzumo, which remained in possession of his family till they resigned in favour of his sister's descendants (*see* Ninigi). While in Idzumo, Susa-no-o performed the Perseus-like deed of delivering a maiden from an eight-headed dragon. He afterwards married her. Then he continued his journey to the underworld.

Swarga. The heaven of Indra, situated on Mount Meru (*q.v.*). A paradise of all conceivable joys; of palaces of gold and diamonds, of exquisite gardens, bright nymphs, music, and song.

T

Tammuz (Dumu-zi). The cult of this Babylonian and Assyrian god is traced back to an extremely ancient past. He was a nature-god and his myth represented the dying of the year and its resuscitation with the spring. A chief feature of his cult was the annual festival of mourning for the death of the young god, when women were hired to weep (*see* Ezekiel viii. 14). The fourth month of the Babylonian year was named after him, and the Hebrews used the same title for theirs. The myth of Tammuz is associated with that of Ishtar (*q.v.*), who slew him after he had become her husband, and for whose sake she descended into Hades. The myth of Adonis and others allied with it are finally identical with that of Tammuz.

Tamu. A culture-deity of the Caribs of Brazil, probably the same as the god Zume (*q.v.*). He was said to have been of light complexion, to have come from the east, and to have instructed the Caribs in the arts of agriculture and refinement, after doing which he disappeared in the direction whence he came.

Taoism. Lao Tzu, a Chinese philosopher, who probably flourished about 600 B.C., formulated a philosophy which is known as Taoism, from the word Tao, signifying the omnipresent and omnipotent principle upon which it is founded. It is a doctrine of passivity or inaction, constant adaptability of self to environment, without effort, all advancement and progress being in the " line of least resistance." The impracticability of such a system is obvious, and it is little short of marvellous that it attained any prominence whatever. Taoism is a philosophy, and regards deity as a principle which exists as intrinsic and operates spontaneously without self-manifestation. An exponent of the system has said : " The ultimate end is God. He is manifested in the laws of nature. He is the hidden spring. At the beginning of all things he was." Those disciples who followed Lao Tzu, however, regarded Tao as the First Cause, that in which everything was ultimately resolved. This power dwelt beyond the limits of the terrestrial universe, and if men desired union with it after death, and immortality, they must achieve freedom from the trammels of the flesh.

Those spirits who had achieved such freedom circled round Tao, a point of glowing light, in the supreme glory of motion for ever and ever. Taoism, like Confucianism, however, evolved a species of degenerate mythology, which embraces not only men who are made into gods by means of apotheosis, but spirits who reside in various natural objects. Sea, river, and star-gods are found in the pantheon of Taoism, the Spirit of the Sea, the King of the Sea, and the God of Tides having temples erected to them by the sea shore. The dragon in many forms is worshipped by Taoists. The Ruler of Thunder and the Mother of Lightning are two of their principal nature divinities. They have also a god of literature, Wen-tsch'ang (q.v.), Tow-moo, a female divinity who dwells in the Great Bear, whilst another part of this constellation is worshipped under the name of Kwei-sing. Chang is another star-god of the Taoists. The entire mythology of the Tao religion has been very much sophisticated by Buddhistic influences. Buddha is represented by Teen-tsun, and Bodhisattwa by Tsoo. Yuh-hwang-shang-te is saviour of the world and lord of creation. The San-tsing, or "Three Pure Ones," are the Taoist trinity. They are a threefold manifestation of one historical person, representing the Buddha past, present, and to come. There are also three beings called the San-kwan, or "Three Rulers," who rule over heaven, earth, and water. In fact in the Taoist pantheon we have a well-marked mythological system, which, like that of Confucianism, was built up by superstition upon the ruins of a philosophical system.

Tashmetu. Wife of the Babylonian god Nabu.

Ta-urt (Thoneris). An Egyptian hippopotamus-goddess, wife of Set.

Tem (Temu, Atem, Atmu). A form of the Egyptian sun-god, and a chief of the company of gods at Heliopolis, said to personify the evening sun. He was the " father of human beings," and came forth from Nu (q.v.), being self-created. Shu and Tefnut were his first offspring. He is invariably figured as a man-god. Tem is one of the forms of Ra incarnate in the bull Mnevis. Pithom (house of Tum) was another centre of his cult.

Tem was associated with a version of the flood legend, according to which he let loose the waters of the primeval abyss over the earth, intending to destroy mankind, and only those who were with the god in his boat escaped with their lives.

Tenjin (or Temmangū, etc.).   Japanese god of learning and caligraphy.   He is a deified man, Sugawara Michizane, of the ninth to tenth century, a favourite with one of the emperors, but banished by his successor.   The cow and the plum-tree are associated with his worship (Chamberlain), the former being the animal on which he rode, figures of it in bronze and stone being placed in the court of his temple.

Tezcatlipoca.   An important deity of the Aztecs of ancient Mexico, in whose pantheon he held a position similar to that of Jupiter in the Roman or Zeus in the Greek.   His name signifies " Fiery Mirror," and he was so called because he wielded a shield of polished metal, in which, as god of justice, he was supposed to behold the deeds of men.   He was primarily the personification of the breath of life.   Savage man regards the wind as the great source of breath and of immediate life, and in many tongues the words " wind," " soul," and " breath " have a common origin.   But although he was a life-giver, Tezcatlipoca had also the power to end existence.   In some cases he appears as the inexorable death-dealer, and as such is termed " The Hungry Chief " and " The Enemy."   One of the names by which he was best known was " The Youthful Warrior," to signify the reserve of vital force which he possessed, and which was boisterously typified in the tempest.   He was usually depicted as holding a dart in his right hand, and his mirror-shield with four spare darts in the left.   The Aztecs pictured him as rioting along the highways as the wind of night rushes along the deserted roads with more seeming violence than by day.   His exalted position in the Mexican pantheon seems to have won for him especial attention as a god of fate and fortune, but it must have been as an afterthought that these attributes were granted him.   Indeed, the place he took as the head of the pantheon forced upon him many attributes foreign to his original character.   At one period in Mexican history, shortly before the Spanish conquest, his worship had become so universal that there are grounds for believing that it might have developed into monotheism, or the worship of one god. He was one of the few Mexican deities who had any relation to the expiation of sin.   To sum up his attributes, it may be said of Tezcatlipoca that he was a wind-god who, through the speedy advancement in fortune of the Aztec people, became their tutelar deity, and the recipient of nearly every attribute that it is possible for a god to possess.   He had several festivals in the year, the circumstances of one of which are worth recording. A war-captive without spot or blemish was selected to play the part of the god for the time being, and was carried through the streets of the city by night as it was supposed the deity himself would be conveyed. He was provided with musical instruments, and instructed to comport himself as it was fitting the earthly representative of a divine being should. Later he had four wives bestowed upon him, each with the name of a goddess, and was feasted as the earthly representative of Tezcatlipoca by the nobility of the country. On the day of the festival he was conveyed to the teocalli or pyramid of Tezcatlipoca, and, having taken a tearful farewell of his spouses, and having destroyed his musical instruments, he was made one with the god by the usual method of sacrifice, that is, he had his heart torn out. Afterwards the body was eaten at a formal repast, the idea being that those who partook of it would also partake of the qualities of the god. In some places we even find Tezcatlipoca playing the rôle of creator, and he was regarded as the power who would ultimately bring the universe to destruction.

Thonaraz, Donar (Anglo-Saxon, Thunar; Norse, Thor). God of the air, of thunder and lightning, of winds and rains, the father of might and strength, strongest of gods and men, the antagonist of giants ; presiding over weather and crops, protector of the earth, the friend of men, god of justice and victory, the guardian of the home. The cult of this god is found among most German tribes ; the Saxons in England set him below Odhin, but in the north evidence remains of the high honour in which he was held in the number of temples dedicated to him, and of places and persons named after him. He was one of the three deities (Thor, Odhin, Frey or Frikko) to whom was dedicated the great temple at Upsala. Groves were consecrated to the god, the oak being considered especially sacred to Thor. Latin writers identified him with Jupiter or Hercules. The Scalds represented Thor as a son of Odhin, his mother being a mountain goddess Fjorgyn, or Jord (the earth), or Hlodyn, perhaps identical with Hludana, a name found in Latin inscriptions in Friesland and Lower Rhine district (*see* Frigg). Thor was gigantic in height, strength, and appetite, young and pleasant of countenance, with a red beard, into which he snorted when angry, while his voice and eyes became terrible. His wife was the giantess Jarnsaxa, or Sif, for whom the dwarfs forged golden hair ; he had children who personified strength

and courage, vehemence or anger, and for companions Loki
and two gigantic young peasants, Thjalfi, the swift runner, and
his sister Roskva. These accompanied Thor on his wanderings,
for the god loved to have intercourse with the dwellers on earth,
and his journeys were often taken on foot with a basket slung
over his shoulders. He went long distances, wading daily
through four rivers, on his way to administer justice under the
World-Ash. Men appealed to him for help in battle and in
peace. His likeness was carved to ensure luck and protection
on the chief seat of the house and on the prow of vessels. He
was concerned with all domestic matters ; many superstitions
regarding the cure of illnesses were connected with him, and no
journey was undertaken, no new home settled upon, before his
guidance and approval had in some way been secured. " Odin
was god of the warrior, Thor of the peasant " (Golther). " Of
the solemn mystery which surrounds the form of Woden, there
is no trace in the simple, vigorous Thunar " (Kauffmann).
The Eddic poem, Harbardsljod, describes a humorous scene
between the two gods. Odhin, in the guise of a ferryman, refuses
to take Thor across the water. Then follows an argument in
which Thor is no match for the witty and cunning Odhin, and he
has no adequate weapons of speech with which to return the
taunts of the other god—it is, in short, an unequal encounter
between peasant and man of wit, which Saussaye thinks may
possess some significance with regard to the history of culture
and religion. Thor's irresistible weapon was the hammer,
Mjolnir (or a fiery axe), which after doing its deadly work
returned of itself to his hand, and as further accoutrements he
had a girdle of strength and iron gloves. Marriage ceremonies
were consecrated, obsequies hallowed, and contracts settled by
Thor's hammer. His mansion was Bilskirnir, in which were
five hundred and forty halls. Thursday (A.S., Thunresdag ;
O. Norse, Thorsdag) was a day set apart in many places for
peaceful and civil affairs, and for the opening of the Thing ; it
was a favourite day for weddings, and the peasant liked to keep
it as a holiday from ordinary work. Thor's chariot was drawn
by goats ; thunder was believed to be the roll of his chariot
wheels. Mogk considers Thor a development of one aspect of
the old sky-god Tiwaz. For myths in association with this god
see Hrungir, Thrymr, Skrymir, Utgardhaloki, Hymir, Geirrödhr,
Thjazi. The word Thor originally meant " extension," and was
principally applied to sound. His fiery red beard is, of course,
the lightning. His hammer is Mjolnir, " the crusher," or

thunder. He is a rain and thunder deity like Indra or Mixcoatl. He sometimes assumes a rôle of omnipotence, as does Indra. He is perpetually at war with the frost-giants. His wife, Sif, is the uncultivated earth, and her hair the grass, burned up by fire (Loki), but restored by subterranean forces (the dwarfs).

Thor. *See* Thonaraz.

Thoth (Tehuti). The " twice " or " thrice great," chief of the eight gods of Hermopolis. The " lord of divine words," scribe of the gods, god of wisdom and learning, inventor of arts and sciences, a personification of the reason and intelligence of the gods. He was self-created and rose with Ra at the beginning of time. With his voice " of just intonation " he spake the word that brought all things into being, and to him was due the ordering of the universe. He was the arbiter between the gods of light and darkness ; he had knowledge of the spells, and of the right way of pronouncing them, necessary to enable the deceased to pass safely through the underworld to his desired haven ; and his words had power to resuscitate the dead. Thoth it is who waits in the judgment hall of Osiris to receive the verdict after the weighing of the heart, communicated to him by the dog-headed ape who is always associated with this god. Thoth is figured with the head of an ibis. The Greeks identified him with Hermes. The name signifies " The Measurer," and as such he is a moon-god, and is represented as wearing the lunar crescent and disk, and holding a pen or stylus and a notched palm - branch. He it was who wrote the sacred books, and was the father of magic.

Thrymr. A Norse giant associated with the tale of the loss of Thor's hammer. The latter awoke one morning and found it gone. Loki borrowed Freyja's falcon garb and flew to the giant's home, who, in answer to the inquiry of Loki, tells the latter that the hammer he had stolen was hidden eight fathoms below the ground ; moreover he refused to restore the stolen object unless Freyja was brought him to be his wife. When Freyja heard of this proposal her anger was such that the earth trembled, and her necklace (Brisingamen) burst asunder. Thor, by Heimdall's advice, therefore dressed himself as Freyja, disguising himself in women's garments and the necklace, and repaired to Thrymr. The giant could not hide his astonishment at the bride's appetite, for Thor had no equal as a trencherman, and on this occasion an ox, eight salmon, and three hogsheads of beer were with ease consumed by him. Loki who had dressed up and accompanied him as a waiting-maid, explained that the bride had not been able to eat for eight days owing to her impatience to reach her lover. Thrymr sent for Thor's hammer, the usual consecration of a marriage bond. Thor laughed when he saw it again, seized it, and quickly slew Thrymr and his whole race of giants. Thrymr and his giants symbolise the forces of winter conquered by Thor, the god of rain and thunder, who breaks up the ice-bound earth and dissipates the frost.

Tien and Shang Ti. In ancient Chinese literature we meet with two terms either of which appears to be used for the name of the supreme cause or god. These are T'ien and Shang Ti, the former meaning the sky or visible heavens, and the other " the Supreme Ruler on High." These names are employed interchangeably for the word " god," but there is no doubt that at some remote period they were used to designate different conceptions of the deity. T'ien is probably the older, as signifying the expanse of heaven and the phenomena of thunder, lightning, and rain which emanated from it, thus proving to the primitive Chinese mind the existence of a deity who set these phenomena in motion. Shang Ti is more the appellation of a personal god, and this is borne out by the circumstance that whereas T'ien is usually associated with fate or calamity of any sort, Shang Ti is sacrificed to as a material being who leaves footprints on the soil and comes into contact with mankind. However, we cannot doubt that whatever the method of their fusion, the two names refer to one and the same being, and may be taken as alluding to his material and spiritual aspects, respectively. It would seem from these premises that the earliest religious ideas of the Chinese were monotheistic, and the canonical books and the methods of worship employed in the imperial court uphold the theory that it has remained so down to the present day. It is interesting to observe that the pictographic script of China, although forty centuries old, still retains traces that the name T'ien alluded to the anthropomorphic or manlike and material conception of God, as the figures intended to convey the name appear as rude drawings of the human form. The earlier Chinese philosophers regarded Shang Ti as synonymous with heaven, and earth as the sphere of his action. Only once, however, does Confucius allude to God as a personality. Chucius in later days proclaimed that the names T'ien and Shang Ti meant nothing more than " principle " or " law," but admitted the existence of a governing power which he called Ti. The reasons for the original worship of a supreme being in China appear to have been thanksgiving and prayer, as we find early records of days for their celebration being set apart by imperial and other authority.

Tiwaz (Anglo - Saxon, Tiw; OHG., Ziu, Zio; Norse, Tyr). (The identity of the name with Greek Zeus and old Indian Dyaus (*q.v.*) has been questioned by some later philologists.[1]) A deity of prehistoric antiquity; originally a sky-god, a god of light, and the oldest form of the storm-god. His worship is traced among the greater numbers of the Teutonic tribes; the Swabians honoured him as their national god, and were known into later times as Ziuwari, Ziumen; the Saxons held him in reverence, and Tacitus relates of the Semnones that they offered human sacrifices to this god, and that none might enter his sacred grove except in chains, and should one chance to fall he might not rise, but had to roll himself away from the holy precincts. Like many old deities, he lost in time his pure cosmic qualities and became an especial god of war and justice, and as such he was known to the Scalds. He led the tribes to battle, and their armies were blessed in his name by the priests. As a consequence he became associated by Latin writers with Mars, and " Martis dies " became in Teutonic tongue Tiwes-daeg (A.S.), Tysdagr (Norse), our Tuesday. Zistag still exists in certain dialects. Other names belonged to this deity: Er, Ear, whence the Bavarian Ertag; and Dings, which signified his lordship of the Thing (the popular assembly), and hence the German Dienstag. In 1883, two Roman altars were discovered in the north of England; they had been dedicated in the third century A.D. by a squadron of Frisians from Twenthe in Holland to " Mars Thingsus," whom they honoured, according to different interpretations, as the god presiding over some popular assembly, or over their particular division of the forces (Lat., Cuneus; Teu., things, Kauffmann). Much scoffs at this latter idea; the root of the verb retained in the word Ding has, he says, gone through such a long course of evolution in meaning, that it is difficult to decide how the god-name Thingsaz is to be understood; anyhow, he adds, the name points to claims above those of a mere god of war; he inclines to the idea which others hold that it may indicate an atmospheric god of some kind—of sky, storm, etc. The Teutonic Mars was also known among

[1] This doubt also makes his character as a sky-god uncertain (Saussaye).

the Saxons as Sahsnot (Anglo-Saxon, Seaxneat), " Sword-bearer " or " Companion of the Sword " (sax was the short sword from which the Saxons took their name), and the sword dances of which Tacitus speaks may have been performed in his honour.[1] Irmin, the mythic ancestor of the Herminones (see Mannus), a chief race of the West Germans, is thought to have been probably identical with Ziu, as their names are found in combination. The word signified the august, or sublime one, and in compound words and proper names had the sense of fullness of power, " universal." The venerated wooden columns or tree-trunks, the mysterious Irminsûl (" column of the world ") of the Saxons, one of which was destroyed in its sacred grove by Charlemagne near Eresburg (now Stadtberg or Marsberg) when at war with this people, are supposed to have been dedicated to some sky or war-god, possibly to Tiw. Even as a war-god, Tyr, in time, had to give place to Odhin, and in an Old Saxon baptismal formula of the eighth century Saxnôt comes after Thor and Woden. Norse legend makes Tyr the son of the giant Hymir. He was nobly associated with the myth of the Fenris-wolf, for he alone had courage to thrust his hand into the monster's jaws, thereby enabling the other gods to bind him, and losing his own arm, like the Hindu Savitri. This tale may point to the original nature of Tyr as associated with light, day swallowed by night, or the sun by the wolf, as related in Norse legend (see Golther). In the last terrible conflict, Tyr and the hell-dog Garm slay one another. Much is entirely at variance with the monotheistic tendency of some scholars, who identify Tyr with the old sky-god or derive from him the other gods, Woden, Thor, Heimdall, Balder, and Freyr.[2]

Tlaloc. Tlaloc was the Mexican god of rain and moisture. It was thought that he made his home in the mountains which surrounded the valley of Mexico. Sculptured representations of him occur more frequently than those of any other Mexican deity. He is usually represented in a semi-recumbent attitude, with the upper part of the body raised upon the elbows, and the knees drawn up, probably to represent the mountainous nature of the country whence the rain emanated. He was espoused

[1] The identification of Tiwaz with Er, Sahsnot, and Irmin is not fully certified. Much thinks Sahsnot was a more fitting name for Freyr, who has a sword in his myth.

[2] The memory of Tiw and Odhin was kept alive formerly in the refrain of verses sung at the common-riding, which used to take place at Hawick in yearly memory of Flodden. It runs, " Teer yebus ye Teer ye Odin " (Teribus ye teri Odin).

to Chalchihuitlicue (Emerald Lady), who bore him a numerous progeny, the Tlalocs or clouds. He manifested himself in three forms, the lightning-flash, the thunderbolt, and the thunder. He was supposed to inhabit the four cardinal points and every mountain-top, and the colours of the four directions of the compass were introduced into his costume, in stripes of yellow, green, red, and blue. In order that he might fructify the crops a vase containing every kind of grain was placed before him. He dwelt in a well-watered and luxurious paradise, called Tlalocan, where those who had been drowned or struck by lightning enjoyed immortal pleasures. He is usually represented in the Aztec manuscripts as having a dark complexion, a large, round eye, a row of tusks, and an angular blue stripe rolled over the lips. This latter appears to have been evolved from the coils of two snakes, reptiles typical of water. A large number of virgins and young children were annually sacrificed to Tlaloc. His chief festival was the Etzalqualiztli, " when they eat bean food," which was held on the 13th of May. At this function the priests of Tlaloc plunged into a pond imitating the sound and movements of frogs. The mountains Popocatepetl and Teocuinani were especially sacred to him, and his teocalli or temple stood on the heights of the latter, and contained his idol carved in green stone to represent water.

Tohil. A god of the Kiche Indians of Guatemala, alluded to in the " Popol Vuh," their religio-historic saga. The divine beings gave him to Balam Quitze, one of the first men, as a god to worship, evidently as a symbol of themselves. It was under his guidance that the Kiches left the district of Tolan, and set forth to their new home in Guatemala. He it was who gave the people the gift of fire by shaking sparks (flints) from his sandals. There can be no doubt that he was a thunder-god, akin to Mixcoatl and other American divinities such as the Peruvian Con-con.

Tsul 'Kalu. Or " Slanting Eyes," a hunter-god of the Cherokee Indians. He is supposed to dwell in a great mountain of the Blue Ridge in North-West Virginia, and to own all the game in the district. From the description of his appearance we may conclude that he resembled a deer, as did several hunter-gods of the American peoples.

Tuat (Duat). The Egyptian realm of the dead. Particulars of the region are given in the Book of the Dead (*q.v.*), of which there are various extant versions. The Tuat was divided into twelve portions corresponding with the same number of hours of the night, and according to the Book of Gates, each portion was divided from the next by a gate, guarded by serpents. Ra in his boat travelled nightly through it (*see* under Ba).

Tuatha de Danann. "Tribe of the goddess Danu." The appellation of the gods of the Irish Celts, who were supposed to be descended from the goddess Danu. They invaded Ireland from a magic cloud, and gave battle to the Firbolgs, who ruled in the land. They drove the Firbolgs into Connaught, and appropriated the best parts of the country. Their principal leaders were the Dagda, Angus, Len, Lugh, Midir Lir, Manannan, Morrigu, Cleena, Aine, and Sinend, many of whom are mentioned under their own names. They were the nature and culture deities of a later race who drove the older inhabitants of Ireland westwards.

Tuisco. A god of whom Tacitus (" Germania," 2) relates that he was " born of the earth," celebrated by the Germans in their songs, and that he had a son Mannus, the progenitor of the three tribes Ingaevones, Herminones, and Istævones. The father and son were thus honoured as the source and founder of the race.

Tupan. The principal deity of the Tupi and other Brazilian tribes. He is supposed by them to exist in the upper regions, across which he flies in the shape of a great bird, watching over the welfare of the tribes under his ægis. On coming to earth he instructed them in the arts of agriculture and endowed them with the gift of fire. He is sharply distinguished from other native gods, and is evidently regarded as a deity all-powerful and invisible than as one with whom the Indians are in direct communion. (*See* art. " Brazil " in " Encyclopædia of Religion and Ethics.")

Tvastri. The divine artisan and architect of the universe of Vedic mythology, " the Hindu Vulcan," believed to be a very ancient deity. All things were thought to have their form from him. He had his forge where he sharpened Brahmanas-pati's axe and moulded Indra's thunderbolts. Even men were shaped by Tvastri, and by his agency husband and wife were framed for each other whilst yet unborn. He furthermore protects the creatures he has made. Though not regarded as divine in the Vedas, he is generally looked upon as such in the

Purānas. He is usually represented as having three eyes and as carrying a club. Nowadays he is regarded as the patron deity of artificers. The Ribhus (*q.v.*) were his pupils; Saranyu (*q.v.*) his daughter. He brought about his own end, for angered at Indra having killed his son, he uttered a curse against him, but in some way pronounced it wrongly, and he himself was slain by it. (*See* Visvakarman.)

U

Uatchet. Tutelary goddess of the north of Egypt (*see* Nekhebet). She gave help to Isis when this goddess had to seek shelter in the swamps of the Delta. Horus was placed in her charge when Isis, his mother, went to seek Osiris. The Greeks knew her as Buto. When figured as a woman she wears the crown of the north, and holds a sceptre, sometimes entwined with a winged serpent. She is symbolised by a winged uræus, and sometimes has the vulture form of the sister goddess Nekhebet.

Ukemochi. Japanese goddess of food, or cereals. Identified by the Japanese with Inari.

Ullr, " the lordly." A Swedish god, born of Sif and stepson of Thor, a famed archer and skater ; men swore by his ring and invoked him when entering on single combat. His dwelling was the dark Ydalir (Yew-valley), said to be either because yew wood is the best for bows, or because green in winter, and a tree of death. He is identical with the Ollerus of northern sources (the Mitothin of Saxo, *see* Loki), who took Odhin's place when the latter was absent, and on the great god's return fled away to Sweden on a bone (skate, or snow-shoes). Kauffmann identifies him with Vidharr and Hoenir, to whom the office of judge belonged, assigned also by Saxo to Mitothin.

Ullr, according to Meyer, is a dull, winterly counterpart to Odhin. His identification with Holler the Frisian god of the dead is uncertain (Saussaye). Apparently at one time a god of considerable importance. . . . As Thor in Norway, Freyr in Sweden, Ullr may have been venerated in North Scandinavia, on the boundaries of Lapland and Finland (Golther).

Uma (Haimavati). The wife of the Hindu god Siva and daughter of Daksha (*q.v.*), known under the further names of Ambika, Devī, Durga, Kali, Parvati, Sati, etc.[1] Like her husband she had both a repellent and gracious side to her character, represented under different forms according to

[1] The sect of the Saktas are worshippers of Sakti—divine energy personified in the woman, more especially in the various forms of Siva's wife.

the above names. She is described as of great beauty and austerity, and was the reincarnation of the self-immolating Sati (*q.v.*), born the second time as the daughter of the mountain Himavat and Menā, according to a post-Vedic myth. Her name signified light, or heavenly wisdom; and she was worshipped later as an embodiment of lofty abstract qualities.

Urdhr (Anglo-Saxon, Wyrd=fate). The most famous of the Norns. Her fountain was at the foot of the ash Yggdrasil, and there the gods assembled daily to administer justice. So purifying is the water of Urdhr's fountain that everything it washes becomes as white as the film within the egg-shell. Urdhr and Hel are identical.

Ushas. The dawn, to whom beautiful Vedic hymns are addressed and many epithets applied. She is the life and breath of all things, speeding men forth to their occupations and awakening the worshippers; she is young, immortal, born afresh each day, and has ruddy steeds yoked to her shining car.

Utgardhaloki. *See* Skrymir.

V

Vach. Goddess of speech. "Mother of the Vedas." She became the wife of Brahmā, and as such was known under various names (*see* Sarasvati). Vach was associated with Prajapati in the work of creation, and identified with Viraj, and called the daughter of Kama (*q.v.*). (*See* also under Soma.)

Vaikuntha. The paradise of Vishnu, a glorious description of which is given in the Mahābhārata. Also a name of Vishnu in one of his incarnations.

Vaivasvata. The present Manu (*q.v.*).

Valhalla. Odhin's hall, where Norse warriors who had fallen in battle renewed their martial life and feasted with the god. The hall was built round the trunk of a tree, Laeradhr, on the leaves of which browsed the stag Eikthyrmir and the goat Heidhrun, from whose udders flowed the inexhaustible stream of mead drunk by the heroes of Valhalla. Five hundred and forty were its doors, through each of which 800 warriors could pass at a time; its roof was composed of shields, its beams of spear shafts, and the gleam of swords and breastplates lit up the interior. On the west wall hung a wolf, surmounted by an eagle. Beyond the hall was a forest of golden foliage (Glasir), and round it a sacred wall. Every day the champions (Einherjar) ride forth to combat with each other on Odhin's field, and each night return to feast on boar and mead. When fresh heroes are expected, Odhin sends to meet them at Asgardh's gate with goblets of mead.

Valkyrie (Old German, Idisi). Female warriors who dwelt in Vingolf, which was under the same roof as Valhalla. Over them reigned the goddess Freyja, and they waited on the heroes of Valhalla. Odhin sent them to the field of battle to make choice of the warriors to be slain, and to turn the tide of victory as he chose. Their steeds carried them through the air and over seas. The Valkyrie were counterparts of the Amazonian women of the Teutonic tribes who took part with their husbands in the field of battle, such as are said to have graced the triumph of Aurelian, and who acted as shield-bearers to the Vikings. They had something fateful about them; " they wove the web of battle," and were in this way allied to the Norns. Their symbol was a swan, and swans were believed to be transformed Valkyries. In the Volsunga saga and other ancient Teutonic tales should a hero seize the " swan-dress " of a Valkyrie she is powerless to leave him. Brynhild and other warrior women alluded to in these old sagas were Valkyries.

Vanir. Shining ones, or friendly ones. Gods of the atmosphere (Uhland). The three Norse deities Njordhr and his son and daughter Frey and Freyja were Vanir. The war between the Aesir and Vanir was the first war in the world. It was brought about by the Vanir goddess Gullveig, who was practised in sorcery and witchcraft; she was ill-treated in the hall of the gods, being thrust through with spears and thrice burnt, but her life was charmed, and she still lived. Then the war began by Odhin hurling his spear into the midst of the Vanir host; the Vanir forced their way up to the citadel of the gods and won the day; peace was concluded, and ratified by each side spitting into a vessel (*see* Odhrerir) and hostages were exchanged, Njordhr being sent to the Aesir and Hoenir to the Vanir.

This war has been variously interpreted as a cult war, as a war between a warlike and peaceful agricultural nation, or as a nature myth, the light breaking through the clouds that originally enveloped the earth, or general opposition of gods of light and darkness, but it obviously belongs to the first category, and displays every sign of a struggle between rival systems afterwards amalgamated. Meyer gives a Biblical explanation.

Varuna. An exalted Vedic deity, " the all-enveloping one," personification of the sky, in whom were combined the divine attributes of the other gods. The Vedic hymns describe Varuna as a god of unparalleled moral grandeur. With law and wisdom he measured out the earth, made a pathway for the sun and stars, guided the rivers in their courses, ordered the winds, sent rain to refresh the pastures, gave fire to men, and set Soma on the mountain. The sun is his eye, the wind his breath. Thousand-eyed, nothing is hid from him; men's secrets are known to him, the winkings of their eyes are numbered. A judge, but a gracious god to sinners, from whom men cannot escape though they fly to the uttermost parts of the earth.

From his dwelling in far supernal regions, beyond which thought cannot reach, he watches as a guardian of the universe; his bliss is shared with the god Yama, and thither the blessed dead hope to be transported when life is over. Nevertheless, Varuna, like other gods, is represented as eating and drinking, and otherwise occupied in a human manner. Indeed his heaven is a place of purely sensual delights. Varuna, in comparatively early times, became more particularly a luminary of the night sky; as his supremacy declined, later mythology honoured him chiefly as a god of the waters, "an Indian Neptune." Prof. Roth says, "When on the one hand the conception of Varuna as the all-embracing heaven had been established, and on the other hand the observation of the rivers flowing towards the ends of the earth and to the sea had led to the conjecture that there existed an ocean enclosing the earth in its bosom, then the way was thoroughly prepared for connecting Varuna with the ocean." Varuna is represented sitting on a composite creature, half-antelope, half-fish, known as a makara. He holds a rope, for sinners were lassoed by him and Mitra, the latter god being associated with Varuna in work and power. Bergaigne, without excluding the idea of the sky as the "enveloper, or emprisoner" of light and of the waters (the former by night, the latter during seasons of drought), demonstrates that the above method of dealing with his enemies affords an interpretation of Varuna's name. The decline of Varuna's supremacy, which was superseded by that of Indra, was due, according to Roth, to the gradual modification of the old Aryan religion after it had been transplanted to India. The Indian faith, as found in the Rig-Veda, contrary to that of the Persian, to which the more supersensuous and spiritual elements of religion appealed, had begun already to give preference to gods representing the powers of nature. It was as a reaction against this tendency, alien to old Indo-Germanic instincts, that the speculative and philosophical spirit arose. (*See* article on the chief gods of the Aryans in "Zeitschrift der deutschen Morgenländischen Gesellschaft," vol. vi.) Prof. Macdonell is of opinion that Varuna's kinship to the Greek Ouranos, "though presenting phonetic difficulties, seems possible." Etymological explanation of Varuna and Mitra is as yet uncertain. Varuna is still worshipped by fishermen, but no images are made of him.

Vasaki. *See* Sesha.

Vasishtha. A pre-eminent Rishi, author of several hymns of the Rig-Veda. One of the mind-born sons of Brahmā. His contest with Viswâmitra, also an author of some of the hymns, is related in the epics.

Vasishthas. *See* Angirases.

Vasudeva. Father of the god Krishna.

Vasus. A group of eight divine beings who attended upon Indra; their names represented natural phenomena.

Vāta. *See* Vayu.

Vayu (Vāta). Vedic god of the wind or air, associated with Indra and offspring of heaven and earth. He (or Indra) formed a triad with Agni and Surya; he dwelling in the air, Agni on earth, and Surya in heaven. A fierce god, the horses of his chariot, which rolled with a " rending and resounding " noise, being at times a thousand in number, but varying with the supposed strength of the wind. In the epic period he became the father of Hanuman and Bhīma, and later myths grew round his name. He is figured riding on a deer. As regards the comparison with the Teutonic Wodan-Odinn, Schrader (art. " Aryan Religion," Hastings' " Ency. Rel. and Ethics ") says, " The etymological connection in this view is not free from difficulty." He is some-times regarded as father of the Maruts (*q.v.*) and is spoken of as the son-in-law of Tvastri (*q.v.*).

Vedic Literature (Veda, " knowledge "). The Vedas compose the ancient sacred literature of India, and were believed to be divinely revealed. They fall into four divisions (Samhitâs): Rig-Veda, Veda of hymns; Sama-Veda, of chants or tunes; Yajur-Veda, of sacrifice; Atharva-Veda, of magic and spells, dealing with popular superstitions rather than with the religious and sacerdotal matters of the other three.

The Rig-Veda is divided into 10 Mandala, the greater number of which are ascribed to certain families of Seers (2-9 are known as the family books). This and the Atharva-Veda are of chief interest as regards ancient religious conceptions.

To each Samhitâ or Mantra is attached a prose writing, of later origin; these are the Brāhmanas, theological treatises, concerned with sacrificial rites. Supplementary to these are the Aranyakas, " Forest treatises," mystical and philosophical, prepared for recluses; and the " Upanishads," of a more speculative character, dealing with Brahma (neuter) and Atman, the " world soul." We have in these, writes Jacobi, " the unique spectacle in the history of religion of the search for a supreme god after the popular gods had proved to be false."

The Sutras (Sutra=string), rule-books on matters of ritual, law, and everyday life, not reckoned as a whole among the divinely revealed scriptures.

The Vedas are among the most ancient writings of the world. Notwithstanding their great age it is now generally acknowledged that they are the product of a period of religious thought that was drawing to its close. Tilak (" The arctic home in the Vedas ") writes : " Though the Vedas are the oldest records of the Aryan race, yet the civilisation or the characteristics and the worship of the deities mentioned therein did not originate with the Vedic bards, but was derived by them from their inter-glacial forefathers and preserved in the forms of hymns for the benefit of posterity." It need hardly be said that Vedic scholars differ as to the number of centuries that may be assigned to these wonderful relics of the pre-historic past.

Verethraghna (or Bairām). In the Younger Avesta the angel or genius of war. His name allies him with the Indian god Indra, who as slayer of Vritra was known as Vitrahan.

Vidharr. A son of Odhin and the giantess Gridh. At the final overthrow of the gods he avenges his father's death by tearing the jaws of the Fenris-wolf asunder with his iron shoe. He is one of the Aesir who survive the catastrophe (*see* Ragnarök). Vidharr's dwelling is Vidhi, " in the forest " (Kauffmann), " low, bushy growth of the heath " (Mogk), or have we not to do with a wind god? (Much). He is the " Silent God." Strength and silence are his special attributes. Kauffmann recognises in him the Deus Requalivahanus of the altar found near Cologne (*see* Freyr), and further identifies Vidharr with Heimdall and Hoenir, all three being originally identical with Tyr, with which idea all scholars do not agree (*see* under Tyr). Vidharr was the only one at Aegir's feast who escaped the venom of Loki's tongue. There is no trace of Vidharr's cult in the north. He belongs chiefly to the Eddic poems.

Virabhadra. A monster, the description of whom leaves nothing of terrific to the imagination, created by Siva as a " form of his anger." (*See* Daksha.)

Viracocha. One of the chief gods of the ancient Peruvians. Although the name Viracocha was the specific appellation of a deity it was also a generic name for divine or supernatural beings. It means " Foam of the Water," from the circumstance that the god had risen from the depths of Lake Titicaca. After he had risen from the sacred waters Viracocha created the heavenly bodies and set them in the sky, at the same time fixing their several courses unalterably. He then created the human race out of stone figures made by himself, and ordered them to follow him to Cuzco, the capital. There he placed them under the rule of Allca Vica, who was the first ancestor of the Incas. He then returned to his home below the waters of Lake Titicaca. This myth clashes with that of the origin of the Incas from Manco Ccapac, and may have been that favoured by an older or more recent priesthood. Viracocha was usually depicted as being bearded with water-rushes, without flesh or bone, yet swift in motion, and from this description it is not difficult to see that we have to deal with a water-god, a fertiliser of plant-life and a guardian of the growth of all things, man included. He was in many respects analogous to the Mexican Tlaloc.

Viraj. *See* Manu and Purusha.

Vishnu. The name appears to be derived from the root Vis, to enter, to pervade, agreeably to the all-pervading nature of the deity. A god of secondary rank in the earlier Vedic period, but later the second deity of the great Hindu triad, Brahmā being the creator and he the " preserver." Vishnu was closely associated with Indra, whom he assisted in his many victorious onslaughts on the evil powers. Together they engendered the sun, " made the atmosphere wide, and stretched out the world " for man's habitation, and performed certain acts of creation. Some of their attributes are interchangeable. Vishnu is chiefly remarkable for his three strides with which he traversed the universe, planting his foot in three places, which have been interpreted as earth, atmosphere, and sky, and as the three positions of the sun at rising, mid-day, and setting. The idea of the three divisions of the universe appears supported by the statement that his " highest step " is " fixed like an eye in the heavens," and that there lies his own high dwelling, and further by the account of his strides in the myth of his dwarf incarnation (*see* Macdonell and Bergaigne). Vishnu in the beginning was the personification of the larger conception of the sun as a source of energy and activity. He was at times identified with Agni and Soma, emerging like the former from a lofty and invisible dwelling to manifest himself in heaven and on earth (Bergaigne). In the Rāmāyana he is unrivalled in power, but Siva has become apparently his rival in the Mahābhārata. As a member of the great triad he has retained his early characteristic and remains the " unconquerable preserver." He is the " all-pervading spirit," a form of the supreme " all-god," one with Brahmā, a philosophical abstraction, the principle of cosmic life. Vishnu's names are many ; his dwelling is Vaikuntha ; he is figured dark in colour, with four hands, clad in yellow, riding on his bird Garuda, holding a lotus, a club, a shell, and a discus, the latter weapon able of itself to destroy and to return to the hand that flung it. During the interval between each Kalpa, or day of Brahmā, while creation pauses, Vishnu reclines on a lotus, or on the coils of the thousand-headed serpent Sesha. His wife Lakshmi sometimes bears him company. " Vishnu," writes Monier Williams, " is the most human and humane god of the Hindu pantheon—a kind of protest in favour of a personal deity, as opposed to the impersonal pantheism of Brahmā."

Vishnu has appeared in several forms; in each case his presence was needed on earth by some existing evil, and he is expected again as a redeemer to abolish the iniquity and tyranny of the present age. The usually accepted avataras of Vishnu are ten in number, but later writings have added to them, and his re-incarnations are even referred to as innumerable. The first four avaratas are supposed to have occurred in the first age, the Satya Yuga.

AVATARAS OF VISHNU.—The first three, the fish, tortoise, and boar, are also ascribed to Brahmā.

1. THE FISH (Matsya).—Associated with the tale of the flood. In the earliest account it says that Vaivasvata, the seventh and present Manu, saw a little fish in his washing water that spoke to him, and asked to be saved, and then he would be a preserver to Vaivasvata ; and the fish proceeds to warn him of the coming flood. Manu follows his directions and builds his ship accordingly, doing what was asked of him for the fish itself. The fish grows larger and larger, the ocean alone being of size to hold it, and when the flood rises Manu ties his ship to its horn, and is then towed safely to where he can fasten his ship to a tree, and so Manu was the only one saved from destruction. (*See* the Babylonian Ea (Oannes).)

2. THE TORTOISE (Kurma).—Associated with the tale of the churning of the ocean (*q.v.*), when Vishnu in this form served

as a pivot for the mountain. When the avatara is of Brahmā it is only stated that the god (Prajāpati), having taken this form, then " created offspring."

3. THE BOAR (Varāha). — Brahmā as the boar raised the earth on his tusks from out the waters, and then began his work of creation. When associated with Vishnu it is related that a demon dragged the earth down under the waters, and Vishnu fought for a thousand years before he slew the enemy and uplifted the earth.

4. THE MAN-LION (Nrisinha).—There was a devout son of a demon, named Hiranyakasipu ; the latter had been granted invulnerability, and no power could destroy him. Angered at his son's worship of Vishnu he endeavoured in every kind of way to slay him, but the great god preserved his worshipper. The son insisting on Vishnu's omnipresence, the father in scornful rage asked if the god was in a pillar of his hall, and being answered in the affirmative, exclaimed, " Then I will kill him," and violently struck the pillar. Whereupon Vishnu stepped from the pillar, in a form half-man, half-lion, and instantly tore the demon in pieces.

5. THE DWARF (Vāmana).—Connected with Vishnu's three strides. There was one, Bali, who had become king of the three worlds, to the detriment of the gods. Vishnu appears before him as a dwarf, with the request that he may have as much land as he can cover with three strides. Bali, looking on his small person, consents without hesitation. Then Vishnu takes his well-known strides, recovering the supremacy of the universe for the gods ; or, according to one version, he took two strides, recovering heaven and earth, and either had nowhere to take a third, or voluntarily left the infernal regions to Bali.

6. RAMA WITH THE AXE (Parasurāma).—Vishnu was manifested in this form in order to suppress the tyrannous Kshatriya, one of the four chief castes. His story is told in full in the Mahābhārata and the Puranas.

7. RAMA CHANDRA.—Hero of the Rāmāyana. Son of King Dasaratha of Ayodhya. The chief theme of the epic is the war waged by him with the demon Rāvana, who had carried off Rama's wife Sita ; Rama was aided by Hanuman, king of the monkeys (q.v.).

8. KRISHNA (q.v.) or Balarama (q.v.).

9. BUDDHA (q.v.).

10. KALKI (The White Horse).—This is the incarnation now expected by the Hindus, at the close of the present Yuga. The

god will appear seated on a white horse, with a gleaming sword in his hand, to restore the world to its primitive purity. The Vishnu Purana gives a long account of the evils awaiting his redemptive advent; righteousness will be restored by him, and the minds of men made clear as crystal.

Visvakarman. Associated with the Hindu myths of creation, identified in the Brahmanic period with Prajāpati. He is stated in one place to have produced creatures from speech. Later he became the artisan of the gods (*see* Tvastri). He was the fashioner of Jagganath (*q.v.*). Prof. Macdonell writes: "It seems likely that the word was at first attached to the sun-god, but in the later Rig-Veda period became one of the synonymous names given to the one god."

Vivasvat. The sun in Vedic mythology. He married the daughter of Tvashtri and became the father of Yama, and later of the Asvins. It is related in the Rig-Veda that Aditi had eight sons, that she approached the gods with seven and cast out the eighth, Martanda. Later details add that the eighth son was born an imperfect lump, and that the brother Adityas altered his shape, and he whom they fashioned was Vivasvat. An elephant sprang from the pieces which they cut off and threw away. It was therefore enjoined that no one should catch an elephant, as it partook of the nature of man (Muir, iv. 15).

Votan. *See* Itzamna.

Vritra. "Encompasser" (Macdonell). The demon of drought slain by Indra (*q.v.*).

Vukub-Cakix. An earth-giant mentioned in the Kiche "Popol Vuh" (*q.v.*). As a punishment for his vanity he was slain by the hero-gods Hun-Ahpu and Xbalanque. He is of the same class of deity as the Titans or the Jotunn of Scandinavian myth.

W

Waukheon (or Thunder-bird). Was a god of the Dakota Indians who personified the thunder-cloud. He strove constantly with Unktahe, the water-god, a cunning magician, the master of dreams and witchcraft. This myth, as do similar others, probably represents the atmospheric changes which accompany the advancing seasons and the ripening harvest.

Wen-Tsch'ang. A Chinese Taoist deity who presides over literature. He was originally a star, which descended and became incarnate, and is identified with a small constellation near the Great Bear. Scholars pray to him to assist them in their labours, and a temple is set apart to him in Chinese cities, usually erected on an earthen mound with six sides, to typify the form of the constellation, which has the shape of a hexagon. This deity is said to have visited the earth at irregular intervals during many generations, and became incarnated in the persons of various gifted men.

Woden. *See* Odhin.

X

Xelhua. A Mexican giant who escaped the flood by climbing the mountain of Tlaloc, the god of water. He was supposed to have later built the famous pyramid of Cholula.

Y

Yacatecutli (or Lord of Travellers).   Was, as his name implies,
the deity and patron of the merchant classes of Anahuac or
ancient Mexico, and was supposed to exercise a special guardianship over those chapmen who did so much to extend the frontiers
of the Aztec people.   These merchants had several peculiar
methods of worshipping or adoring Yacatecutli.   Having arrived
at the place where they intended to pass the night, they piled
all their staves in a bundle, and drawing blood from their
tongues, limbs, and ears, they sprinkled it upon the heap of
sticks.   The staff of the traveller was indeed symbolical of
Yacatecutli.   Before it incense was burned as before a god.
They prayed to it to protect them from the dangers of the road
and the wilderness.   On returning from a long journey or a
more than usually perilous sojourn in distant lands the merchants were wont to give a great feast in honour of Yacatecutli.
Those who were invited made a number of genuflections to the
baton or staff which had assisted the traveller upon his peregrin-
ations, and it was finally placed with every sign of reverence
in a neighbouring temple.   Before it were placed offerings of
meats, of flowers, and of fragrant tobacco, after which the feast
in its honour was duly celebrated by those invited, and the staff
deposited in the private oratory of the merchant.   Slaves were
frequently sacrificed to Yacatecutli, and to his five brothers and
sister, Chiconquiauitl, Seven Rains; Xomocuitl, Goose; Nacxitl,
the Four-footed; Cochimetl, Sleeping Maguey; Yacapitzauac,
the Pointed Nosed; Chalmecaciuatl, the Roped Woman, his sister.
The slaves so sacrificed wore the insignia and ornaments of the
god, " as if they were his very images."   A fair was held at
intervals at Azcaputzalco for the sole purpose of buying and
selling these slaves, who were when purchased fattened up for
the sacrifice, and afterwards served up at the repast which
followed their immolation.

Yakshas.   Attendants on the post-Vedic god Kubera, and
guardians of his treasures.   They are represented at different
times as harmless or the reverse.   Their name probably means
" possessed of magical power " (Jacobi).

Yama. In the early Vedic period Yama was the chief of the dead, the son of Vivasvat and Saranyu, or of the Gandharva, and the mythic progenitor of the human race. He is represented as a deified human being rather than a god; as "the first of mortals who found out the way" into the celestial world, to the home that is not to be taken from men. With him, in the highest heaven, dwelt the departed fathers, and thither Agni was besought to convey the soul after death, where it hoped to be reunited to a shining and perfect body. Yama's chief messengers were two grim dogs, who are also described as guarding the approach to his abode, "possibly to exclude the wicked" (Macdonell); at times he sent a bird (owl and pigeon) as herald. In the paradise where Yama and Varuna reigned together in light, every kind of enjoyment awaited the blessed dead; Yama played on his flute as they gathered round him under the shade of the celestial tree; there they drank the soma that rendered them immortal as the gods. In the earlier myth he appears neither as a judge nor a god of the nether world; in the Purānas he is represented as the lord of death, meting out punishments, according to the account of the dead read out to him by his recorder Chitragupta, or Chandragupta, and as supreme over the infernal regions his pleasanter aspect is lost in that of the king of terrors. Those who die appear before him, and the virtuous are sent to Swarga (Indra's heaven) whilst the wicked go to Naraka or Hades. He is figured of a green colour, with red garments; he holds a club and a noose (for drawing the soul out of the deceased's body), and rides on a buffalo.

Yama had a twin sister Yami, and the two have been thought to represent the first human pair, but a Vedic hymn describes Yami as endeavouring to draw Yama into a sexual relationship, which he refuses. There have been various cosmic interpretations of the twins. He is prayed to for an entire month by unmarried females who desire husbands.

NOTE.—We have no description given us in the Vedas of any particular place for the wicked, but we infer they were cast into some dark depth whence they could not escape, for Indra throws evil-doers into a prison apparently of this kind. A hell was only developed in post-Vedic times, and in the Vishnu Purāna the names of the various hells are mentioned. The soul, it seems, was thought by the Hindus to wander about for awhile in the neighbourhood of the living before going to its final dwelling. As with other primitive peoples the proximity of the spirits of the dead was looked upon with fear and dislike. Oldenberg shows that this intermediate condition is proved by the fact that individual offerings were not offered to the deceased for about a year after his death, when he began to be honoured with the customary monthly offerings to departed fathers, grandfathers, and great-grandfathers. In later literature we find that the dead were believed to leave Yama's realm and revisit their friends on certain days during the celebration of the feast for the dead, and to demand food, when it was advisable to give them what they required. (*See* " Religion des Veda.")

Dresses and ornaments were laid with the dead for use in the next world, and the ceremony at cremation of taking the bow and the gold from the hand of the deceased seems to be a survival of an ancient custom of giving these things to the dead to take with them (*ibid.*).

Yazatas. In Zoroastrian belief the celestial beings who rank next to the Amesha Spentas, or archangels (*see* Ahura Mazda) ; they are many in number, and are genii of the elements, protecting spirits, and representatives of abstract ideas, etc.

Yen-lo-wang. A Chinese adaptation of Yama, the Hindoo god of the dead. " His name is perpetually on the lips of the people when death and future judgment are mentioned." He is thought to determine the manner and time of the death of every individual, as well as the future condition of his soul. A popular verse, expressing the inevitable nature of death, says that " King Yama, having decided that a man shall die at the third watch of the night, will certainly not permit him to live till the fifth." The reign of this deity, however, is only within the lower sphere of existence, and he has no power over the person who by his own striving after purity and goodness passes out of the regions of life and death and enters those of dispassionate thought. With Yen-lo-wang nine other gods are associated, and the entire group is known as " The Ten Kings."

Yggdrasil. Horse (or gallows) of Odhin. The ash Yggdrasil (ash in which is Odhin's horse, the wind (Saussaye) ; on which Odhin had hung as a sacrifice (Kauffmann and others)) was the great world tree, representative of all living nature ; or of the physical and moral laws of the world (Rydberg) ; the fate of the world depended upon it. Its branches spread over the universe ; of its three roots, one reached to the Aesir, another to the giants, the third to Niflheim. Under this last root, which is everlastingly gnawed by the dragon, Nidhogg, was Hvergelmir (*see* Niflheim); Mimir's well was under the second root; the Urdhr fountain under the first, and here daily the gods assembled to deliver judgment.   On the tree sat an eagle, with a hawk between its eyes, and a squirrel, Ratatösk, ran up and down it to breed discord between the eagle and the dragon at its foot. Four harts gnaw off the shoots, and one side of the tree decays; but it is nourished by the purifying waters of Urdhr's fountain, which are sprinkled over it by the Norns. In Yggdrasil we have, according to some, a survival of the ancient belief in the sacred character of trees, which led to tree-worship. Bugge and Golther, on the other hand, see in the Teutonic tree an imitation of the cross, but this is no more reasonable than the idea of the Spanish conquerors of Central America, who discerned in the native symbols for the four winds an imitation of the emblem of Christianity.

Yi King.   An ancient Chinese classic, the meaning of which signifies " The Book of Mystery." The text of this work, besides the appendices, added by Confucius, consists of two portions, one by King Wan, 1143 B.C., and the other by the Duke of Chow, his son. It is based on diagrams or lineal figures, ascribed to Fu-hsi, and composed of whole and divided lines.   There are sixty-four of these figures, and exactly what their inventor meant to convey by their use is unknown.   The work obviously deals with action and reaction, however, and " the vicissitudes in the world of sense and society have their correspondences in the changes that take place in the lines of the diagrams."   Good and bad fortune are also indicated by the trend of the lines.   These lines were systematically altered by changing the stalks of a certain plant, and seem to have been intended to typify the fluctuations in the cosmos, or perhaps to serve the purposes of divination.   The entire lines are called " the strong " and the divided lines " the weak."   The two represent matter, and under one form are known as yang, and under the other yin (*see* Yin and Yang).   The strong and active influences are yang, the weak and passive yin.   The concealed workings of nature are designated kwei shan, or operations of spirits.   The Yi King is undoubtedly a book of physical speculation, but so little is known concerning it that ts exact purport is still doubtful.

Yima.   A mythic figure of Persian mythology whom Ahura Mazda requests to carry his law down to men.   Yima refuses the task that Zarathustra finally performed, but he is willing to act as protector of Mazda's creatures, and to guard them from evil powers, such as disease and death, and help them in the way of life and prosperity. By degrees he enlarges the earth, and when it became known to him that a terrible winter followed by overwhelming flood was approaching, he built an enclosure, and conveyed into it the best specimens of animals and plants, and then he and his people dwelt in millennial happiness. (*See* Deluge and Cosmology—American.)

Yin and Yang. These are the male and female principles in Buddhistic Chinese mythology, the two elements which pervade all nature. The life of man and of living things generally depends upon the union of these two principles and ceases with their separation. Various natural objects are labelled by the Chinese in quite an arbitrary way as Yin and Yang. For example, they say that the sun is yang, the moon is yin; man is yang, woman is yin; the rational soul is yang, the physical soul yin; heaven is yang, earth is yin, and so forth. (*See* Yi King.)

Ymir. A primeval giant of Norse mythology, formed of fire and water. The rivers, known as Elivagar, froze as they flowed far from their source Hvergelmir (*see* Niflheim), and ice formed covered with layers of congealed vapour. When the hot air from Muspelheim, on the farther side of Ginnungagap, reached the river so that it melted, the drops took life and formed a being called Ymir, or Örgelmir, as he was known to the frost-giants. He was the progenitor of the race of giants. Out of the drops was also formed a cow, Audhumla, and Ymir was fed by four streams of milk which flowed from her; the cow herself licked the stones that were covered with salt and hoar frost ; the first day she licked there appeared the hair of a man, the second day a head, the third an entire being. This was Buri, father of Borr, who was father of Odhin. Meanwhile Ymir, when sleeping, had engendered a man and woman from his sweat, and also a son from his feet, and from the latter descended the frost-giants. The sons of Borr (Odhin, Vili, and Ve) slew Ymir, and the blood that flowed from his wounds drowned the whole race of frost-giants except one, who saved himself in his bark with his wife, and he was known as Bergelmir. Ymir's body was thrown into Ginnungagap, and from his blood was created the sea and waters, from his flesh the earth, from his bones the mountains, from his skull the sky, from his brain the clouds, and from his eyebrows Midhgardh for the race of men. (*See* also Cosmology and cf. Purusha.)

Yomi. The Japanese Hades, to which in ancient times access was had in a corner of the province Idzumo. The Shintoists have no very definite idea of a future world, beyond the fact that the gods reside in some far height of heaven, and that the dead pass into a vague region.

Yuga. In Hindu mythology an age of the world. Three Yugas have already elapsed, and at the present time we are living in the fourth. Each Yuga is shorter than the one before. The first (Krita) lasted 4000 divine years, being preceded and followed by a twilight of 400 divine years ; the second (Treta) 3000, with twilights of 300 ; the third (Dwāpara), 2000, with twilights of 200 ; the fourth (Kali) is to last 1000, with twilights of 100. As the Yugas become shorter, man deteriorates. The four Yugas altogether, a period of 12,000 divine years, make a Maha-Yuga. Each divine year is 360 years of mortals, the Maha-Yuga consisting therefore of 4,320,000 mortal years. A thousand Maha-Yugas make a Kalpa (*q.v.*).

Z

Zoroastrianism (or, Mazdaism). The religion of the Persians introduced by the reformer Zarathustra, the earliest form of Zoroaster's name as given in the Avesta. Uncertainty hangs over the date and place of his birth. The Greeks spoke of him as belonging to a remote age, but modern scholars assign the period of his life to the latter half of the seventh and early sixth century B.C. (Jackson). It seems certain that he was not a Persian, but a Mede or a Bactrian, either supposition being supported by indications of one kind or another. From the whole tenor of the Gāthās, the most ancient part of the Avesta (*q.v.*), we are led, says Dr. Haug, their translator, to feel that he was a man of extraordinary stamp acting a grand part on the stage of his country's history. Zarathustra speaks of himself as a messenger from God sent to bring the people the blessing of civilisation and to destroy idolatry. Many legends grew up around his memory, of miraculous signs at his birth, of his precocious wisdom, whereby even as a child he confounded the Magi, of his being borne up to the highest heaven and there receiving the word of life from Deity himself, together with the revelation of all secrets of the future. He retired as a young man from the world to spend long years of contemplation before he began his teaching at thirty, and he lived to the age of seventy seven. The religion he taught was the national religion of the Persians from the time of the Achæmenidæ, who dethroned Cyaxares' son, 558 B.C., to about the middle of the seventh century A.D. It declined after Alexander's conquest under the Seleucidæ and the succeeding dynasty of the Arsacidæ, but was revived by the Sassanian rulers and flourished for the four centuries A.D. 226-651. Then followed the Mahometan conquest, accompanied by persecution, before which the faithful followers of Zarathustra fled to India, where they are now represented by their descendants, the Parsis of Bombay.

The religious belief taught by Zarathustra is based on the dual conception of a good principle Ahura Mazda (*q.v.*), and an evil principle, Anra Mainyu (*see* Ahriman), and the leading idea of his teaching is the constant conflict between the two, which must continue until the end of the period ordained by

Ahura Mazda for the duration of the world, when evil will be finally overcome ; until then the god's power is to some degree limited, as evil still withstands him. Zarathustra's doctrine was essentially practical and ethical ; it was not in abstract contemplation, or in separation from the world, that man was to look for spiritual deliverance, but in active charity, in deeds of usefulness, in kindness to animals, in everything that could help to make the world a well-ordered place to live in, in courage, and all uprightness. To build a bridge or dig a canal was to help to lessen the power of evil. As Reinach has concisely expressed it, " a life thoroughly occupied was a perpetual exorcism."

The two figures of Ahura Mazda and Anra Mainyu, the one with his attendant archangels and angels, and the other with his archdemons and demons, or Divs, compose the Zarathustrian celestial hierarchy, as represented in the earlier sacred writings ; in the later ones other figures are introduced into the pantheon (*see* Mithra and Anahita). The sacred writings that have been preserved are of different periods, and outside the range of Zarathustra's moral system of religion there are traces in them of revivals of an older primitive nature worship, and of the beliefs of an early nomadic shepherd life, as, for instance, the sacredness in which cow and dog are held (Lehmann), as well as reminiscences of general Indo-Germanic myths.

Ahura Mazda was the creator of the universe for the duration of which he fixed a certain term (*see* Cosmology). It seems uncertain whether the Persians pictured the world as round or flat, but according to their idea it was divided into seven zones, of which the central one was the actual habitable earth. Between these zones and enveloping the whole was the great abyss of waters. Between earth and heaven rose the celestial mountain whence flowed all the source of all rivers upon earth, and on which was deposited the Haoma (*q.v.*).

The central feature of Zoroastrian ritual was the worship of fire, an old-established worship which had existed before Zoroaster's time (Lehmann). In the oldest period images were forbidden, and holy rites could be performed without temples, portable fire-altars being in use. Temples were, however, built in quite early times, and within these was the sanctuary from which all light was excluded, and where the sacred fire was kept alight, which could only be approached by the priest with covered hands and mouth. The Persians carried the fear of defilement to an extreme, and had even more elaborate regulations than most easterns concerning methods of purification and avoidance of defilement, both as regards personal contamination or that of the sacred elements of earth, fire, and water. Even hair and nails could not be cut without special directions as to how to deal with the separated portions. But this perpetual and exhausting state of caution and protective effort against contact with defiling objects, and rigorous system of purification, had an ultimate concern with the great struggle going on between good and evil. Death and everything that partook of death, or had any power of injury, were works of the arch-enemy. It was owing to the fear of contaminating the three elements named above that the Persians neither buried nor cremated their dead, and looked upon it as a criminal act to throw a corpse into the water. The old mode of disposing of the dead was similar to that now practised by the Parsis of Bombay, who carry the body to one of the Towers of Silence. So the Persians exposed the corpse till one or other devouring agent, birds of prey or the elements, had reduced it to a skeleton. As regards man himself he was thought to be a reasonable being of free will with conscience, soul, and a guardian spirit or prototype of himself who dwelt above, called a Fravashi—his own character, indeed, put into a spiritual body, almost identical with the amei-malghen or spiritual nymphs of the Araucanian Indians of Chile. He had the choice of good and evil, and consequently suffered the due punishment of sin. For the first three days after death, the soul of the dead was supposed to hover about its earthly abode. During this time friends and relatives performed their funerary rites, their prayers and offerings becoming more earnest and abundant as the hour drew nigh when the soul was bound to start on its journey to the beyond. This was at the beginning of the fourth day, when Sraosha (*q.v.*) carried it aloft, assailed on the way by demons desirous of obtaining possession of his burden. On earth everything was being done to keep the evil spirits in check, fires being lighted as particularly effective against the powers of darkness. And thus assisted Sraosha arrived safely with his charge at the bridge that spanned the space between earth and heaven. Here at the entrance to the " accountant's bridge " (Cheyne and Black) the soul's account was cast up by Mithra and Rashnu ; the latter weighed its good and evil deeds, and even if the good deeds turned the scale, the soul had still to undergo immediate penance for its transgression, so strict was the justice meted out to each. Now the bridge may be crossed, and a further automatic kind of verdict takes place, for to those fit for heaven the bridge appears a wide and easy way, to the unfortunate ones doomed to destruction it seems but of a hair's breadth, and stepping on to it they straightway fall into the yawning gulf beneath. . The blessed ones are met at heaven's gate by a radiant figure who leads them through the anti-chambers that finally open into the everlasting light of the celestial abode. This is the triumph of the individual soul; but there is "a far-off divine event" awaiting, which will be heralded by signs and wonders. For 3000 years previous to it there are alternate intervals of overpowering evil and conquering peace. At last the great dragon is let loose and the worst time comes, but Mazda sends a man to slay it. Then the saviour Saoshyant is born of a virgin. The dead arise, the sheep and goats are divided, and there is lamentation on the earth. The mountains dissolve and flood the earth with molten metal, a devouring agent of destruction to the wicked, but from which the good take no hurt. The spiritual powers have now to fight it out. Mazda and Sraosha overcome Ahriman and the dragon, and "then age, decay, and death are done away, and in their place are everlasting growth and life."

Zu. This is an old myth only in part preserved, of how Zu stole the tablets of destiny from En-lil (*q.v.*), supreme power being offered to one who would recover them.

Zume. A deity worshipped under various names over a wide tract in South America. The Paraguayans called him Zume, the Caribs Tamu, the Arawaks Kamu, and the Carayas Kaboi (*q.v.*). He is a deity of the "culture-hero" class, and gave the knowledge of the various arts and crafts to the peoples he visited. In the Caraya legend he appears as the hero who led his people from the under to the upper world. The widespread character of his worship shows that the original civilising agency of these countries must have progressed from a common centre. The fact that Zume was said to have come from the place of sun-rise together with that of his being a culture-bringer is good evidence that he emanated from the sun, that indeed, like Quetzalcoatl, in Mexico, he was a "man of the sun." (*See* Ehrenreich, "Die Karayastämme," p. 39, and his article on South America in "Encyclopedia of Religion and Ethics.")

ILLUSTRATIONS
OF
DEITIES, TEMPLES
AND
RELIGIOUS SYMBOLS

ACKNOWLEDGMENTS

THE Illustrations of Agni, Jagannath, Brahma, and Lakshmi on page 208, and Surya, Indra, and Siva's Temple on page 209, are reproduced from *Hindu Mythology*, by W. J. Wilkins, by permission of Messrs. W. Thacker & Co., and those of Aah and Pakt on page 210, and Apis and Nut on page 211, from *A Concise Dictionary of Egyptian Archæology*, by M. Broderick and A. Anderson Morton, by permission of Messrs. Methuen & Co. Ltd.

We are also indebted to Messrs. Lippincott & Co. for permission to reproduce the Thunderbird on page 214.

BAS-RELIEFS AT SANCHI.
The Sacred Tree Pipal with Hindu worshippers.

DAGOBA AT
AMRAVATI
WITH
BUDDHISTIC
SYMBOLS.

a

b

a. Amravati.

b. Siddartha.

WORSHIP
OF THE
CHAKRA
(OR
SACRED
WHEEL).

KRISHNA HOLDING UP MOUNT GOVARDDHANA.

Saraswati
सरस्वती

Ganēsa
गणेश

MONKEYS BUILDING A BRIDGE BETWEEN INDIA AND CEYLON.
See Hanuman.

SIVA.   VISHNU.

BRAHMA.

SIVA (MAHADEVA) AND PARVATI.

CAVE TEMPLE
AT
AJUNTA:
VISHNU
AND
SARESWATI.

CHAITYA
CAVE:
BUDDHA
GIVING
ALMS.

ALTAR IN CHAITYA CAVE.

CAVE TEMPLE OF THE JAINA GROUP,
THE INDIAN SUBHA.

EASTERN GATEWAY OF STUPA OR TOPE AT SANCHI WITH RELIEFS
ILLUSTRATING THE LEGEND OF BUDDHA.
(Mixed Hellenic and Indian character.)

AGNI.

JAGANNATH.

BRAHMA.

LAKSHMI.

SURYA.

INDRA.

SIVA'S TEMPLE AT BENARES.

AAH.

THE PHOENIX OR EGYPTIAN
BENNU BIRD.

SEB.   OSIRIS   SERAPIS.
APIS.

PAKT OR PASHT.

FORMS OF HATHOR, EGYPTIAN
SKY GODDESS.

FORMS OF ISIS, THE WIFE OF
OSIRIS.

HORUS, SON OF OSIRIS.

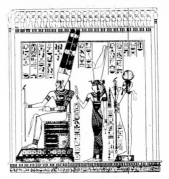

THE THEBAN TRIAD,
AMEN, MUT, AND KHENSU.

APIS.

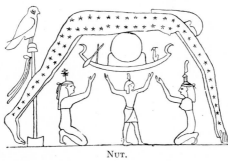

NUT.

BES, EGYPTIAN GOD OF
PLEASURE.

TANAITIS, THE BABYLONIAN
VENUS.

CREATION TABLET (Nineveh).

BABYLONIAN SUN GOD TABLET.

213

BABYLONIAN PRIESTESS INTRODUCING A VIRGIN TO THE TEMPLE OF
MYLITTA TO RECEIVE THE PRIEST'S BENEDICTION.

THE AZTEC CALENDAR
STONE.

THE THUNDERBIRD OF THE
NORTH AMERICAN INDIANS.

QUETZALCOATL, THE MEXICAN
GOD OF AIR.

LETCHWORTH
THE TEMPLE PRESS
PRINTERS

EVERYMAN,
I·WILL·GO·WITH
·THEE,
&·BE·THY·GVIDE
IN·THY·MOST·NEED
TO·GO·BY·THY·SIDE